Teaching and Learning in Changing Times

Edited by

Martin Hughes

BLACKWELL
Publishers

Copyright © Blackwell Publishers Ltd, 1996

First published 1996

2 4 6 8 10 9 7 5 3 1

Blackwell Publishers Ltd
108 Cowley Road
Oxford OX4 1JF
UK

Blackwell Publishers Inc.
238 Main Street
Cambridge, Massachusetts 02142
USA

British Library Cataloguing in Publication Data

A CIP catalogue record for this book is available from the British Library.

Library of Congress Cataloging-in-Publication Data
Teaching and learning in changing times / edited by Martin Hughes.
p.   cm.
Includes bibliographical references and index.
ISBN 0-631-19277-8 (alk. paper). – ISBN 0-631-19278-6 (pbk.: alk. paper)
1. Education–England. 2. Education–Wales. 3. Teaching–England.
4. Teaching–Wales. 5. Learning. 6. Educational change–England.
7. Educational change–Wales. I. Hughes, Martin.
LA632.T42 1996
370′.942–dc20
95-9403
CIP

Printed in Great Britain by
Hartnolls Ltd, Bodmin, Cornwall

This book is printed on acid-free paper

Teaching and Learning
in Changing Times

Contents

Contributors

Peter Aggleton   Institute of Education, University of London
Rosalyn Ashby   Institute of Education, University of London
Paul Black   King's College, London
Ezra Blondel   King's College, London
Margaret Brown   King's College, London
Christopher Brumfit   University of Southampton
Paul Cooper   University of Cambridge
Charles Desforges   University of Exeter
Alaric Dickinson   Institute of Education, University of London
Sandra Duggan   University of Durham
Richard Gott   University of Durham
Susan Harris   University of Sheffield
Cathie Holden   University of Exeter
Janet Hooper   University of Southampton
Martin Hughes   University of Exeter
Peter Lee   Institute of Education, University of London
Fred Lubben   University of York
Donald McIntyre   University of Oxford
Robin Millar   University of York
Rosamond Mitchell   University of Southampton
Penny Munn   University of Central Lancashire (Preston)
Ian Plewis   Institute of Education, University of London
Gabrielle Rowe   University of Cambridge
Jean Rudduck   Homerton College, Cambridge
Rudolph Schaffer   University of Strathclyde (Glasgow)
Shirley Simon   King's College, London
Marijcke Veltman   Institute of Education, University of London
Gwen Wallace   University of Derby
Geoff Whitty   Institute of Education, University of London

Acknowledgements

We would like to acknowledge the support of a number of individuals and institutions, without whose help the book could not have been written. Our main acknowledgement is undoubtedly to the Economic and Social Research Council (ESRC), who funded all the research reported here. We should point out, however, that the views expressed here are those of the authors and do not necessarily reflect the views of the Council. We would also like to thank our Steering Committee – John Gray (chair), Rosalind Driver, Alan Gibson, Francoise Leake, Virginia Makins and Gill Pinkerton – who have provided substantial help and guidance throughout the lifetime of the programme, and the ESRC officers (Amy Cavanagh, Peter de Vries, Andrew Lester, Peter Linthwaite and Stephen Schwenk) for their efficient and helpful support of the programme. The editor would like to add particular thanks to the programme secretary, Margaret Bown, for her valuable and unstinting work in support of the programme. In addition, the authors of chapter 1 would like to thank the heads and staff of their project schools for all their help and cooperation, and Andrew Pollard and the PACE team for the use of their data. The authors of chapter 2 would like to thank Caroline Smith, Christabel Owens and Tricia Nash for their assistance in collecting and analysing the data reported in the chapter. Finally, the authors of chapter 4 are most grateful to Basil Bernstein for his help and encouragement with their project.

Introduction

Martin Hughes

The education system in England and Wales has for the last few years been experiencing a radical and unprecedented programme of reform. This programme includes the introduction of a National Curriculum for all pupils aged between 5 and 16 years, the standardized assessment of pupils at ages 7, 11 and 14 years, major changes to the way schools are funded and managed, and a greatly increased emphasis on parental choice and accountability. The assumption behind these reforms is that they will significantly improve the quality of teaching and learning in schools, and that this in turn will lead to higher educational standards for all children.

The educational reforms have generated a great deal of public debate, both nationally and internationally. At home, the views of politicians, teachers' leaders and other educational experts are regularly reported in the media. Abroad, there is much interest in whether the reforms will have their desired effect, and whether the underlying ideas should be adopted by other countries. Meanwhile, those most directly affected by the reforms – such as teachers, pupils and parents – attempt to make sense of a rapid, and at times bewildering, process of change.

At a time when education is receiving such intense public scrutiny, it is clearly desirable that discussion of the underlying issues should be informed as far as possible by careful and dispassionate research. This was the thinking behind the launch in 1991 of a major programme of research by the Economic and Social Research Council (ESRC), the UK's leading funder of research in social science. The programme was entitled 'Innovation and Change in Education: The Quality of Teaching and Learning', and its overall aim was:

> to increase our understanding of teaching and learning
> at a time of unprecedented change in education.

This book reports some of the main findings arising from the ESRC research programme. Each of the ten project teams has contributed a chapter, in which they set out their findings and discuss the implications of their research. These ten chapters form the core of the book. The purpose of this introductory chapter is to provide a brief overview of the educational reforms, to describe how and why the research programme was set up, and to outline the main themes that will be explored in the book. These themes will be returned to in the concluding chapter.

A Brief Overview of the Educational Reforms

The educational reforms have been introduced in England and Wales through a series of White Papers, Education Acts and other pieces of legislation over the last decade. While there are many aspects to the reforms, four features in particular can be singled out. These are the National Curriculum, standardized assessment, changes to the management of schools and an increased emphasis on parental choice. Each of these four features will be briefly summarized here.

The centre-piece of the reforms is undoubtedly the National Curriculum itself. Introduced by the 1988 Education Reform Act, the National Curriculum sets out what will be taught to all children from the ages of 5 to 16 years in all publicly funded schools in England and Wales. Particular emphasis is given to the three *core* subjects of English, mathematics and science, with Welsh providing a fourth core subject in Wales. There are also seven *foundation* subjects, consisting of history, geography, design and technology, art, music, physical education (PE) and (for secondary pupils only) a foreign language. Religious education is not part of the National Curriculum, but all schools are required by law to teach it.

The National Curriculum has brought with it a whole new set of terminology, some of which may be unfamiliar to some readers. Thus the main phases of education are now referred to as *Key Stages*, and cover the following ages:

> Key Stage One – pupils aged 5–7 years
> Key Stage Two – pupils aged 7–11 years
> Key Stage Three – pupils aged 11–14 years
> Key Stage Four – students aged 14–16 years

The details of the curriculum are specified in statutory documents known as Orders. These spell out, for each subject, both the *programmes of study* (what is to be taught) and the *attainment targets* (what is to be learnt). In all subjects other than art, music and PE, the attainment targets are organized in a hierarchy known as the *ten-level scale*. This scale provides a ladder of achievement ranging from level 1 (which might be expected of an average 5-year-old) to level 10 (which will only be reached by an exceptional 16-year-old). Within each attainment target, written *statements of attainment* attempt to specify what a pupil should know or understand at each of the ten levels.

One of the main criticisms made of the National Curriculum in its original form was that it was too complicated and elaborate. As a result, Sir Ron Dearing was asked by the government in 1993 to undertake a full-scale review of the National Curriculum and the associated assessment arrangements. Dearing consulted widely amongst teachers, educationalists and other interested groups, and published both an interim report (Dearing, 1993) and a final report (Dearing, 1994). His main recommendations were that the National Curriculum should be slimmed down and be less prescriptive, that there should be a reduction in the number of attainment targets and statements of attainment, and that more time should be available in the school day for teachers and schools to use at their discretion. Dearing also proposed that, after these changes had been made, there should be no further changes to the curriculum for a period of five years.

The second main feature of the educational reforms – and undoubtedly the most controversial one – has been the introduction of standardized assessment for all children aged 7, 11 and 14 years. The original intention of the 1988 Education Reform Act was that all children would be assessed in all National Curriculum subjects at the end of each Key Stage, and that the assessments would be carried out using a mixture of Teacher Assessment (TA) and Standard Assessment Tests (SATs). It was also intended that the assessment results for each individual child would be reported to their parents, while the aggregated results of all children in each school would be published in the form of 'league tables', thus allowing the performance of individual schools to be directly compared.

As with other aspects of the reforms, there have been substantial modifications to the assessment programme since it was originally conceived. Thus assessment was first introduced in 1991 at Key Stage One, but only in the core subjects of English, mathematics and science. Some league tables of Key Stage One results were published in 1991 and 1992, but these have since been dropped at this stage. In 1993, the attempt to introduce assessment at Key Stage Three was opposed by a major boycott by teachers (supported in some cases by parents and governors) and little assessment took place that year. The Dearing review of the National Curriculum recommended that SATs should continue to be used for assessing the three core subjects, but that TA would be sufficient for the other subjects. Dearing also recommended that the SATs should be simplified, and that the amount of teacher time taken to administer assessment should be reduced as far as possible.

The third main feature of the reforms has been the changes made to the management and funding of schools. The main aim of these changes has been to loosen schools from the control of local education authorities, who were seen by the government as being resistant to the general thrust of the reforms. Under the new arrangements for the local management of schools (LMS), individual schools have been given far greater control than previously over the management of their own budgets. The size of a school's budget is now directly related to the number of pupils on roll, with the intention being to reward popular (and presumably successful) schools at the expense of those that are unpopular. In addition, arrangements have been made to allow schools to 'opt out' of local authority control altogether and obtain 'grant-maintained' (GM) status, if the majority of parents wish this to happen. Any school obtaining GM status receives its funds directly from the government, and ceases to come under the jurisdiction of the local authority.

The fourth main feature of the reforms – and one that is directly related to the previous one – has been the increased emphasis placed on parental choice and accountability to parents. This enhanced role for parents was developed through a series of Education Acts during the 1980s, which aimed both to increase parents' rights in choosing schools and to increase the role parents could play on a school's governing body. Further obstacles to parental choice were removed by the 1988 Education Reform Act. These pieces of legislation were followed by the publication in 1991 of the Parent's Charter, which sets out in some detail the rights and responsibilities of parents. Central to the Parent's Charter is the parent's right to information about his or her child's school, through such documents as an annual written report on the child, regular reports on the school from independent inspectors, and the publication of 'league tables' comparing the performance of local schools.

The overall aim of the measures described above is to raise educational standards throughout the country. Whether this aim has been achieved is another matter. At the time of writing (early 1995) there is relatively little evidence, in either direction, as to whether there has been a substantial long-term improvement in standards. Indeed, many would argue that we will have to wait for several more years before there is firm evidence concerning the extent to which the reforms have succeeded. It is clear, however, that the reforms have already succeeded in raising public awareness about the importance of education, and have led to much greater public discussion about central educational issues. At the same time, the reforms have also raised a number of issues and questions that require the attention of research.

The ESRC Research Programme

The Economic and Social Research Council (ESRC) is the UK's leading funder of social science research. Its mission is to promote and support research that aims:

to increase our understanding of social and economic change ... thereby enhancing economic competitiveness, the effectiveness of public policy and public services, and the quality of life.

One way in which the ESRC attempts to meet its aims is by funding programmes of research on topics of particular relevance and concern. It was therefore quite appropriate for the ESRC to set up a research programme aimed at increasing understanding of teaching and learning in the context of the recent educational reforms. This programme, it should be pointed out, was not intended to carry out an evaluation *per se* of the government's reforms. Rather, it was intended to use the reforms as a 'natural laboratory' in which to investigate some issues of fundamental concern to teaching and learning. In so doing, it was intended to contribute to the ESRC's stated concern 'to increase our understanding of social change'.

The ESRC research programme consists of ten projects based at different centres within the United Kingdom. The projects were selected in an open competition involving over 250 researchers, all of whom had submitted outline proposals. The projects finally chosen drew on a wide range of academic disciplines – including psychology, sociology, linguistics and education – and between them covered all phases of compulsory education, from preschool to the end of Key Stage Four. As will be seen, the projects adopted a range of theoretical and methodological approaches, and focused on a variety of issues and problems. At the same time, the editor of this book was funded to act as part-time coordinator to the programme.

This book represents one of the first products of the ESRC programme. It is to some extent an account of work 'in progress': some projects had not completed their work at the time the chapters were written, and their accounts present only interim or partial findings. Nevertheless, the work reported here constitutes a substantial body of evidence on some issues of central educational importance.

The book is intended for a wide readership. The contributors all believe that their research should be of interest and relevance to many different groups – including policy-makers, academics, teachers, students, parents, governors and the general public. They have therefore attempted to write in a way that will make the research accessible to such a wide-ranging audience. At the same time, the contributors have inevitably drawn on the conceptual tools of their trade – such as theoretical frameworks and methodological techniques – which are an essential part of doing research. It is hoped that readers will see the relevance of these conceptual tools for increasing their understanding of what is happening in schools.

It should be emphasized that, as researchers funded by a public body, the contributors are not writing from any personal or political motivations concerning the educational reforms. Their role is to provide evidence on issues that they believe are of fundamental public importance, and to spell out the implications for policy-makers and practitioners. If their evidence leads them to question a particular piece of policy or practice, then it is their responsibility to indicate their concern. The aim, however, is to illuminate and inform, not to criticize or condemn.

The Main Themes of the Book

Like the reforms themselves, the chapters in this book encompass a wide range of issues, subjects and age-ranges. Underlying this diversity, however, are three main themes that cut across the individual chapters and that appear and reappear in several different forms.

The first theme is the need to *understand the changes currently under way in schools, and the effects they are having on those most directly involved.* As indicated above, the programme is not attempting to carry out an evaluation of the reforms. Rather, it makes the assumption that there may not necessarily be a congruence between, on the one hand, the aims and aspirations of those who design a new piece of policy, and on the other hand, the ways in which that policy is interpreted, understood and implemented in practice. This theme is particularly prominent in the first three chapters of the book. Thus in chapter 1, Ian Plewis and Marijcke Veltman look at the extent to which the time spent on particular activities in infant classrooms has actually changed as a result of the introduction of the National Curriculum. In chapter 2, Charles Desforges, Cathie Holden and Martin Hughes look at the views of one group who have been given particular prominence within the reforms – parents – and consider how the introduction of standardized assessment is seen from the parents' perspective. Chapter 3, by Susan Harris, Jean Rudduck and Gwen Wallace, focuses on the pupils' perspective, and particularly on the way in which their school careers have been influenced by the reforms. At the same time, the theme of understanding change is also prominent in other chapters, such as chapters 4 and 7.

The second main theme is the desire to *understand what makes for effective teaching and learning, particularly as this is experienced by teachers and learners.* The concern here is not so much with whether certain teaching approaches are more or less effective for teaching specific parts of the curriculum (for example, whether it is better to teach reading through a 'phonics' or a 'real books' approach), important though such questions are. Rather, the contributors are interested in the actual processes of teaching and learning as they take place in the classroom, and in the ways in which teachers and pupils perceive what is happening at such times. This theme is particularly prominent in the middle third of the book – although again, not exclusively so. Thus in chapter 4, Geoff Whitty, Peter Aggleton and Gabrielle Rowe look at the role of cross-curricular themes (such as health education, citizenship and economic awareness), and describe how the themes are presented and perceived within an almost exclusively subject-based National Curriculum. In chapter 5, Christopher Brumfit, Rosamond Mitchell and Janet Hooper examine another cross-curricular issue – 'Knowledge about Language' – and look at how this is presented and perceived within English and foreign language classrooms. Chapter 6, by Paul Cooper and Donald McIntyre, looks specifically at what pupils and teachers think makes for 'effective teaching and learning' in English and history classes, and at the possible congruence between the perspectives of teachers and pupils. Some of the ideas developed in chapter 6 are continued further in chapter 7, by Penny Munn and Rudolph Schaffer, who look at teaching and learning in the preschool period: this chapter, it should be noted, describes research carried out in Scotland, where the educational reforms have taken a direction slightly different from that of England and Wales.

The third main theme is that of *pupils' understanding – and the way it progresses – both within and across specific subject areas*. The issue of progression has been made particularly salient by the ten-level scale underpinning the National Curriculum, and the associated need to draw up models of progression within each attainment target and each subject area. This issue is addressed primarily in the last four chapters of the book. Thus in chapter 7, Penny Munn and Rudolph Schaffer look at the development of numeracy and literacy in preschool children, while in chapter 8 Paul Black, Margaret Brown, Shirley Simon and Ezra Blondel look at progression in two related areas of science and mathematics. Chapter 9, by Sandra Duggan, Richard Gott, Fred Lubben and Robin Millar, looks at pupils' ability to carry out scientific investigations, and in particular at their underlying concepts of evidence. The last contribution is from Peter Lee, Alaric Dickinson and Rosalyn Ashby, who look in chapter 10 at progression in children's understanding of second-order historical concepts, such as evidence, explanation and cause.

These three main themes are returned to in the final chapter of the book. This concluding chapter summarizes what the research of the ESRC programme has revealed about pupils' learning and understanding, about the nature of effective teaching and learning, and about the effects that the reforms are having on schools. From these conclusions, a number of important issues are highlighted for attention. These issues include the need to link the curriculum more closely to progression in pupils' understanding; the need to go beyond the subject-centred nature of the National Curriculum and address the problem of coherence in the curriculum; the need to give serious attention to the issue of differentiation; the need to rethink the role of parents; and finally, the need to pay more attention to social, emotional and motivational factors in education. We believe these issues deserve close attention from researchers, policy-makers and practitioners – indeed, from anyone who is concerned with improving the quality of teaching and learning in our schools.

1

Where Does All the Time Go? Changes in Pupils' Experiences in Year 2 Classrooms

Ian Plewis and Marijcke Veltman

Editor's Introduction

We start by looking at what has actually changed in classrooms as a result of the current educational reforms. This first chapter, by Ian Plewis and Marijcke Veltman, investigates the effect that the National Curriculum might be having on a fundamental aspect of schooling – the length of time pupils spend on particular activities. The chapter focuses on Key Stage One (5–7 years), as this has been one of the stages most affected by the reforms. The project is unusual in that it can make direct comparisons with data collected in the same classrooms before the National Curriculum was introduced. Plewis and Veltman report that 7-year-olds are now spending more time on science, history and geography, but much less time on art, craft and construction activities. There is virtually no change in the amount of time children spend on the '3Rs': indeed, children are on average spending only eight minutes a week reading aloud to an adult. These findings suggest that while classrooms in the 1990s are different from those in the 1980s, they are not radically so. Indeed, there may still be a considerable gap between the aspirations behind the current reforms and the realities of what is actually happening in classrooms.

Introduction

The 1988 Education Reform Act (ERA) was expected to wreak great changes in the way schools function as institutions, in the way teachers behave as professionals, in the way parents respond to and influence the outcomes, organization and control of education, and in the way pupils experience school. It was on the last of these issues – the extent to which pupils' experiences at school have changed – that we focused in our research, and we present some of our findings in this chapter. We concentrated on pupils passing through Key Stage One in primary (or infant) schools. This was the period of schooling intended to be affected first by those aspects of the legislation concerned with the introduction of the National Curriculum and compulsory assessment.

In what ways might the school experiences of pupils of this age have changed? For example, would the division of the curriculum into core and foundation subjects lead to more emphasis being given to the core subjects, in particular the basics, or 3Rs, at the expense of some of the foundation subjects such as music and art? Or might the reverse hold, with the increased curriculum load at Key Stage One leaving less time for the basics? Would the introduction of the National Curriculum lead to fewer differences between schools in what pupils of a particular age are taught? Might compulsory assessment at age 7 lead to changes in teacher practices such that they start to 'teach to the test'? Each of these questions has been addressed by research. It is the first of them – in particular, the allocation of time to different parts of the curriculum – that receives most of our attention in this chapter.

New legislation is not, however, bound to change practice at the levels of the school and the classroom. On the one hand, a National Curriculum is in place, with programmes of study set out at the various Key Stages for the core and foundation subjects, and with prescribed assessment procedures. And from our reading of some accounts of education in infant schools before 1988, in conjunction with the legal requirements of the Act, we might be led to expect that pupils in infant classrooms in 1993 were being nourished by a different diet of educational experiences from the one provided for their predecessors ten years earlier. On the other hand, the notion that life in a typical 'progressive' post-Plowden infant classroom was all play and no work was never supported by the research evidence. As Tizard et al. (1988) put it, 'the great majority of children were, in fact, being taught a rather narrow range of subjects in a fairly traditional way'. Also, the original concept of the National Curriculum, and more especially national assessment, was substantially modified as a result of pressure from the teaching profession. Teachers, although generally sympathetic to the basic idea of a National Curriculum, resisted some of the assessment procedures, especially at Key Stage One, which went against long held and cherished views about how young pupils should be educated. Primary teachers' views about the National Curriculum and assessment at age seven are described in more detail in the following chapter by Desforges, Holden and Hughes, and also by Pollard et al. (1994).

Hence the transition from pre-ERA to post-ERA was not smooth. There were many shifts in the definition of the National Curriculum, culminating in the report by Sir Ron Dearing (Dearing, 1994), some of the implications of which we discuss later. There were also changes in assessment procedures, and in the way assessments are to be reported. Thus, not all the intended effects of the Act were necessarily going to be found when subjected to the close scrutiny that educational research can provide. It is the purpose of this chapter to report on just such a scrutiny.

Our research spotlight was directed onto the way in which Year 2 pupils, most of whom are 7 years old, spent their time at school in 1993, compared with the time assignments reported from previous research. We concentrated on the way time was assigned and used because we believe it is a good indicator of the opportunities available to pupils for learning. It is reasonable to suppose that, other things being equal, the more time pupils spend working in a particular curriculum area or subject, the more they will learn. Also, time use, both within and outwith the classroom, provides us with some evidence about the importance that teachers and schools attach to different areas of the curriculum. Hence changes in the way school time is used will tell us something about change in educational opportunities, and in teachers' and schools' priorities. This, in turn, will inform us about the effects of changes in educational policy brought about by the ERA. Of course, we recognize that time use is only one facet of young pupils' educational experiences – their interactions with their teachers and their peers, the appropriateness of the tasks assigned to them and so on – are all important. But, as in most research, we could not cover everything in one project. As well as looking at time use, we did look at curriculum coverage in maths as described in Plewis and Veltman (1994). These findings are described in Plewis and Veltman (forthcoming).

Just what sort of changes did we expect to find between the mid-1980s and mid-1990s in the amount of time spent in different school activities by pupils in Year 2? Of the three core subjects, two – English and maths – have always been the predominant activities in infant classrooms, but the third – science – has not. Clearly, with the designation of science as a core subject, we expected to find more time devoted to activities that could be labelled explicitly as science. Also, we expected to find changes within a subject or curriculum area, with perhaps more emphasis on, for example, reading within language, and on design and technology within art and craft activities. But, assuming that the length of the school day is fixed, if some activities become more prevalent, then either others become less prevalent, or else more time during the school day is devoted to classroom-based activities and less to activities such as assembly, PE and playtime.

In order to answer questions about change with any conviction, we needed a good empirical baseline with which to compare any new findings. Fortunately, we were able to draw on just such a baseline. A longitudinal study of pupils entering 33 inner-London multi-ethnic infant schools in 1982 provided data on how those pupils spent their school day when they were in Year 2 (i.e. top infants) in 1985, well before the content of the ERA was known. The design of this earlier study, the methods of data collection and the results were reported in Tizard et al. (1988). The relevant points to note for this chapter are that 90 pupils were observed in 26 schools for one full day in the spring term. In addition, we were able to draw on unpublished data collected the following year from 40 Year 2 pupils who were observed over two full days. Thus we have comparative data for 130 pupils (and 170 school days) spanning the two years 1985 and 1986. Continuous observations were made throughout the day, except at playtime, by one observer. The observer scanned all the target pupils (a maximum of four pupils) in the class, noting the activities in which they were engaged, and the times at which they changed from one activity to another. Observations were carried out on days selected by the class teacher as being predominantly classroom based. The findings are given alongside the results from the 1993 study.

The 1993 Study

The sample for the 1993 study consisted of pupils from 22 of the 33 schools in the Tizard et al. study just described (we did not have enough resources to return to all 33). Only two of the schools were infant schools, the rest were primary schools, although three of those were on split sites. Eight pupils were selected from one Year 2 class in each school. Three of these classes were mixed-age (or vertically grouped) classes. All the pupils were either white or black. (By black we mean black British children of Afro-Caribbean origin, a small proportion of whom had one white parent. By white we mean children of white parents born in the UK.) We restricted our sample to white and black pupils, mainly because the earlier study had done so to allow it to examine the relative educational progress of the two ethnic groups, and also so that we could see whether opportunities for learning, as given by time spent in different activities, were different for black and white boys and girls. Within each school, an attempt was made to select equal numbers of white and black boys and girls, but this was not always possible. Each school was visited twice and two sets of four pupils were observed, one set on each day. However, in one school, it was possible to observe only one target child on the second visit. The breakdown of the observed sample was 45 white boys, 44 white girls, 42 black boys and 42 black girls, a total of 173 pupils. The teachers were not told which pupils we were observing.

The observation method was essentially the same as in the earlier study, except that the data were collected on a palm-top computer and then downloaded to a personal computer for analysis, rather than using pencil and paper as before. The observation categories were, however, refined to take account of the new requirements imposed by the National Curriculum. Thus we explicitly coded time spent in the classroom doing science, history, geography and religious education (although the latter category was never, in fact, observed). And, within science, we had sub-categories such as energy and forces. If pupils were working on a topic, then we coded their activities according to the subject area they were actually engaged in at the time. The data were collected during the spring term in 1993.

It is important to recognize that we observed pupils rather than teachers. (Campbell et al., 1991, studied teachers' use of time since the introduction of the National Curriculum at Key Stage One.) The way a teacher assigns his or her time to different curriculum areas is not necessarily the same as that experienced by the average pupil. For example, a teacher could, in principle, spend nearly all day hearing individual pupils read, whereas most pupils could be doing maths worksheets for most of the day. Also, we did not attempt to code whether pupils were actually 'on task' when engaged in a curriculum area, only that they had either been assigned, or had chosen for themselves, a task in that particular area.

In addition to our observation data, we interviewed the classroom teachers and the heads of our sample schools at the end of the summer term. These were relatively unstructured interviews, using open-ended questions, but they were focused on teachers' and heads' perceptions of change over the previous decade. However, we did not ask directly about time use. We draw on the data from these interviews in the final section of this chapter.

Results

First, to emphasize a point we made earlier: we were interested in *changes* in pupils' time assignments over the period from 1985–6 to 1993. Thus we do not describe the 1993 position in great detail. Table 1.1 summarizes our most important findings.

First we consider the length and balance of the school day. We see from table 1.1 that, averaging across schools, 69 per cent of the school day was, in principle, available for teaching, with 29 per cent devoted to breaks and dinner time and 2 per cent to registration and collecting dinner money. (In practice,

Table 1.1 Proportion of time spent in different activities

Working time in class	% School day		% Working time in class	
	1985–6	*1993*	*1985–6*	*1993*
Writing	9	8	20	20
Oral language	9	7	19	18
Maths	8	7	17	16
Art/craft/construction etc.	10	4	21	9
Reading	3	3	6	8
Science	} 1	2	} 2	4
History		1		2
Geography		1		2
Being allocated activities	2	6	4	15
Permitted 'free' play	1	1	2	2
Miscellaneous	4	2	9	6
Total	47	42	100	100
Other work time				
Music/PE/rehearsals etc.	4	8		
Assembly	3	7		
TV etc.	1	1		
Other out-of-class work	2	4		
Total	11	20		
Non-work activities				
Outside play/dinner time	28	29		
Lining up/tidying up etc.	6	5		
Toilet visits/errands etc.	4	1		
Register/dinner money etc.	3	2		
Other	3	2		
Total	43	38		

of course, time is also needed for procedural activities such as tidying up.) The mean length of the teaching day in our sample was about four hours 25 minutes. This figure is somewhat higher than the minimum of four hours 12 minutes recommended by the Department of Education in circular 7/90 on the management of the school day. However, the recommended length (called 'lesson time' in the circular) excludes time devoted to acts of collective worship, whereas our figure includes the time given to assemblies. The circular is, in fact, rather ambiguous about the position of assembly in the taught day; we chose to include assembly in our figure because it is often an occasion for other collective activities, such as presenting pupils' work, as well as for worship.

In terms of balance of the day, we found a shift away from both working time in the classroom, and from non-work activities such as lining up, towards what we call other work time – activities like assembly and PE. In 1985–6, pupils were engaged in work four times as much in the classroom as they were out of it; in 1993 the ratio was only two to one. Certainly, assembly and, to a lesser extent, rehearsals for assembly absorbed a good deal more time in 1993 than they had in 1985–6; assembly was observed on both days in 19 of the schools, and on one day in the other three, and lasted from ten to over 40 minutes, with a mean length of 28 minutes. Also, there was more 'other out-of-class' work, more than a third of which was infant story time, a collective activity not seen in 1985–6.

Turning now to the assignment of time to different curriculum areas within the classroom, we see from table 1.1 a good deal of consistency between the observation years for writing, for oral language, for maths and for reading. The 3Rs of writing, maths and reading (rows one, three and five of table 1.1) accounted for 44 per cent of classroom time and 19 per cent of the school day in 1993, the corresponding percentages being 43 and 20 in 1985–6. On the other hand, there are some marked differences too. Much less time was being spent on art, craft and construction activities – down from over 20 per cent in 1985–6 to less than 10 per cent of classroom time in 1993. However, more time was being devoted to science (4 per cent) and, to a lesser extent, history and geography; these activities accounted for 8 per cent of classroom time altogether in 1993, having been rarely observed in 1985–6. Within science, over a third of the time was assigned to electricity and magnetism, with 'life and living processes' (such as growing beans) accounting for a further 16 per cent.

Another substantial difference is in the category 'being allocated activities', which was much higher in 1993 than it was in 1985–6. This category refers to occasions when pupils are sitting on the carpet and the teacher is explaining the task – in maths, language or whatever – to be done that session. It specifically refers to situations when a task is being allocated and *not* to instruction related to that task. However, the distinction between allocation and whole-class or group instruction is not always easy to make, and it is possible that we have overestimated 'allocation' at the expense of some areas of the curriculum. We discuss this issue later in the context of classroom organization. For now, we show what the distribution of classroom time looks like if we reassign 'allocation' to subjects. This was not difficult to do because we coded allocation in terms of maths, language and other activities, and we could make reasonable assumptions about the smaller amount of allocation observed and coded in 1985–6. Table 1.2 gives the adjusted results. Most of our conclusions are unaffected by this adjustment. However, the proportion of working time in class devoted to the 3Rs rose in 1993 to 54 per cent from 45

Table 1.2 Proportion of classroom time spent in different activities after reassigning 'allocation'

Working time in class	% Working time in class	
	1985–6	*1993*
Writing	21	26
Oral language	19	18
Maths	19	21
Art/craft/construction	21	11
Reading	6	8
Science		5
History	3	2
Geography		2
Permitted 'free' play	2	2
Miscellaneous	9	6
Total	100	100

per cent in 1985–6, although the corresponding proportions of the *school day* (not shown in table 1.2) are closer: 23 per cent and 21 per cent.

Up to this point, we have shown that there were some changes in Year 2 pupils' use of time at school between 1985–6 and 1993, but that there was a lot of consistency over the period as well. Now we look more closely at particular areas of the curriculum – maths, language etc. – to see whether the balance changed within those areas. For example, although the percentage of time assigned to maths work appeared not to have changed over the period in question, it is possible that more maths time was being devoted to number work. In fact, this was not so; for both years, the maths time was roughly equally divided between number and other maths work. However, within other maths work, there was a shift away from tasks involving time (14 per cent of all maths tasks in 1985; 1 per cent of maths time in 1993) to tasks involving area and volume (4 per cent of all maths tasks in 1985; 25 per cent of all maths time in 1993). This perhaps reflected the topics that teachers expected to be covered by the SATs in the Summer term. (In the event, many of our sample schools boycotted either the administration or the reporting of the SATs.)

One of the most striking findings from the 1985 observations was how little time pupils read, either to their teacher or to any other adult in class – about eight minutes a week on average. Although the amount of time devoted to reading in 1993 was a little higher than it was in 1985–6, all this increase was accounted for by an increase in pupils reading to themselves. Again, we found that Year 2 pupils read aloud to an adult in class for eight minutes a week. (It is possible that some reading at school took place outside the class, which we were unable to observe.)

Turning to writing, we found a shift away from descriptive writing (topic and 'news' writing) towards creative writing (writing stories) compared with 1985. There was about twice as much descriptive writing as creative writing in 1985, whereas, in 1993, 39 per cent of all writing was creative and 25 per cent was descriptive (the rest was comprehension, work cards etc.). Finally, within those activities called art, craft and construction, about half of the time was spent drawing, crayoning and tracing, just as were half the tasks in 1985. Certainly, there was no evidence of a shift towards activities of a more technological nature over the period.

Up to now, we have broken down pupils' activities into essentially the same categories that were used in the Tizard et al. study in order to be able to make comparisons over time. However, these categories do not correspond directly with the subjects set out in the National Curriculum. We could, however, rearrange our 1993 data to fit more closely with the National Curriculum. Thus we combined writing, reading and oral language to form an English category, we separated music and PE, and we based our percentages on all the time spent in work, but excluding time in assembly and rehearsing for assembly. Altogether this amounted to about 54 per cent of the school day (see table 1.1).

This reorganization of our data enabled us to compare our results with those obtained by Pollard et al. (1994) in their study of primary schools, known as PACE. The two studies are not directly comparable: Pollard et al. observed in nine Year 2 classes scattered across the country, two of which were in Catholic primary schools (there were no church schools in our sample); there were six target pupils per class; and their observations were carried out over three days during the Autumn term of 1991. (The PACE team also observed in nine Year 1 classrooms.) Also, the systematic observation method used in PACE was somewhat different from ours. These differences in method must be borne in mind when looking at table 1.3, which gives results from the two studies. There are some differences – Pollard et al. found more religious education and science, we found more English, music and PE. But the similarities outweigh the differences and increase the confidence we have in our results.

We found that the core subjects of English, maths and science accounted for 58 per cent of work time. This figure is in the middle of the range found in an official study of Key Stage One classrooms in 55 primary schools in 1993–4 (OFSTED, 1994). We also found that English dominated the time devoted to the core subjects just as it had in 1985–6, that the foundation subjects accounted for 24 per cent of time, and so the National Curriculum as a whole

Table 1.3 Proportion of work time spent in National Curriculum activities

National Curriculum activity	% Work time	
	Plewis and Veltman	Pollard et al.
English	38	32
Maths	16	15
Science	4	10
History	2	1
Geography	1	1
Art	} 9	5
Technology		5
Music	6	4
PE	6	3
Religious education	–	5
Other, curriculum	6	7
Other, non-curriculum	12	13
Total	100	100

The figures for Pollard et al. are based on their table 7.10. Because they categorized their observations by 'main' and 'part' curriculum, these two categories were combined in the ratio 3:1 and rescaled to 100 per cent.

accounted for over 80 per cent of work time. We return to the implications of these results later.

Finally, we come to the issue of equal opportunities – did time assignments vary between boys and girls, between black and white pupils, and between the four ethnic group and sex combinations? This is not an easy issue to judge; certainly there were some differences, but they could have arisen by chance, given the relatively small group sizes. Our criterion for deciding whether or not the group differences were due to chance was based on the extent to which any difference was found consistently across the 22 schools. Using this criterion, the only marked difference we found was for maths: white pupils spent more time doing maths than black pupils. Excluding allocation to maths, we found white pupils spent 19 per cent of working time in class doing maths, compared with 15 per cent for black pupils. We found white pupils doing more maths in 14 out of 19 schools; no maths was observed in two schools, and one school had no white pupils eligible for our sample. (Technically, the difference was statistically significant at the 0.05 level, as judged by a Wilcoxon signed rank test.)

Discussion

There is enough evidence in the previous section to lead us to the conclusion that the school day of Year 2 pupils was not quite the same in 1993 as it was a decade or so earlier. The differences are not dramatic but they are, we believe, real. They can be summarized as follows. More of the school day was devoted to work, especially to work outside the class, and less to administrative and procedural activities, although the periods for outside play and dinner time did not change. Seven-year-olds were doing more science at school, but they were spending much less time on art, craft and construction. However, time devoted to the basics, or 3Rs, did not fall. White pupils continued to spend a little more time on maths than black pupils. We now reflect on these changes, on whether they were predictable, and on what they mean for education at Key Stage One. We also consider how far the observed changes were congruent with teachers' perceptions of change, and we look at the 1993 position alongside contemporary official statements about the curriculum. We end with some brief comments about our methods.

It does seem that school days for 7-year-olds became rather more 'academic', and a little more structured by 1993, compared with what they were in the mid-1980s. Not that substantially more time was being devoted to the basics (although neither did it fall, as suggested and feared by some commentators). But we did find much less time given to art, with only 9 per cent of working time in class devoted to art, craft and construction, and probably half of this being activities of a technological, rather than of an aesthetic, nature. In 1985–6, more time was given to art and associated activities than to any other activity. However, the figure of 9 per cent does not account for all the time pupils were engaged in those kinds of activities because, for example, they would sometimes have been drawing as part of a story (coded as writing) or drawing a flower as part of science. (This was also true in 1985–6.) This move to a more academic school day is not, however, supported by all our data. Thus we found the time given to music and PE, rather than falling, seemed to be a little higher. Also, within writing, there was more, rather than less, emphasis on creative writing. The changes that we observed were certainly not so marked as to support the idea that the introduction of the National Curriculum has had a 'Gradgrind' effect on pupils' school experiences.

Our evidence on structure comes from the finding that, whereas the time given to permitted free play did not change, and was still very small (2 per cent of working time in class), there was a fall in the time spent lining up, running errands and in other miscellaneous activities – down from 19 per cent of the school day to 12 per cent (table 1.1). However, we did not find, as we thought we might, a reduction in the time allowed for outside play and dinner time. This contrasts with the Office for Standards in Education finding that 80 per cent of all schools they inspected had increased lesson time since 1989 (OFSTED, 1994). They do not, however, give a figure for Key Stage One.

Our result on the small and unchanged amount of time pupils spent reading aloud to an adult in class needs to be seen in the context of the concern about reading standards expressed by, for example, Turner (1990) and investigated by the House of Commons Education, Science and Arts Committee in 1991. If reading aloud to an adult is the most effective way of teaching a child to read, then the introduction of the National Curriculum is unlikely, by itself, to raise reading standards. However, it is worth bearing in mind that Plewis et al. (1990) found, for a sample very similar to the one studied here, that 6-year-olds read aloud twice as much at home as they do at school. Hence strengthening home–school links might be a more effective way of raising reading standards than trying to find more time within a crowded school day for hearing pupils read.

How far is this interpretation of our data about the changing nature of the school day supported by heads' and teachers' perceptions? In our sample, all the relevant comments were in that direction – less time for cooking, for choosing in the home corner, for PE and for playtime – together with a recognition that time was precious. As one teacher put it:

> We have to be really tight on getting up and down for assembly to make sure we fill up our time properly.

Interviews with a larger sample of 80 teachers in the PACE project gave a similar picture. They believed less time was spent on art, which our data support, but also on music and, to a lesser extent, on PE, which we did not find. The PACE researchers also reported teachers believing they did less creative writing with their pupils, which, again, we did not find. However, these perceptions about writing may be related to perceptions about choice; we do not know whether pupils had more or less choice about the topics they could write about. Neither do we know whether the more 'academic' school regime led to a reduction in pupils' enjoyment of school. However, a theme that emerged from our study, as well as from PACE and from Campbell et al.'s study of teacher time, is that teachers and heads thought that teaching infant pupils was a less inspirational and joyful activity than it used to be. To quote another of our Year 2 teachers:

> There's just less time now. I mean, we used to do some exciting things, but now there's less time.

One reason for the reduction in teachers' enjoyment could be that teachers saw less opportunity for an integrated day, and for topic work. Our observation data do not bear on this issue, because we coded activities in both studies in terms of subjects, but it was a trend mentioned by many of our teachers and heads. As two heads put it:

> When I was teaching, 90 per cent of my teaching was done on topic-based work . . . Now there is much more pressure to move into discrete subject areas.

and

> I think that the integrated day, all the things that were recommended by the Plowden report – well, there just isn't the time for that now.

But not all heads saw things that way:

> In a sense, the idea of an infant integrated day still carries on because we still fit the National Curriculum into topics.

A second change that emerged from our data relates to the organization of the school day. We found, rather surprisingly, that pupils spent more of their learning time in school out of the classroom in 1993 than they had in 1985–6. There seem to be two reasons for this. The first is that assembly took more time than it did in the mid-1980s. This, in turn, is probably explained by the fact that religious education in schools has been given more official attention since the introduction of the National Curriculum, although it is not a foundation subject. In our inner-city, and hence multicultural and multifaith, schools, the response to this attention appeared to have been to deal with religious education in assembly rather than in the classroom, where it was never observed during our visits. The second reason is that pupils were doing more out-of-class work, which could be accounted for by the fact that some of our Year 2 teachers were given some non-contact time for record keeping and assessment.

The other evidence we have on the way the day was organized comes from our 'being allocated activities' code, the problematic nature of which was raised earlier. Although the increase in 'allocation' could be artefactual, we believe it could reflect changes in classroom organization. First, the PACE research suggests an increase in the extent to which teachers determined which tasks a pupil should do, rather than the pupil deciding for themselves, which would imply that more time was needed for allocation. Second, PACE found that pupils were involved in 'whole-class interaction' for 36 per cent of their classroom time, whereas Year 2 pupils in the Tizard et al. (1988)

Table 1.4 Work time in National Curriculum activities: comparisons with Dearing

| | Minutes per day | |
National Curriculum activity	Plewis and Veltman	Dearing
English	79	60
Maths	34	42
Science	9	18
History	3	12
Geography	3	12
Art	} 18	12
Technology		12
Music	12	12
PE	13	12
Religious education	14	12
Total	185	204

1 Dearing also recommends that 12 minutes English per day is taught through other subjects.

2 Our data on religious education are estimated by assuming that half assembly time is devoted to RE.

research were in teacher-led situations for only 26 per cent of the time. Moreover, the PACE sample teachers believed that whole-class interaction had increased, although this was not a trend often remarked on in our teacher interviews.

A third important issue when thinking about change concerns the move to a more scientific and technological curriculum. To some extent, this was inevitable once science became a core subject. If we define the scientific curriculum as science, technology and maths, then we found about one-quarter of working time in class could be classified as scientific. But most of this is, of course, maths – we estimated that pupils spent four times as much time doing maths as they did science. So, although pupils were doing more science in 1993 than they were in 1985–6, science was very much the poor relation within the core curriculum.

This discussion of the relative amounts of time given to maths and science brings us rather naturally to a discussion of the 1994 Dearing report, where, for the first time, concrete proposals were made about time use. In table 1.4, we compare the time allocated to the National Curriculum subjects in our study with those put forward by Dearing for Key Stage One. (For convenience, the figures are given as minutes per day; this is an average figure, not a prescription for *each* day.) A number of points emerge from this comparison. First, Dearing appeared to underestimate the amount of time taken by miscellaneous administrative and procedural activities – about 8 per cent of the school day in our sample (excluding registration – see table 1.1). Although his putative official day, or lesson time, is a little shorter than we actually found – 252 minutes as opposed to our 263 minutes – his recommended time allocations take up 204 minutes, whereas ours used only 185 minutes. Thus it may be difficult for teachers to meet Dearing's time allocations, and to restrict the work on National Curriculum subjects to 80 per cent of teaching time, as he suggests. Second, following the Dearing recommendations would mean less time being given to English, and more to maths and science within the core curriculum, although the total time devoted to the three core subjects would stay the same at two hours per day. Third, a little more time would be given to the six foundation subjects, especially history and geography, which we observed so rarely. Finally, Dearing recommended that nine minutes a day are taken up by information technology within other subjects; this would represent a considerable increase over our observation of less than two minutes a day for all computer work.

We now turn to the issue of equal opportunities. On the whole, our data are reassuring on this issue; pupils from our four sex and ethnic groups appeared to spend their school day in essentially the same way. The one exception to this is in maths, where white pupils spent more time than black (Afro-Caribbean) pupils. There are a number of possible explanations for this difference; it could be that teachers were assigning more maths tasks to white pupils than they were to black; it could be that white pupils might have chosen maths more often than black pupils; or it could be that white pupils took longer than black pupils to complete their maths work. More research is needed properly to understand this difference, but there is no reason to suppose that it emerged after the ERA, as a difference of the same magnitude was found by Tizard et al. It is, however, a worrying difference when we consider that Plewis (1991) showed that the maths attainment of black pupils, especially black boys, fell further and further behind that of white pupils over the primary school period.

We end this chapter with a few comments about our sample and our methods, and how they might have affected our results, especially our inferences about change. There was considerable overlap between the schools in our sample and the schools observed in the earlier studies, but, of course, the schools had experienced many changes in personnel over the intervening period, and the characteristics of their catchment areas might also have changed. Also, although observation took place during the Spring term in both studies, the rhythm of the school year has changed since the ERA, affected as it now is by the need to conduct the SATs in the Summer term. Hence it is possible that, if we had observed over all three terms in each study, the observed differences would have been smaller. Also, our results can only be generalized to multi-ethnic schools in London. On the other hand, the changes we have highlighted are substantial and are likely to be genuine.

Finally, we must remember that the ERA was not an intervention introduced as a scientific experiment – we cannot necessarily attribute change in time use to the introduction of the National Curriculum. Change might have happened anyway, or it might have happened as a result of other changes in the education system such as local management of schools (LMS). In the end, soundly based conclusions about the effects of the ERA on education in infant schools, and elsewhere, will come, not from just one study, but from a series of studies on the same theme. And, if there is real interest in monitoring what is happening in the education system, as we believe there should be, particularly at a time when there are so many changes in government policy, we need a continuing programme of research to try to unravel the effects of these policy changes.

2

Parents, Teachers and the Assessment of 7-year-olds

*Charles Desforges, Cathie Holden
and Martin Hughes*

Editor's Introduction

The next chapter, by Charles Desforges, Cathie Holden and Martin Hughes, continues our concern with the reforms at Key Stage One, and with how the reforms are perceived by those most directly affected by them. The chapter focuses on the standardized assessment procedures introduced for 7-year-olds, and in particular, on the argument that standardized assessment will help to raise standards by providing valuable information for parents. Desforges, Holden and Hughes present findings from a study in which interviews were carried out with the parents and teachers of over 120 children about to undergo SATs at Key Stage One. While the parents were mostly satisfied with their own child's school, they expressed concerns about standards in primary education more generally. Most parents wanted to know more about their children's progress, but were divided as to whether formal assessment was necessary for this purpose. The teachers, for their part, underestimated parents' interest in and support for assessment. The authors conclude that most parents would value a relationship with schools that offered them both information and involvement, and they provide examples of schools that are attempting to do this.

Introduction

The introduction of standardized assessment for all children aged 7, 11 and 14 years has become one of the most controversial aspects of the current educational reforms. It has been vigorously promoted by politicians and policy-makers on the grounds that it is an essential part of raising educational standards. For example, John MacGregor, then Secretary of State for Education, wrote in 1990 that:

> If people do not grasp the power of assessment – when properly integrated with the curriculum – to raise standards, then they are missing half the point of the National Curriculum ... A National Curriculum without assessment would have been lop-sided and incomplete. It would have lacked the dynamism – the potential to lever up standards – that assessment provides. (DES, 1990b)

The arguments put forward by the government to support standardized assessment have fallen into two main categories. First, it has been argued that assessment will raise standards by providing *teachers* with new information about the children in their classes (e.g. DES, 1990b, p. 12). In other words, it is argued that standardized assessment will provide teachers with more detailed information about children's strengths and weaknesses, and in particular, how these relate to the statements of attainment embodied in the National Curriculum. As a result, their teaching can be better tuned to the needs and capabilities of individual children.

The second main argument is that assessment will help to raise educational standards by providing information for *parents*. This information can take two different forms. On the one hand, standardized assessment can provide parents with more detailed information about their *own child's progress*, and in particular about how their child is performing in relation to agreed national standards (e.g. DES, 1991f, p. 2). This means that parents can, if necessary, provide appropriate help at home that is sensitive to their child's particular strengths and weaknesses. At the same time, standardized assessment means that information can also be provided about the performance of *individual schools*, through the publication of aggregated assessment results in the form of local or national 'league tables' (e.g. *The Parent's Charter*: DES, 1991e, 1994). The mechanism through which this kind of information is expected to raise standards is through the exercise of parental choice (enhanced by the commitment to open enrolment in the 1988 Education Reform Act) and by relating school budgets directly to pupil numbers (through the introduction of Local Management of Schools, or LMS). Schools, it is assumed, will thus be sensitized to parents' wishes for higher standards, and will endeavour to provide these for their pupils.

The response of the teaching profession to the introduction of standardized assessment has generally been less than enthusiastic. In particular, criticism has focused on the use and form of standard assessment tests (SATs), and on the publication of aggregated results in the form of league tables. According to surveys carried out by the National Union of Teachers in 1991 and 1992, teachers who administered SATs at Key Stage One reported that the SATs had been unduly time-consuming, that normal teaching had been disrupted, and that the results told them little they did not already know. In 1993 the SATs were due to be introduced at Key Stage Three (14 years), but a massive boycott by teachers ensured that very little assessment actually took place. In some schools, teachers used SATs to obtain information about their pupils, but refused to pass on the results for publication in league tables. Partly in response to this action, the government decided to abandon the publication of league tables at Key Stage One, and the 1994 Dearing review advocated the use of 'short, written tests', to be set and marked by external assessors. However, at the time of writing (early 1995), the precise future of standardized assessment in England and Wales remains unclear.

In view of the importance of the issue, one might expect the debate on the role and value of standardized assessment to be well informed by evidence. But in fact, there are relatively few empirical studies of the effect of assessment policies on classroom practice (see reviews by Ellwein et al., 1988; Desforges, 1989). The impact, or more accurately the presumed impact, of standardized assessment on the quality of teaching and learning is frequently debated more in terms of slogans and rhetoric than it is in terms of evidence (Desforges, 1992). Our overall aim in this chapter is therefore to contribute some empirical evidence on the issue.

Our particular focus in the chapter will be on the views of *parents*. As we indicated above, the introduction of standardized assessment has been justified – at least in part – on the grounds that it will raise standards by providing parents with information about their own child's progress and about the performance of individual schools. However, as we have argued in more detail elsewhere (Desforges et al., 1994a; Hughes et al., 1994), this argument is based on a number of assumptions about parents that are not necessarily supported by the available evidence. As with the issue of assessment, there is a clear need for empirical evidence on parents' views to inform current debate.

In this chapter, we focus on four main areas. First, we look at parents' views concerning *standards* in schools. We are interested in whether parents are satisfied with the standards that prevail at their own child's school, whether they are happy with standards more generally, and how they think standards might be improved. Next, we focus specifically on *assessment*: we ask what value parents place on standardized assessment for their children, and whether they feel that assessment can play a central role in raising educational standards. Following this, we look at the extent to which *teachers* are aware of parents' views; our interest is based on the assumption that if schools are to be responsive to parents' views, then they must at least be aware of what those views are. Finally, we consider ways in which schools might *work more closely* with parents in these areas, and describe three schools that are attempting to do just this.

The Study

The evidence we will use to answer these questions comes from a study in which we followed two cohorts of 7–year-old children through the standard-ized assessment procedures in 1991 and 1992. These were the first two years in which standardized assessment was undertaken for all 7–year-olds in England and Wales. Each cohort consisted of around 120 children drawn from 20 schools in London, Bristol and the South West of England. The schools varied on factors such as size, urban/rural and ethnic composition. Six children (three boys, three girls) from a Year 2 class within each school were selected for the study. Each group of six children contained two high-attainers, two medium-attainers and two low-attainers.

The children's parents and their teachers were interviewed individually on two occasions: in the Spring term before the introduction of standard assessment tests (SATs), and in the Summer term after the teachers had reported the SAT results to parents. The parents were interviewed in their homes, while the teachers were interviewed at their schools. The interviews covered a wide range of issues to do with teaching, learning and assessment. All interviews were tape-recorded, and the responses were subsequently coded into categories derived from the data.

In this chapter we will draw on the initial parent and teacher interviews from the 1992 cohort. Findings from the 1991 cohort can be found in Holden et al. (1993) and Desforges et al. (1994b), while a more detailed account of the 1992 findings can be found in Desforges et al. (1994a).

Parents' Satisfaction with Schools

The great majority of parents were evidently satisfied with their children's schools; 88 per cent of parents said they were either 'happy' or 'happy with reservations', and only 6 per cent of parents said they were 'not happy'. Such findings, it should be noted, are by no means exceptional. We found similar levels of parental satisfaction in our 1991 cohort (Holden et al., 1993), and similar findings have also been reported in other studies carried out both before and after the introduction of the current reforms (e.g. Tizard et al., 1988; Mortimore et al., 1988; Public Attitude Surveys, 1989; West et al., 1992; Hughes et al., 1994). Overall, these findings do not suggest widespread parental dissatisfaction with their children's schools: rather, they indicate an enduring sense of satisfaction with the education their children are receiving.

When asked which features they were most happy with, parents tended to emphasize the social and emotional aspects of school life. They frequently referred to features such as whether the school had a friendly atmosphere, whether the teachers seemed caring, whether there were good home–school relationships, and whether their child was happy. There was a similar focus on non-academic criteria when parents were asked which features they were least happy with; they were more likely to mention physical defects of the school (such as the state of the grounds and buildings) or lack of supervision in the playground than they were to criticize teaching methods or standards.

The importance attached to non-academic factors can be illustrated by the following two parents. The first parent had two children at the school. She had chosen it because it was small and friendly, and the head seemed to know every child by name:

> Yes, I'm happy. I like the way everyone cares about the children – even the dinner ladies. The teachers are very friendly towards parents, and the children are happy. It's a good environment.

The second parent, in contrast, was less happy. She was concerned about teaching methods, discipline, lack of supervision in the playground, and headlice. However, her underlying concern with her child's happiness emerges clearly from the following comment:

> Basically, once they turn five, you're handing them over. Once they walk through that door, they're the teachers' responsibility for the day. You want to know they're taken care of as well as educated. A happy child equals a happy education!

Parents and Standards

The parents were asked a number of questions about standards in education. They were asked what they thought about the standards that prevailed at their own child's school, and what they based this judgement on. They were also asked whether standards in primary schools generally were rising, falling or staying the same, and what they thought might be done to improve standards.

The results showed a distinct contrast between parents' views on standards in their own child's school and parents' views on standards more generally. Thus the great majority of parents were happy with the academic standards that prevailed in their own child's school. Over 70 per cent of parents thought that standards were 'good overall' or 'good in parts', while only 9 per cent thought that standards were 'poor'. In contrast, parents were less happy about standards in primary education more generally. When asked whether standards generally were rising or falling, the most frequent answer (given by 37 per cent of parents) was that standards were falling. Only a fifth of the parents (20 per cent) felt that standards were rising; the remainder said either that standards were staying the same (22 per cent), or that they did not know (14 per cent).

Why were parents more concerned about standards in the country as a whole than about standards at their own child's school? The most likely explanation is that parents were drawing on different sources of information when answering these questions. Thus when asked about their own child's school, parents were drawing primarily on their direct experience of how their own children were progressing. Those parents who had regular access to the school (for example, those who went in to hear children read) could also draw on their experience of working with other children at the school. In contrast, when asked about standards more widely, the parents appeared to be drawing on other areas of experience as well – such as the media, their own educational experiences, or in some cases their experiences as employers. As the following examples show, parents were particularly likely to mention these sources if they considered that standards were falling:

When I was at junior school myself, I was learning French at her age. The teachers made you work harder.

I was horrified to hear [in the media] that 7-year-olds can't read. But it's not just the school's fault – they haven't got time for one-to-one.

We employ teenage girls. Things like their spelling and maths are astonishingly poor. Even very simple things.

Such views, however, were not universal. Some parents commented that things had improved since their schooldays, or that they couldn't remember what they had been taught at particular ages. Other parents said that they did not necessarily believe what they read in the papers, or commented on the discrepancy between what they were told about standards more generally and what they knew about their own child's school:

The media implies that they're not learning anything. I can only judge from what I see here and I think the standard is pretty high. The approach is better than when we were at school. Children are encouraged to learn and find out for themselves and discuss things – it's not just talk and chalk.

When asked what could be done to improve standards, parents favoured additional resources rather than changes in teaching methods. The most frequently mentioned remedies were for smaller classes, more teachers and classroom assistants, more equipment and more money spent on schools. In contrast, there were fewer calls for a return to traditional methods or for more attention to the basics.

Parents' Knowledge about School

While parents were generally happy with their children's schools, there was one area where they were less than fully satisfied. Nearly two-thirds of the parents (64 per cent) felt they did not know enough about what was happening to their child in school, compared with just over a third (36 per cent) who did. In particular, parents wanted to know more about the curriculum, about their child's daily routine, about the teaching methods used and about their child's progress. They also wanted to know more about their child's strengths and weaknesses so they could provide help where necessary at home. In some cases, it seemed, the communication of such information was left very much to chance:

> *What would you like to know more about?*
> Everything! A teacher who is not my daughter's teacher came up to me and said she was giving her extra help with reading and writing, and that it would help if I gave her more encouragement at home. I was amazed! It was the first I knew about it. I didn't know she had a problem with her writing. A definite lack of communication.

Our finding that a substantial number of parents did not feel well enough informed about their children's progress is by no means new. Similar findings have been reported in a range of other studies, carried out both before and after the introduction of the current reforms (e.g. Munn, 1985; MacBeath and Weir, 1991; Hughes et al., 1994). As we shall see in the next section, this finding is particularly relevant to understanding their views on assessment.

Parents' Knowledge about Assessment

During the period leading up to our interviews, parents had been the intended recipients of a large amount of information and opinion on the subject of assessment. The major source of information was the government, which had attempted to inform parents about various aspects of the current reforms through a series of nationally distributed pamphlets and leaflets. Many schools had also attempted to inform parents about the assessment procedures, using methods such as meetings, letters and handouts. In addition, the media regularly reported the views of politicians and teachers' leaders on assessment and other topics, and gave considerable coverage to individual parents who were considering withdrawing their children from the SATs.

In order to find out what effect this information had been having, we asked the parents how much they knew about the forthcoming assessment procedures, and whether they wanted to know more. Despite the large amount of information that was potentially available, the parents appeared to know very little about how their children were to be assessed. Over half the parents (57 per cent) were considered to have 'very little' knowledge about the assessments, while a further third (36 per cent) had only 'partial' knowledge. Less than one in ten of the parents were considered to have any 'detailed' knowledge of what was involved. Despite the apparent efforts of many schools to inform parents about assessment, nearly half the parents (47 per cent) said that the school had told them nothing at all about what was happening.

This lack of apparent knowledge among parents did not, however, seem to reflect an underlying lack of interest in the topic. When asked if they would like to know more about the assessments, virtually all the parents said that they would. Their main request was for more information about how the assessments would be carried out, although some parents wanted to know more about what would happen to the results. For many parents, their desire to know more was explicitly linked to a desire to help their child through what might be a difficult time:

> Yes, I'd like to know more. I'd like to prepare him for it. I don't agree with it, but if he's got to be tested I'd like to make it as painless as possible for him.

Parents' Attitudes towards Assessment

The parents were asked whether they thought that the formal assessment of 7-year-olds was a good idea, and whether they would like to be involved themselves in the assessment process. Despite their limited knowledge of the assessment procedures, all the parents were prepared to offer an opinion on whether the formal assessment of young children was a good idea. Just under half of the parents (49 per cent) either approved of assessment or approved with some reservations, while just over a third (38 per cent) did not approve; the remaining parents (13 per cent) were considered to have mixed feelings. The main arguments put forward in support of assessment were that it would help in the early diagnosis of children's strengths and weaknesses, and that it would provide useful information about children's progress for parents and teachers. The following comment was typical of many:

> I'm in favour of some testing to see how well children are doing and to sort out problems earlier. Otherwise children can slip by and be missed. It's beneficial for the teacher and the pupil.

Those parents who were opposed to formal assessment were not actually opposed to the early diagnosis of children's weaknesses or to receiving useful information. Rather, their opposition stemmed from the view that such information could be provided without the need for a formal system of assessment. Thus the main arguments raised against assessment were that continuous assessment was more appropriate for children of this age, that assessment might put too much pressure on children or label them failures, and that assessment was a waste of teachers' time. As one parent put it:

> The teachers know how a child is developing, and they should be able to feed that to parents without the child having to sit tests.

A common factor underlying most parents' views on assessment, then, was that they wanted more information about how their children were getting on at school. Where they differed was that some parents felt this information would not be provided unless a formal assessment system was in place, while other parents felt that such a system was unnecessary and even counterproductive.

The parents' desire to help their children also emerged when they were asked if they would like to participate in any way in the assessment process. We had expected that most parents would simply want to be passive recipients of assessment information, and were somewhat surprised when nearly half the parents (43 per cent) said they would like to be actively involved in some way. These parents had different ideas about how this might happen. Some parents thought they could work towards the assessments with their child at home, others thought they could contribute their knowledge of the child's ability, while others again thought they could actually assess their child at home. Several of the parents' comments indicated that they felt they had some particular knowledge or perspective concerning their child that would be relevant to the assessments, and that this should be taken into account:

> I would like the teacher to ask my opinion about his reading and writing, because we do a lot of it at home.

> I could help with the reading – I can understand what he's saying when some people don't.

These parents, it would seem, saw the forthcoming assessments as a valuable opportunity to get directly involved in helping their children learn.

Teachers' Perceptions of Parents

How do teachers see parents? In order to explore this issue, the teachers in this study were asked a number of questions about the views and opinions of their parents. Specifically, they were asked how much the parents knew about assessment and whether the parents wanted to know more. They were also asked whether their parents were in favour of the formal assessment of children at this age, and whether they thought that parents wanted to be involved in the assessment process. Finally, the teachers were asked if they themselves were in favour of assessment. The results are summarized in table 2.1.

The teachers accurately judged that the parents were not very knowledgeable about the assessments. When asked how much parents in general knew about assessment, almost all the teachers (19 out of 22) replied that parents knew 'very little'. One teacher commented:

> We send information home as it comes out, but it doesn't mean a great deal to them. One parent thought her son had to pass the 7+ tests before he could go up to juniors. They're very mixed up.

In contrast, the teachers seriously underestimated the extent of parents' interest in the issue. While almost all the parents said they wanted to know more about

Table 2.1 Comparison of parents' and teachers' views

Topic	Parents' views	Teachers' views
Parents' knowledge about assessment	57% of parents had 'little knowledge'	86% of teachers thought parents had 'little knowledge'
Parents desire to know more about assessment	90% of parents 'wanted to know more'	18% of teachers thought parents 'wanted to know more'
Parents' attitudes to formal assessement	49% of parents 'in favour' of assessment	23% of teachers thought parents 'in favour' of assessment
Parents' desire to be involved in assessment	43% of parents 'wanted to be involved'	18% of teachers thought parents 'wanted to be involved'

assessment, only four teachers thought this would be the case. Several teachers made explicit reference to what they saw as parents' lack of interest in the subject. One teacher, for example, remarked that:

I don't think they think about it very much at all.

Another teacher, however, thought the issue was more complex than just a lack of parental interest:

They're very interested in what the children actually do, but they haven't shown any interest in the actual assessment procedure or SATs. I don't think, deep down, that they're uninterested. I think there's some barrier there at the moment, some reason why they don't come in to find out more. And we don't push it, because we don't want to get them wound up about the tests.

As well as underestimating parents' interest in assessment, the teachers also underestimated parents' support for assessment (see table 2.1). Less than a quarter of the teachers (23 per cent) thought that parents were in favour of formal assessment, while virtually half the parents (49 per cent) were actually in favour. In particular, the teachers seemed unaware of the value that parents placed on assessment as a means of diagnosing children's strengths and weaknesses. Only one teacher thought that parents would support assessment for this reason, yet it was mentioned by nearly a third of the parents.

One possible reason for the teachers' underestimating parents' support for assessment is that the teachers themselves were predominantly opposed to assessment. Over two-thirds of the teachers (68 per cent) thought that the formal assessment of 7-year-olds 'was not a good idea', and not a single teacher was prepared to say unreservedly that it 'was a good idea'. The main arguments that the teachers raised against assessment were that it had damaging effects on children; that it served no useful purpose; and that continuous assessment was more appropriate at this age. Very few teachers thought that formal assessment would provide either the parents or themselves with useful information, and only one teacher thought that formal assessment would raise educational standards. The following comment was typical of many:

Formal assessment is counterproductive. It puts the children under some stress. It's something quite different, and it's hard to explain to them why you're doing it. It takes up an awful lot of time and involves an awful lot of money, which could be spent on things more useful to them. And at the end of the day it doesn't tell you any more than you could have found out by teacher assessment.

The teachers also underestimated the extent to which the parents wanted to be involved in the assessment (see table 2.1). Only four teachers thought that parents wanted to be involved, compared with nearly half the parents who actually did want to be involved. As before, several teachers commented that parents were not generally interested in such things, and that for the most part they were happy to leave it to the teachers. There were some exceptions, however. The following teacher, for example, could see that parents might want to be involved in the assessment process, and that this might be beneficial all round:

> In SATs, yes. They'd like to see how their child coped. Any parent is interested in what their child is doing, especially in competition with other children. Also in informal assessment, if they had the format for doing it. If they had specific criteria, it would be very helpful. It would help the parents as much as the teacher. They'd realize where their child was, and would notice if the child couldn't do something.

Overall, then, it appears that the teachers had only a partial awareness of their parents' views. While the teachers correctly perceived that parents knew very little about assessment, they underestimated the parents' interest in assessment, their support for it, and their desire to be involved in it. We have suggested that one possible explanation might be that the teachers themselves were strongly opposed to assessment, and so ascribe to parents views that they themselves held. Whatever the reason, our findings suggest that schools need to reflect on whether they are sufficiently aware of how their parents feel, and to consider ways in which they might increase their knowledge of parents' views.

Building Better Partnerships with Parents

In a small extension to the project, we have been working closely with three schools that are attempting to build closer relationships with parents along the lines indicated above. These three schools are very different from one another. School A is a small village primary school, School B a large inner-city first school serving a deprived estate, while School C is also a large first school, but with a socially mixed catchment area. Inevitably, the approach taken by each school reflects its particular circumstances and history. Nevertheless, they have all been attempting to develop a closer understanding of their parents' views and to consider seriously how far they can provide what parents want. Each school started with its Year 2 classes, and focused initially on the issues of assessment and learning.

School A, having consulted its parents on ways to improve home–school links and parental understanding of assessment, invited all Year 2 parents into the classroom (in groups of three) to shadow their children at work. The school also revised its assessment records to provide a space for parents' comments, and instigated a programme of home visits for all parents of Year 2 children. The purpose of the visits is twofold: they provide the teacher with a fuller picture of each child's capabilities, which can be used in teacher assessment, and they enable the teacher to advise parents on ways in which they can help their children at home.

School B also consulted its Year 2 parents on what they wanted from the school. As a result, folders were provided that travel between home and school, containing anything from children's work to comments from parents and teachers about things the child has done in each location. School B has also provided parents with specific suggestions of ways in which they can help their children at home. For example, at the beginning of each term parents are given a description of the forthcoming topic with ideas on 'how you can help'. Parents have also been given their own guide to the Attainment Targets in English, written by the teachers in 'Childspeak'.

School C has been focusing on ways in which they can make parents better informed about the assessment process. Meetings about the SATs have been held class by class rather than across all Year 2 classes (as was previously the case), thus enabling parents to have fuller discussion of the issues and actually handle the SAT materials. The school has also sent out information on the term's topics at the beginning of each term, and has instigated class 'coffee mornings' to enable parents to meet teachers more informally.

Early responses to these innovations indicate that parents are very pleased to have been consulted about what they want, and that additional information provided by the school has been valued. For example, all Year 2 parents in School A have taken the opportunity to 'shadow' their child in the classroom. Subsequent interviews reveal that this has been greatly valued by parents, both in terms of learning about their own child and learning about teaching methods. The teacher in School A who carried out the home visits has commented on how much she has learnt from these visits about the learning that takes place at home.

In School B, the teacher has reported that up to a third of the children bring work or drawings done at home in their folders on a Monday morning. One parent commented that now she knew what the term's topic was, she was happy that her daughter was spending so much time on these drawings – she now realized their relevance to what she was learning at school. The parents were particularly pleased to receive the 'Childspeak' Attainment Targets; as one said, 'now I'll know what those levels mean'.

All three schools have reported that the Year 2 teachers made a significant impact in terms of increasing parents' understanding of assessment and learning, and that the teachers have gained greater understanding of the parents' views.

As a result, all three schools intend to broaden the scope of the innovations from Year 2, to become whole-school policy.

Conclusions

Standardized assessment has been introduced in England and Wales as part of an explicit attempt to raise educational standards. Standardized assessment results, it has been argued, can provide valuable information for teachers and parents about the performance of individual children, as well as providing aggregated information about the performance of individual schools. These arguments, as we have seen, rest on the assumption that parents share the government's concern with standards in education, and that parents will value SAT results as a way of keeping informed about their children's progress. The research reported here allows us to look more carefully at these assumptions about parents. In this final section we summarize our findings and put forward some implications.

The overwhelming majority of parents were clearly happy with their children's schools. The findings from this study – together with those from other research – do not support the kind of widespread parental dissatisfaction that is frequently portrayed in the media. At a time when the teaching profession has been subject to repeated public criticism, it is important to remind teachers that they appear to have the support of the great majority of their parents. This support, however, is neither universal nor unqualified. In particular, nearly two-thirds of the parents felt they did not know enough about what was happening to their children in school.

Parents' desire for more information about their children also appeared to underpin their views on standardized assessment. The parents in our study knew very little about the assessments, but almost all of them wanted to know more. They wanted to know how their children were doing, about their strengths and weaknesses, and about how they as parents could help them at home. They supported formal assessment if they felt this was needed to supply this sort of information; however, a substantial minority felt that such information could be supplied just as well through continuous informal assessment. In addition, nearly half the parents wanted to be directly involved in some way in the assessment process.

The teachers were only partially aware of their parents' views. They were correct in thinking that their parents knew very little about assessment, but incorrectly assumed that this reflected an underlying lack of interest. They also underestimated parents' support for assessment and their desire to be more closely involved. It is possible that the teachers were heavily influenced by their own negative feelings about assessment, and incorrectly assumed that the parents would hold similar views.

There are some important implications here for practitioners. While it is heartening to know they have the support of most of their parents, there is clearly much more they could do if they are genuinely seeking to provide what parents want. In particular, schools need to address parents' desire both for more information and for more involvement. They need to reflect on what they currently provide in each area and whether this is adequately meeting their parents' needs. In the preceding section we provided some examples of schools that are attempting to do precisely this.

Finally, there are some important implications for policy-makers. The current reforms have frequently been justified on the grounds that they have the full support of parents. Yet our results suggest that this is only partly true. While parents share some of the government's concerns about educational standards in general, they appear to be almost entirely happy with what is provided by their own child's school. Similarly, while parents welcome the opportunity to receive more detailed information about their own child's progress, they are by no means totally convinced that the full machinery of standardized assessment is necessary for this purpose. Our research suggests that what parents would most value is a genuine partnership with schools in which their views are listened to and taken account of, and which offers them both information and involvement. The dilemma for policy-makers is whether to press on with the reforms in their current direction, or whether to alter course and encourage schools to develop the kinds of partnerships that their parents really want.

3

Political Contexts and School Careers

Susan Harris, Jean Rudduck and Gwen Wallace

Editor's Introduction

Chapter 3 continues and extends our concern with the effects that the reforms are having on the realities of school life. However, the focus now shifts from Key Stage One to Key Stage Three (11–14 years). This chapter, by Susan Harris, Jean Rudduck and Gwen Wallace, reports findings from a longitudinal qualitative study that is following pupils from three contrasting comprehensive schools through their last four years of compulsory education. The chapter describes the pupils' experiences in Year 9 (13–14 years), and in particular their experiences of assessment, setting and options. The findings from this study suggest that the current reforms, which were ostensibly intended to increase competition and differentiation *between* schools, are in fact increasing competition and differentiation *within* schools; as the authors point out, this is sometimes at odds with the schools' own commitment to equality of educational experience. Harris, Rudduck and Wallace conclude that 'the reforms do not seem to be giving teachers the support they need for dealing, in school and classroom, with issues to do with students' motivation, their sense of fairness and their sense of self-worth'.

Introduction

In planning the study presented here – 'Making Your Way Through Secondary School' – we opted for a longitudinal design that would allow us to track, in real time, students' careers during their last four years of compulsory schooling. The value of the concept 'career', as Goffman (1961, p. 119) points out, is its 'two-sidedness': one side is linked to the development of image of self, self-identity and sense of future, while the other concerns the progress of the individual through institutional time and his or her movement within the academic and social structures of the institution.

Over 80 students are involved in the study (the numbers fluctuate slightly as families move in and out of areas). The students were 12 years old when the study started in 1991 and 16 when it ended in 1995. It would have been methodologically comfortable for us if the students themselves – as they progressed through Years 7 to 11 – were the major source of 'movement', with the background maintaining some stability, but this has not been so. The reforms of the 1988 Education Reform Act, and subsequent extensions and revisions, have created turbulence and uncertainty. Indeed, Esland's comments (1971) could well have been made today: he writes of the anomie experienced by people who are 'confronted by uncontrollable change' and who find themselves searching for identity. Our data suggest that these words could apply to schools as institutions as well as to many of the people who work in them. Thus, although the main focus of our research is students, we have a layered agenda: we must take into account changes in national policy and try to understand their impact on school 'identity' and structures, and then consider how these changes are affecting the careers of the students and their sense of self-as-learner.

We have been working with three comprehensive schools. In each of the three schools one form group was chosen from the 1991–2 Year 8 cohort. In each school the headteacher ensured that parents and governors were consulted about the study; there were no objections. Each term the students were interviewed for 15–20 minutes – initially in pairs but thereafter individually. The interviews were fully transcribed. We also interviewed the year tutor and form tutor of the target groups once a term, and the headteacher two or three times a year. Once a year we interviewed other members of the senior management team and some subject teachers who had contact with members of the target group. Additional data came from our reading of students' school reports. We also collected policy documents, 'mission statements' and information material prepared for students and parents, and we attended occasional events in which the target students were involved (such as options evenings).

Unlike most of the other studies reported in this book, ours was only part way through at the time of writing. Instead of presenting overall outcomes, we have chosen to focus on one segment of the study, the students' experience of Year 9, which was characterized for most of them as the year of SATs (Standard Assessment Tests), setting and options. We see our data as illustrative of a general trend that other writers (some of them cited in this chapter) have written about more fully: the way in which schools' commitment to equity of provision for their students may give way, under the pressure of the recent reforms, to greater differentiation. While differentiation is intended to match provision to students' capabilities, in practice it is still likely to create 'winners' and 'losers' in terms of the resources that support learning and students' experiences of learning. Our particular concern is with the effect of greater differentiation on students' feelings about school and about themselves as learners.

At the national level the principle of differentiation among schools is being actively promoted; the preferential budgets offered to schools opting out of local authority control into grant-maintained status have clearly been a means of breaking down the former 'monopoly control' exerted by local authorities (see Wallace, 1992, 1993). Indeed, diversity, under the provisions of the 1993 Education Act, creates a 'career structure' for schools that allows those that wish to, to 'improve' their status and become more selective. Jonathan, whose analysis supports the 'winners' and 'losers' theme, comments:

> it is probable that some schools will get better and others worse, with those parents who are most informed and articulate influencing and obtaining the 'best buy' for their children, thus giving a further twist to the spiral of cumulative advantage that results when the state is rolled back to enable 'free and fair' competition between individuals and groups who have quite different starting points in the social race. (Jonathan, 1990; cited in Codd, 1993, p. 80)

In a climate where 'winning' and 'losing' is related to formula funding, there is pressure on schools to demonstrate 'superiority' in terms of image, style and results. For example, two of the three schools in our study have either introduced or intensified the use of uniform in a bid to improve their appeal to parents – although in neither school was this a move that commanded the full support of the staff. Glossy brochures, active recruitment in local primary schools and image-making events have multiplied in all three schools. Thus 'school career' is not only about what happens to students as schools redefine the structure of opportunity; it is also about what happens to schools in a market climate that promotes diversity of provision in the name of choice and competition.

The new financial arrangements for delegating budgets to schools have led to uncertainties over funding and staffing at a time when teachers are trying to cope with the demands of the National Curriculum and with the national requirement to improve standards. In a climate of general anxiety about student numbers – which relate directly to income – much of the management activity in schools is currently focused on recruitment strategies and strategies for stalling financial crises. A degree of disequilibrium is likely in some schools as a result of panic measures – the introduction of numerous initiatives that bring either cachet or finance, but that may be pulling the school in different directions. Other schools are confronting the issue of shedding teachers through voluntary redundancies and the consequent problems of staffing the curriculum.

The data that we draw on in this chapter were collected in 1992–3. Had teachers not boycotted the first round of publicly reported tests at Key Stage Three, our students would have sat them. They expected to sit them, and the interviews suggest the disorientation that many were feeling as the political battle over testing was played out at national level. Our students were the first – and, after the recommendations of Dearing (1994), probably the last – to face such a restricted set of option choices in Year 9 as a result of the acknowledged overcrowding of the curriculum. Our students also experienced the side-effects of the intricate (1993) structure of 'levels' and 'attainment targets': even teachers who were fundamentally committed to mixed-ability teaching felt it necessary to group students.

The word 'political' in the title of this chapter is not unduly significant for, as Apple (1993, p. 40) says, 'as an act of influence, education is profoundly ethical and political by its very nature'. We are concerned with the effects, as far as we are able to discern them, of recent policies that have sought to extend that influence in a systematic and profound way. Recalling the rhetoric of 'entitlement' that accompanied recent reforms, we asked ourselves whether, in Bastian et al.'s words (1985, p. 2), 'the democratic promise of education' had been enhanced. This question provides a focus for the analysis of our data. In the central section of this chapter, we look at our three schools individually in order to underline the importance of institutional context as central policies interact with the different traditions, cultures and conditions of particular institutions.

Students' Experiences of Testing, Setting and Options in Three Comprehensive Schools

School A

School A is an 11–19 split-site comprehensive in a relatively prosperous middle-class area of a city. The school has undergone radical change in recent years, moving from a grammar school that catered mainly for white, male, middle-class students to an increasingly multi-ethnic comprehensive that now draws students from right across the city and from more diverse social, cultural and economic backgrounds. The school continues to enjoy a good reputation for its academic excellence and also for its involvement and success in music, drama and sports activities. The headteacher, who joined the school in the late 1980s, sees the new diversity as one of the school's strengths. Of the three schools involved in the research, this is the only one (at the time of writing) where rolls are rising, although such an indicator of 'success' is proving double-edged as resources are being stretched to the limit and pressures on staff are increasing.

While many staff are in favour of changing the traditional identity of the school, there are different views of what constitutes a positive environment for student learning. The tensions are most apparent in the efforts the head and some staff have made to encourage all staff to be more aware of their pastoral responsibilities to all students. Although in theory this principle operates right across the school, in practice it operates more fully at the lower end of the school, where examination pressures are less intense; in Years 10 and 11, in contrast, teachers continue to define their responsibility to the students mainly in academic terms.

Setting in School A

In the early 1980s the school, which had been streamed, started to move towards a policy of setting in some subjects and mixed-ability teaching in others. In the year of the interviews with Year 9 students (1992–3), setting operated in science, maths, French and English. The practice of setting in some subjects and maintaining mixed-ability teaching in others tends, as is often the case in schools where the academic tradition is strong, to suggest that subjects where students are set have a higher status. Some members of staff were in favour of an even stronger setting policy and a more competitive framework for academic achievement. We noted that many Year 9 students in school were sharply aware of the implications of setting, were consequently anxious to be in the top sets and wanted to be separated from students whose behaviour sometimes 'stops them working'.

An indirect consequence of the practice of setting in the early years of secondary schooling is that the form group becomes a less important social unit. As one student said:

> You don't really spend much time with certain members of your class . . . some of my friends [in the same form] I don't see all morning . . . You see them for about ten minutes in the morning and then you see them at lunchtimes and break, but that's about it. (Year 9/Female)

While in Schools B and C the sense of belonging to a form was strong, in School A there was less camaraderie among members of the same form, and friendship groups were much more likely to be based on ability. One girl, not in the high-ability sets, commented that it was difficult to get on with everyone in the form and that some students 'all hang around together and they never, like, help us. Because they are, like, the brainy ones' (Y9/F). Apart from registration and a handful of classes (personal and social education, craft, design and technology, and music) the form did not work together.

SATs in School A

Given the particular traditions of the school, it is not surprising that students generally appeared to accept the competitive ethos at an early stage in their secondary school career; this may have influenced their attitudes to SATs. SATs seemed to be more important to students than options and there was a strong sense of the 'seriousness' of the Summer term tests:

> Last year we didn't have any tests – well we did have some tests, but ... SATs tests are more important. (Year 9/Male)

> You have these SATs exams and there wasn't anything like that last year, no serious exams. (Y9/M)

> It's more important [in Year 9] because we've got our SATs tests and you've got to learn everything. Instead of going out at weekends you've got to learn the things that you do. (Y9/F)

In this school students were also keenly aware of the way in which doing badly in the expected tests might affect the sets they would be in next year:

> *What do you think will happen if you don't do well in the SATs?*
> ... if you don't do well you'll be in lower sets next year so you won't get taught as well. (Y9/M)

Some students also thought – perhaps rightly – that there was a direct link between the set you were in and the grade you could achieve in that subject at GCSE: 'I think like the SATs set you up for your GCSE studies and everything, all part of your future' (Y9/M). Students in the other two schools had less understanding of the way that current events were shaping their individual and collective futures. All students seemed to be aware, however, that preparation for the tests was causing them to lose out on some things that they enjoyed – such as trips or residential visits.

Although staff were at pains to reduce any worries students had about sitting the tests, a few students felt that the additional pressure had affected their work. One student vividly expressed the complex reactions that the tests (and the uncertainties surrounding them) were engendering:

> It's 'cause they're new and that. I think that makes you feel worse ... They're really rushed. It's about 12 weeks and to do your GCSEs you get two years ...

> It's putting me off work, actually. I mean, I want to work hard, but then I think I can't be asked to, it's the SATs. And then you think that sometimes they're not going to be doing them and then we are, then we're not, then we are. (Y9/F)

On the whole, more girls than boys expressed anxiety about the SATs; more boys tended to accept the fact that they had to be done, but thought that they were not worth too much worry. The following two quotations are selected to typify the responses of female and male students:

> I'm dreading them ... There's a right load of pressure put on us to do them and that. And some teachers say, 'Oh, it's not really that important, but just do your best', and other teachers say, 'It's right important, it's important that you do good in them'. (Y9/F)

> I'm not really bothered about them. (Y9/M)

One student commented, astutely, that SATs were important because they affected the school's reputation. His view was that the SATs were not so much about how well individual students were progressing, but a simple measure of how efficient the school would look to the consumer: 'It's to do with the National Curriculum organized by the government. Your school will do better if you do better' (Y9/M). In this school, attended by substantial numbers of students from professional and academic families, students were perhaps more likely than in the other two to have heard parents talking about such things as 'league tables'.

Options in School A

The system for choosing options was taken very seriously by the teachers in School A, as it was in the other two schools. A lot of teacher time was spent talking to students about options and interviewing students and parents, and options evenings were held for students and for parents. Students were given a Year 10 *Curriculum Booklet* which said, 'This booklet is for you ... For the first time in your school career, you have to make some really important decisions about your studies and perhaps your future'. The booklet contained detailed information about the structure of courses, the breakdown between final examination and assessment work, and an explanation (for relevant subjects) of the different levels of attainment. Some information was also included about the content of courses, but this was less prominent than the information about the Year 11 examinations.

For the 1993 options, students had to choose one humanities course and one language (from French, German, Latin or Spanish), and then they had to choose two further courses from a list of sixteen. These were written in two columns with the traditionally 'academic' choices (history, geography, French, German, Latin and Spanish) in one column and, in the other, art, drama, music, economics, religious studies, design and communication, design and realization, home economics (food), practical studies, and Community Link Catering Course (CLCC). The last two courses were not GCSE courses.

Despite the highly organized and efficient management of the options process, many students seemed to experience it more as a task required of them by the school and less as an individual, empowering moment in their school life – something that some staff at the school would like them to feel. On the whole, students were non-committal about their options. Some made negative choices: for example, geography is not quite as bad as history, so geography is chosen, or French is a bit easier than German, so French is taken. On the whole, options were less of an event for students in School A than they were for students in Schools B and C.

School B

School B is an 11–16 comprehensive in an economically disadvantaged area where unemployment is high. The school population, like the local community, is predominantly white and working class. Students who want to continue in full-time education at 16 can go to a Further Education College or to another secondary school a few miles away (the former grammar school, which has kept its sixth form). Since the early 1980s, School B has built up a strong equal opportunities programme and has seen it as important to encourage a more articulate confidence among its students. Over time, the head was able to appoint new staff who were in sympathy with these policies, but attitudes and practices in the community are slow to change. On the whole, parents do not have high aspirations for their children. They have not, traditionally, seen it as any of their business to worry about what schools do or do not do, and there is a habit, in some families, of condoned non-attendance.

The form group involved in our study was, overall, remarkably cohesive and mutually supportive. In terms of class and background the group was fairly homogeneous and there were no sharp sub-group tensions. The disruptive behaviour, mainly coming from boys, was a source of irritation to students who wanted to work reasonably hard, but quite often all members of the group were drawn into the antics and there was a high level of communal enjoyment. As teaching in form groups gave way, in Years 8 and 9, to cross-form, mixed-ability groupings in some subjects, so the sense of form identity became somewhat diminished, but a general spirit of openness and camaraderie survived. The school's commitment to music, the arts and technology – performance and display are a good means of acknowledging the talents and achievements of different students – may well contribute to the spirit of goodwill that has generally prevailed in the school.

The last headteacher took early retirement a few years ago, anticipating that the present reforms in education were unlikely to support the principles of equity that he had tried to place at the heart of his school. The new head has experienced some anxiety that, as parents are encouraged to think seriously about choice of school rather than to rely on family custom, local conservatism may well lead them to think that the comprehensive in the next small town must be better because it used to be 'the grammar', has a sixth form, and because the students there wear a uniform. A high priority for the new head was, therefore, to strengthen the school's links with local families, and recent initiatives have been successful in bringing parents into the school who had before tended to leave everything to the teachers unless there was a crisis. A uniform has been introduced for younger students, but it is intended ultimately for the whole school. Clearly, as the school feels increasing pressure to conform to a particular image in order to maintain its recruitment targets, tensions within the staff are likely to emerge. A school that, until recently, reflected the principle that effective organizations are built on a shared sense of purpose and a common commitment to defined values, was beginning to experience some internal division. The new head was trying hard both to ensure the survival of the school and to achieve a resolution of the tensions. She was seeking a reunification of the staff around a position that was politically realistic, but one that entailed some compromise on the school's earlier philosophy.

Setting in School B

For the last decade or so, students at School B have been taught in mixed-ability groups, with one exception – maths – where it was argued that the special nature of the subject required setting. Students first experience setting in maths in Year 9. The students we interviewed all understood that their performance in the maths test at the end of Year 8 would determine which groups they would be placed in – but the groupings had been presented to them in terms of 'pace' rather than 'capability'. By the end of Year 9, however, their language had changed – perhaps because the educational climate generally was more explicit about differentiation. Now they were talking more about 'top', 'middle' and 'bottom' groups. Some students used both vocabularies simultaneously: 'Like in the top group there are some who are faster than others, faster learners' (Y9/F); '. . . top group, that's the fluent class. You work faster' (Y9/M).

It seemed that where setting is a minority practice, students are likely – initially, at least – to be less compliant about it. For example, some members of the 'bottom' maths group were quite articulate about their desire to be regraded and to move up:

> I think I would like another test at the end of the year to see who can get in t' top group out of bottom group. And I am not going to copy off anybody to try and get in t' top group. (Y9/F)

> Like you are in the bottom group and you have got to like try and achieve somat. You have got to try and achieve stuff, like to get you into the top group and get a better education. Like if you are the bottom group all t' time you would just be stuck there if you did nowt to attempt to get out of it. (Y9/M)

Although some students were battling to get out of the bottom group, the image that was reflected back to them – ironically by fellow students – was not helpful: 'Well, I'm in the bottom group now and I feel horrible because people are saying that you are dumb' (Y9/F); 'Everybody calls it "duggy" group' (Y9/M). As setting spreads to other subjects, the effect may well be, over time, an easier acceptance of the sorting and an increase in the kind of peer group labelling that can, ultimately, diminish the dignity of young students and their desire to do well. A comment made by one student in the bottom maths set suggests that as setting becomes more widespread, differentiation may be accepted by students as the natural order of things:

> You get used to it after a bit and you just think, 'Oh, right, this is my class, this is our class what we are in'. (Y9/M)

SATs in School B

The students had some sense that the tests were part of a national programme and not something relating only to their school: 'I think it's for National Curriculum thing' (Y9/M); '. . . teachers have to make us take them, don't they? They're being helpful towards us to help us pass' (Y9/F). Students noticed that the usual internal tests seemed to be taking place more often and decided that the teachers must be giving them some practice for the tests that lay ahead, which were clearly more significant: 'You have to write on paper and all that lot, right quiet' (Y9/M). Students were also aware of the pressure on teachers: 'You go along and then at the last minute, a few weeks before, they [the teachers] go, "Oh, we have a test coming up. You have got to do all this and all this"' (Y9/F); 'Everything's rushed because they have to get it all [done] really quick' (Y9/F).

Some students thought the tests might help them to concentrate, and no student was greatly dismayed. Some students didn't see the point: 'I don't know what it's all got to be done for, because it's not going, like, to get you a better [job]' (Y9/F); 'I think they are fobbing us off, because you can't, like, get a job with them. It's your final exams at the end of school that makes the difference, isn't it?' (Y9/M). Others thought that they were getting in the way of their 'real work': 'We haven't been doing any proper work. We've just been doing about SATs all the time and we haven't been able to do us ordinary work' (Y9/M). The majority of students, however, thought that they needed something like a test to make them focus on learning:

> Well, it's made me settle down a lot more because . . . if these hadn't come in I think I'd have still, like, have been not getting on with my work much and that. But now, like, I've concentrated more with all these happening. (Y9/F)

> I'm looking forward to some of the tests what's coming up because, like, when I know what sort of tests they are and I know what to study on't, then I can start studying on that, and that will be interesting. (Y9/M)

We have yet to see whether this increased motivation endures beyond the period of the test itself – and whether it serves the principles of longer-term learning rather than just short-term revision.

Options in School B

In School B, options were eagerly anticipated by almost all the students interviewed: 'We've been talking about them since first year' (Y9/F). Options function here as a symbol of power-sharing; many students said, in interview, that they feel much older in Year 9 – and they want more responsibility and to be trusted by teachers to do things on their own. Options offer them some sense of ownership: '[I] just like picking my own thing' (Y9/F). Even though the choices were restricted, students were still excited by the opportunity to take responsibility for shaping part of their Y10 curriculum. They could choose *either* geography *or* history, and they could choose *two* of the following: art, drama, music, business studies, social science; they were asked to name a third course as a reserve. The limited scope for choice was compensated to some extent by their prioritizing of 16 different activities in PE so, overall, the students did not feel cheated of the experience of saying what they wanted to do.

Students tended to choose what they liked and/or knew they were good at: most wanted a course that was not reputed to be too 'hard'. Some students chose 'new' courses because they wanted a change; some chose courses that would take them out of school on visits. Students were clearly choosing courses rather than teachers. Older friends or siblings were listened to – even if the advice was rough and ready: 'Drama's embarrassin'', or 'Business Studies is right hard' (Y9/F). The choices do not reflect strong gender stereotyping: male as well as female students said they chose social sciences because they liked 'looking after bebbies'.

Very few students failed to get the options they had listed (although, interestingly, where there was some oversubscription and teachers had to accept some and turn away others, the basis of the selection was not always apparent to the students). In this school there is little evidence of pressure on 'bright' students to take more academic courses (perhaps because there is little status difference among the few courses that were on offer: in 1993 they all led to GCSE, although this was about to change). The school's options leaflet is straightforward and easy to understand, there are 'taster' sessions for subjects that are new, and a well-designed consultation evening for students and their parents. Students felt that they had made their own minds up – and this seemed generally to have been the case.

School C

School C is a community school with a strong sense of community values. About a quarter of the students are from ethnic minority backgrounds and the school has, until recently (when the policy changed), attracted Section 11 money for additional language support. The school is situated between a long-established housing estate and a commercial development that provides an attractive alternative venue for students in the lunch hour. The council-built estate was refurbished in the late 1980s when individual gardens were carved out of the communal space and properties were sold to tenants who elected to purchase. A new housing development is raising the status of the area generally. Within easy reach is a new City Technology College and a well-regarded comprehensive with aspirations to become grant maintained. In School C, the skew in the student intake towards lower ability is being exacerbated both by the tendency for the socially aspiring parents in the area to look to the alternatives, and by the local authority's policy of placing students (generally boys) excluded from other schools into schools, like School C, which have not met their recruitment quotas.

As government policy requires that local authorities delegate funding to schools on a formula based largely on pupil numbers, School C faces the prospect of a progressively declining budget. The 1993–4 intake fell by 50 and the head expected a fall of a further 40 in 1994–5. The annual intake was expected, following 'a blip in the birth rate', to stabilize at 120. However, as the local education authority responds to government policy on age-weighted formula funding, the school finds that not only does it lose additional payments that its low socio-economic catchment attracted, but it is also facing the loss of the Section 11 money. The head predicted (from a total budget in 1992 of just under £2 million – of which approximately £1.5 million went on teaching staff salaries and approximately £150,000 on premises) a budget loss in 1994 of £80,000, and a further £100,000 the following year. Three staff took early retirement in summer 1993 and the reduced budget meant that more were likely to leave in summer 1994. The possibility of redressing growing imbalances in the staffing profile is slight, but criteria for compulsory redundancies are being drawn up that will take staff specialisms into account.

Setting and SATs in School C

In the first three years of the school all classes are of mixed ability and there is considerable emphasis on promoting cooperation and good social relationships through the form group. It is not uncommon for students to help one another and to work in small friendship groups. As in School B, the form has had the same form tutor since they entered the school, and the tutor recently rejected an opportunity for promotion in order to remain with the students. Grouping by ability is not a concept with which students are familiar. In mathematics, for instance, they make their way through the graded Schools Mathematics Project (SMP); they tend to judge their ability and progress not in relation to other students, but by the colour of the book they are currently working on. (Some, however, confessed to actively avoiding moving onto a 'harder' book.) At the end of Year 9 students were still vague about how they would be affected by the new grouping in mathematics that was to be introduced in Year 10, although some were interpreting the colours of the different groups (rightly so) in terms of ability – the yellows and reds, they decided, were in the top groups, and the greens and blues were students who were not so good at the subject.

Students had only a vague sense of what the SATs might mean for them: 'We've just had these tests and then he tells us which levels we're on and which group we're going in, I think. That's what he said, I think' (Y9/F). Many students said that what happened in Year 9 would affect their future prospects in the job market, and they had some sense that the SATs might affect which options they would get and their prospects for GCSE, and also that the SATs might lead to their being 'sorted out' from one another. There was evidence of growing concern:

Do you know anything about [the SATs]?
No. I know nothing about them.
But you're still worried?
That's why I'm worried because I don't know anything. I don't know how we're going to get assessed or if we're going to get kind of what subjects. I know

what subjects we're going to get assessed in, but I don't know what kind of . . . what we're going to be doing in these. (Y9/M)

Students had different ways of handling this concern. Some seemed to have decided that in the face of this mystery, with its elements of uncertainty and surprise, the best strategy was to follow teachers' advice and just 'try hard':

Anything you're worried about?
Exams, because I don't think I'll pass.
You don't think you'll pass?
Yeah. So I'm going to try harder in the tests we get.
It's important to pass?
Yeah. This year, if you don't pass or somat you probably don't get a better job, do you? (Y9/M)

Indeed, the need to 'try hard' and to 'work hard' in Year 9 was often related to students' thinking of abandoning certain kinds of behaviour:

I've got to stop messing around now, just put my mind to it. I can do it if I put my mind to it. (Y9/M)

You've got to work hard this year to get, to be sure of getting a place into the subject you want. Because if you misbehave then if they look at your record and say this boy has messed around then . . . (Y9/M)

The thought of the consequences left him lost for words.
Students who had missed school for some reason had an additional source of anxiety:

I came [to this school] half way through the second year, and so most of them I won't get, you know, I won't get right and I won't, you know, I couldn't answer them. (Y9/F)

And a few students who were in the middle of producing a clamp for the technology SATs said that the time constraints prevented them from achieving the quality they were capable of and that the knowledge of it being a test situation was also working against them:

Like [my friend] says she does better in classroom work than she does in the test because she goes to pieces in tests. So if they'd done it in the classroom work and assess you in that it probably would have been better and more fairer. (Y9/M)

As the year progressed, students began to come to terms with the idea of the tests, but the element of surprise continued to worry them:

> You revised one bit and then they'd get the test sheet with different questions than you'd expect. (Y9/F)

> They sometimes spring them on you and you . . . are really worried because you don't know hardly anything about it and then all of a sudden they spring it on you. (Y9/F)

Some students, however, admitted that some of the surprise might be of their own making: 'Well, we were told about it, but I must have been talking or something' (Y9/M). What became clear from the interviews – across the three schools – was that many students were uncertain what strategies to use to revise effectively. In fact, the anxiety generated by the tests made some students more dependent on their teachers just at the time when teachers were preoccupied with administration and marking; one student complained that one of his teachers was too busy on other things to teach them properly.

Options in School C

The options system in School C is influenced by both financial constraints and the school's view of what it values in the curriculum. Uncertainties about money and staffing delayed the finalization of the options lists and the consultation sessions for students and parents. In the event, students were offered four blocks of subjects. The school has a high regard for public performance as a community activity and art, music and drama featured in two blocks. Block one set four periods of technology against three of technology and one 'expressive art' lesson. Block two allowed students who had selected four periods of technology to choose either an expressive art or one of the following: business studies, French, geography, German, Japanese or a nation-ally certificated 'Youth Award Scheme'. Block three offered one choice from geography, history and religious studies, and block four offered one choice from French, German, Punjabi or Urdu. Students generally felt that they had some control over their option choices, although they were conscious of the limited range of choice. One student, for instance, compared the meagre choices of 1993–4 with the more varied programme offered to his sister in the previous year. A number of students regretted the little time they would have for PE.

There was some evidence of teacher influence on students' options choices. For instance, some potential GCSE candidates were discouraged from taking the Youth Award Scheme – an attractively packaged 'Community Skills' option with a nationally validated certificate: 'It's got all these places you can go to. It means you can do, like, horse riding and everything. It's, like, a challenge. And you get certificates or medals at the end if you achieve them' (Y9/F). The student, attracted by the publicity material for this option, explained why she later changed her mind about taking it:

> I did have the Youth Award Scheme but Miss X came and she had a list of people she thought, like, could do better so, because Youth Award Scheme isn't GCSE. So, I've changed from Youth Award Scheme to geography. Business studies – I didn't really need that so I did geography instead. (Y9/F)

At the end of Year 9, students generally expressed satisfaction with their option choices. The interviews in Year 10 suggested that this sense of satisfaction was persisting; dissatisfaction was growing, however, among students in the bottom set for mathematics – as happened in School B, where students also experienced setting in only one subject.

Discussion

In earlier papers arising from this project (Harris and Rudduck, 1993, 1994), we discussed the challenge for the teacher of establishing, among Year 7 students, a sense of the seriousness of learning in the face of the personal anxieties and social excitements of joining the new school. We also noted the relative lack of identity of Year 8, sandwiched as it is between the novelties of Year 7 and the distinctive features of Year 9. For students whose involvement and investment in schoolwork is fragile, Year 8 can be experienced as a fallow year, where motivation easily flags, and we suggested that schools might wish to find an identity for Year 8 that would help students hold on to their commitment to learning. In this chapter, however, we have focused on students' Year 9 experiences. The three features that give Year 9 its distinctive identity – setting, testing and options – were not new to the system, although they were new experiences for the students.

As Moore (1995) says, we must not fall into the 'naive trap of assuming that there was a pre-Thatcherite, educational golden age of successful, progressive reform' that was brought to 'a cataclysmic close' by the pressure groups from the right and their influence on national policy. Moore's reminder is timely; these things are not new. Tests have long functioned as a mechanism for binding students into schoolwork and the SATs, as we have seen, were beginning to operate in much the same way – as a normative device for ensuring that students were committing themselves to working harder. A number of students said that preparing for the tests focused their minds and gave a sense of occasion to their learning – although others thought that the tests were stopping them getting on with the 'real' work; and one student (Y9/F) shrewdly observed: 'You are not going *to know any more* by doing them tests'. But there is a sharper sense of competition abroad now, and this is having its effect on schools as well as on students. Indeed, some students had a sense of the tests being part of a larger mechanism for separating them, sorting them, labelling them and preparing them for their futures. As Connell (1994, p. 134) says:

> Schools are literally power-full institutions . . . School grades, for instance, are not just aids to teaching. They are also tiny judicial decisions with legal status, which cumulate into large authoritative decisions about people's lives – progression in school, selection into higher education, employment prospects.

Our data suggest that in such a context the socially disadvantaged students are the ones who will find it hardest to compete on equal terms. Apple (1993), commenting on similar moves in education in the USA, argues that traditional working-class groups used to a 'more collective' culture may find it difficult to operate in the mode of 'competitive individualism' that now prevails in schools.

Setting, an offshoot of streaming, has a similar history of advocacy and opposition. Streaming became widely practised after the 1944 Education Act and it was in the 1960s and 1970s that setting – seen as a more flexible and less rigid way of organizing young people – became more common. Mixed-ability teaching increased, especially for 12- and 13-year-olds, after the publication of the Plowden Report in 1967. Policies on grouping have tended to reflect the traditions and values of particular schools. There has been no common practice; setting, for instance, might be introduced – if at all – for different age cohorts and for different subjects according to each school's perception of what is necessary in the particular context that it finds itself working in.

Our interviews suggest that in schools where there is a tradition of formal grouping by ability, and where the climate is already receptive, then the explicit external legitimation that we have at the moment is likely to enhance the tendency for students to accept their lot. But where, as in School B, setting is at odds with the prevailing ethos of the school, students who encounter it for the first time and are placed in the bottom sets are restless and keen to be reassessed so that they can move up. Even here, though, we saw that, over time, students who were not moved up adopted a coping strategy of 'not caring' – and this attitude can easily extend to their schoolwork generally.

Interestingly, in the two schools where the system of mixed-ability teaching is losing ground, the new system of grouping has been presented, at least initially and by some teachers, as being about 'pace of learning' rather than 'ability': groups provide 'faster' or 'slower' rates of learning. The logic seems to be that students may feel less humiliated by being categorized by speed than by ability. Indeed, in the interviews, a number of students said that they needed to work slowly and to go over things more than once. However, we can also see that such a basis for differentiation could, if it became widespread, harden into a routine that fitted with an 'assembly-line' image of schoolwork. We shall see whether, during the period of stability promised by the 1994 Dearing review, schools will step back from grouping by ability or whether the prevailing market climate, which endorses competition and selectivity, will provide an environment in which formal systems for differentiating students will be adopted fairly widely. In some schools, as we can see from the data presented in this chapter, a policy of grouping by ability may be introduced or extended mainly as a strategy for institutional survival in the context of policies that directly advocate a competitive market ethos. We are also aware, however, that in the day-to-day interactions of the classroom, the corridor and the playground, any system that sharply points up the differences between children runs the risk of strengthening the impulse to label those who are different or those who are faltering or those who are weak (see also Harris, 1994).

Options have also had a chequered history. Sir Edward Boyle, Conservative Minister for Education from 1962 to 1964, wanted 'to get away from the situation in which boys and girls are allowed to write themselves off below their true potential of ability' (as quoted by Kogan, 1971, p. 65); he wanted to see 'as many young people as possible going up the ladder as far as their potential abilities can carry them'. One strategy for sustaining aspiration in the final years of compulsory schooling was to give students more choice over their courses of study. Indeed, in the early 1970s there was international support for the 'multi-option' school that would, it was thought, 'reduce inequalities of opportunity while developing autonomous conduct and encouraging the emergence and expression of individual ability' (Ader, 1975, p. 6). Following the raising of the school leaving age to 16, choice was seen as offering young people an experience of being 'citizen consumers'. By the late 1970s, however, Her Majesty's Inspectorate was arguing (DES, 1977) that options gave students a freedom to opt out of important educational experiences that should be theirs as of right – an argument that supports the idea of a common curriculum. Now, as a result of the space taken up by the common features of the National Curriculum, the area where students can exercise choice (the Year 9 options) has diminished in importance. Ironically, this move has occurred at a time when the concept of choice has become central to government policy. While the exercising of choice has diminished for students, it has ostensibly increased for parents (although see Ball, 1993; Bowe et al., 1994; and Gewirtz et al., 1993, for a critique of the way that social class intersects with the principle of choice).

In one of our schools, the one with the strongest academic tradition, choosing options seemed a less significant process for students than the preparation for the SATs. In the other two schools, however, options still represented an important arena for student autonomy. Moreover, it seemed that some students who had been on the edge of disengagement were recommitting themselves through the interest generated by the courses of study that they had chosen to take. This commitment seemed to be sustained well into the Year 10 work. We saw, however, that choice was not entirely open: for instance, in all three schools there were resourcing problems that limited group sizes and some students could not therefore be placed in their 'first choice' courses; and in the two schools where some courses led to GCSE and some did not, teachers' 'advice' could be a means of 'warming up' or 'cooling out' students who had chosen courses that teachers deemed to be inappropriate to their academic capability (see Ball, 1981; Woods, 1971). We believe that genuine opportunities for the exercise of autonomy and responsibility in school are an important aspect of students' motivation and engagement, given both their social maturity and the extent of the responsibilities that many carry in domestic and social contexts out of school.

Our interviews suggest that the majority of Year 9 students really want to learn; they want to do well at school. Disengagement is sometimes the result of genuine boredom, and sometimes a strategy for masking loss of self-esteem. What many students need, in addition to conditions of learning that respect their maturity, is a better strategy for learning: for catching up on the work they have missed; for checking out, without loss of face, their understanding of difficult sequences of learning; for finding out more about the things they are curious about; for contributing, without fear of ridicule, what they know from their own experience of life. Above all, they want a fair chance of developing their confidence as learners.

It is not, as we suggested earlier in this section, that the reforms as such have created problems for a 'previously successful liberal education system', but rather 'that they have not effectively identified and addressed the problems that in fact already existed' (Moore, 1995). The reforms do not seem to be giving teachers the support they need for dealing, in school and classroom, with issues to do with students' motivation, their sense of fairness and their sense of self-worth. These are issues that lie at the intersection of learning, class, culture and control. Indeed, during the fieldwork, we became increasingly aware that, despite differences of traditon and social context, all three schools involved in the research were caught, at some level, between a 'desire ... to serve the competitive demands of a stratified society, and a desire ... to play a social integrative and democratic role, serving the right of all children to develop to their fullest potentional' (Bastian et al., 1985, p. 1).

4

Competing Conceptions of Quality in Social Education: Learning from the Experience of the Cross-curricular Themes

Geoff Whitty, Peter Aggleton and Gabrielle Rowe

Editor's Introduction

This chapter, by Geoff Whitty, Peter Aggleton and Gabrielle Rowe, is directly relevant to two of the main themes of the book. First, the chapter continues the focus – established in the first three chapters – on the relationship between the aspirations of the current reforms and the way in which they are being realized in practice. In addition, the chapter raises issues concerned with our second theme – that of understanding the processes of teaching and learning – and how these processes are perceived by teachers and pupils. The chapter addresses these broader issues through a specific concern with the implementation of cross-curricular themes, such as health education and citizenship, at Key Stages Three and Four. Whitty, Aggleton and Rowe report that these themes, which are important elements of the 'broad and balanced curriculum' advocated by the 1988 Education Reform Act, are frequently being submerged within a curriculum organized increasingly along academic subject lines. One consequence of this, noted by the authors, is that opportunities for pupils to relate the themes to their everyday lives are extremely limited. More generally, the chapter raises concerns that the National Curriculum pays insufficient attention to social education in secondary schools, and that the cross-curricular themes do not adequately compensate for this deficiency.

Introduction

Section One of the 1988 Education Reform Act required schools to provide a balanced and broadly based curriculum that 'promotes the spiritual, moral, cultural, mental and physical development of pupils . . . and . . . prepares such pupils for the opportunities, responsibilities and experiences of adult life' (DES, 1988a). The Act defined the mandatory National Curriculum in terms of academic subjects – the ten core and other foundation subjects. Schools were subsequently advised to teach five non-mandatory 'cross-curricular themes' – namely, health education, citizenship, careers education and guidance, economic awareness and environmental education. (In addition to the five cross-curricular 'themes', the National Curriculum Council (1990a) identified a number of cross-curricular 'skills' and 'dimensions', but the present chapter focuses only on the themes.) The guidance issued by the National Curriculum Council suggested that, although these themes could be taught in a variety of ways and discrete provision might prove necessary for certain elements, most aspects of the themes could be taught through the core and other foundation subjects or through religious education (RE).

Official comments on the relationship between subjects and themes reflected an ambivalence about two contrasting traditions of social education in the English secondary school curriculum. The social education of the elite has usually been based upon a 'liberal education' in a variety of academic subjects, while that of the masses has often taken the form of direct preparation for citizenship and work. The traditional notion of a 'liberal education' assumes that exposure to a broad range of specialist subject discourses will produce an 'educated person'. Such a person will then, almost by definition, be an employable, environmentally friendly, responsible citizen and taxpayer, pursuing a healthy lifestyle. From this point of view, it makes sense for the cross-curricular themes to be taught through the core and other foundation subjects. For schools, it relieves pressure on the curriculum to cater directly for every fashionable political imperative. It also seems to provide a way of meeting such demands, while avoiding charges of 'indoctrination' and 'social control' often associated with more explicit attempts to prepare pupils for adult life (Gleeson and Whitty, 1976; Whitty, 1985).

However, the 'permeation' approach to the teaching of the cross-curricular themes assumes that subjects and themes are essentially different ways of organizing the same curricular elements. It also assumes that the same elements can be used for different educational purposes at the same time. For example, health education may involve the acquisition of subject knowledge and understanding, the development of life skills associated with the making of sound choices, and the fostering and adoption of particular attitudes and lifestyles. Yet, each of these different educational purposes entails different criteria of quality, and this has important implications for the nature of classroom activity and associated modes of assessment. Traditional secondary school subjects tend to privilege the acquisition of knowledge and understanding. There are therefore likely to be tensions between provision for subjects and themes in the secondary school curriculum. The government's view that the educational aims associated with themes could easily be achieved by mapping them on to mainstream subjects was either naive or cynical.

Indeed, the inherent difficulties of the permeation approach to social education have been exacerbated in the case of the cross-curricular themes by a concurrent narrowing of what counts as knowledge in mainstream school subjects as a result of the work of the National Curriculum subject working parties and interventions by successive Secretaries of State. The National Curriculum Council's claim that, in due course, it is likely that schools will 'throw all the attainment targets in a heap on the floor and reassemble them in a way that provides for them the very basis of a whole curriculum' (NCC, 1990a, p. 1) fails to acknowledge that the particular attainment targets identified by the subject working parties have mainly been driven by the requirements of individual academic subjects.

This chapter draws upon the findings of a research project entitled 'Assessing Quality in Cross-curricular Contexts', which explored the implementation of cross-curricular themes at Key Stages Three and Four. The project involved a survey of one in four secondary schools in England and Wales (N = 1,431) and detailed observation in eight schools. (A fuller account of the research can be found in Whitty et al., 1994a.) The chapter demonstrates that, in both teaching and assessment, criteria of quality associated with individual academic subjects have generally taken precedence over those that might have been used to evaluate the rather broader notion of social education that seemed to be implied in Section One of the 1988 Act. In doing so, it also points up some more general issues that will need to be faced in any attempt to develop an approach to social education that combines rigour and relevance.

The study was informed theoretically by Bernstein's work on the classification and framing of educational knowledge (Bernstein, 1971). Bernstein originally defined 'classification' as 'the *relationship* between contents', so that 'where classification is strong, contents are well insulated from each other by strong boundaries [and] where classification is weak . . . the boundaries between contents are weak or blurred' (Bernstein, 1971, p. 49). The concept of 'framing' referred to the 'strength of the boundary between what may be transmitted and what may not be transmitted, in the pedagogical relationship'. Where there is strong framing, 'there is a sharp boundary, where framing is weak, a blurred boundary, between what may and may not be transmitted' (Bernstein, 1971, p. 50).

A curriculum comprised of individual subjects with strong classification between contents was described by Bernstein as a 'collection code'. He suggested that the traditional subject-based English grammar school curriculum approximated to this model, but that there had been moves during the 1960s and 1970s towards what he termed 'integrated codes' – where there was weaker classification between subjects, for example through the development of integrated humanities courses (Whitty, 1992). However, it seemed to us that the Education Reform Act's model of the National Curriculum favoured a strongly classified subject curriculum – that is, a reassertion of the collection code. The subsequent detailed specification of official programmes of study for the core and other foundation subjects also seemed to herald a strengthening of 'framing' in Bernstein's terms, especially in view of his statement that 'where framing is strong, then the acquirer has little control over the selection, organization and pacing of the transmission' (Bernstein, 1977, p. 179).

Yet the very idea of using cross-curricular themes as a basis for social education, as proposed in the National Curriculum Council's various booklets of non-statutory guidance on the themes, seemed to require a weakening of the boundaries between subjects and entail a weakening of framing in the pedagogic relationship as a result of the need to relate school knowledge to pupils' own lifestyles and concerns. We were therefore interested to see how these apparent tensions between different models of curriculum and pedagogy, and their associated modes of assessment, would actually be resolved in school policy and classroom practice.

The National Survey

Our questionnaire asked headteachers or their curriculum deputies whether their schools had made changes in cross-curricular policy and practice following the NCC Guidance on themes in 1990. By the time of our survey in 1992, 82 per cent of schools claimed to have changed their approach. One-third of these stated that the change was due to the National Curriculum, but about a quarter attributed the change to developments of previous practice and were keen to make it clear that change was internally generated and not entirely due to NCC Guidance. However, 84 per cent of all those who had changed their approaches claimed to have referred to the NCC Guidance documents.

The questionnaire responses showed teaching of the various themes to be spread across the core and other foundation subjects in different ways. Some heads ticked every subject on the grounds that themes were by definition permeated. But most were somewhat more discriminating in their responses and the responses as a whole showed different patterns for the different themes. When we looked at the areas in which at least 50 per cent of schools claimed to be teaching the themes, we found that economic and industrial understanding appeared in the most subjects, and could thus be defined as the most fully permeated theme, whereas health education and careers education and guidance were the least permeated of the themes. (The notion of permeation here does not necessarily imply that the boundaries between subjects were permeable, merely that the teaching of the themes was distributed across a variety of separate subjects.)

Health education and careers education were also the themes having the clearest visibility in schools. They had existed long before they were defined as cross-curricular themes, and they were more likely than the others to have discrete curriculum slots or be part of a personal and social education (PSE) programme. Even when this was not the case, they tended to be taught through relatively few core and foundation subjects. They were also more likely than the other themes to have written policies and were amongst those most likely to have designated coordinators backed by a responsibility allowance. In recent years, they had been supported by nationally funded advisory teachers. Thus health and careers had some of the attributes in terms of status, time and resources that Goodson and others have argued are necessary to 'becoming a school subject' (Goodson, 1983, 1985). The closer a theme was to a conventional subject in these respects, the stronger and more tangible its presence seemed to be. It seems from our findings that those themes (i.e. health and careers) that Rowe (1993) has suggested are *least* like academic subjects in terms of their substance are also those *most* likely to have some of the key sociological attributes of subjects.

This has implications for the capacity of these themes to employ distinctive criteria of quality in that it seems likely that having some of the attributes of a subject in terms of its form may allow a theme to deviate from other subjects in terms of its substance. Thus, for example, health educators and careers educators often pride themselves on the links they make to everyday life, on their participatory approaches to learning and on their concern with affective as well as cognitive outcomes. They also tend to make more extensive use of pupil self-evaluation techniques than most other school subjects. The opportunities they have to do these things may actually be dependent upon the relative insulation of their work from the rest of the curriculum and their occupation of curriculum slots in their own right. In Bernstein's terms, their capacity to maintain weak framing in the classroom and weak boundaries in relation to the outside world may result from their strong classificatory relationships with other subjects. As Fowler (1992) points out in relation to liberal studies in post-compulsory education, weak framing is acceptable in an area of work strongly classified from other subjects only because the dangers of polluting high-status knowledge are thereby minimized.

However, the opportunities for careers and health education to maintain their unusual character, either in their own right or in the context of PSE, are far from secure. As well as our own research, there is other evidence that the time allowance for these activities has been eroded or threatened in many schools by the pressure of curriculum overload brought about by the National Curriculum (HEA, 1992; Harris, 1993). Their survival as themes is therefore increasingly dependent upon the adoption of a permeation approach, which is likely to emphasize those aspects of their work that are closest in substance to mainstream school subjects.

Where the teaching of a theme relies on a permeation model, any distinctive features are likely to become casualties at classroom level of the strong classification and strong framing associated with conventional academic subjects, which are now being reinforced by the demands of the subject-based National Curriculum. Rowe (1993) suggests the other three themes are less different than health and careers from mainstream subjects in their substance, and it may be that there is less of a problem in those cases. Yet, even if he is right that the knowledge content of those themes is closer to that of other subjects, the purposes to which it is to be put still differ and this is likely to have consequences for the criteria by which it is to be assessed.

The 'Permeation' Model in Practice

The second phase of our project involved visiting eight secondary schools identified as having different approaches to cross-curricular work. Briefly, the themes were not much in evidence in the work we saw, even in those schools that claimed to have given them some priority in whole-school curriculum planning. Most schools were feeling constrained by the pressures of the National Curriculum to adopt an approach that put an increasing emphasis on the delivery of themes via the core and other foundation subjects with RE. When we looked at what was going on in those subjects, we found that the newer themes, and even the older themes where a permeation model was being adopted, were difficult to identify at classroom level and they were rarely 'visible' to pupils.

We have tried to make sense of what we saw in terms of Bernstein's work on evoking contexts, recognition rules and realization rules (Bernstein, 1981). Different contexts evoke different responses, and one of the marks of competence is knowing the rules that enable you to produce appropriate responses in a particular context. According to Bernstein, 'recognition rules create the means of distinguishing between and so *recognising* the speciality that constitutes a context' (Bernstein, 1990, p. 15). In our context, recognition rules may be the clues that pupils need to determine what counts as a specialized discourse, in other words, a subject. One of the first recognition rules derives from how subjects or themes are divided up. Other salient clues for novices are gained through having to bring specialist equipment such as books, aprons and PE kits to some lessons. Other recognition rules will be given by what form or forms schoolwork takes. Of particular importance when considering themes are the recognition rules that govern talk. These are given either explicitly or tacitly through the rules of classroom discourse. Teachers at the beginning of a year often tell pupils what, in general terms, constitutes acceptable talk.

Realization rules are the rules that tell pupils what constitutes appropriate practice in a lesson. In Bernstein's terms, 'realisation rules regulate the creation and production of specialized relationships internal to the context' (Bernstein, 1990, p. 15). They tell pupils what can and what cannot be done to demonstrate knowledge. They suggest acceptable forms in which subject principles may be demonstrated and this is particularly important in the context of assessment. Realization rules give the form that pupils' written work may take, acceptable methods of oral communication, types of movement in PE and forms of artefact that may be produced in technology and art. More sophisticated realization rules may refer to the structure of arguments or the acceptable sequences of a process.

During lessons teachers will control discourse in order to demonstrate what can literally be said and not said according to the subject code. Sometimes the parameters, or form, of the discourse are given explicitly, as for example with the rules of a formal debate, and sometimes pupils infer them, as for example when talking individually with a teacher. As pupils become used to the ways of working in a subject, they will start to take teachers' accepted discourse rules for granted. When pupils break these tacit rules, teachers will be forced to articulate them again and they will, for a period, become visible.

One of the key problems about using subjects to teach themes lies in the rules that relate to the use of talk in different contexts. We found that all pupils made a strong distinction between subject discourses and talk that they perceived as not directly related to subjects. We asked pupils 'Where do you do a lot of talking?' They indicated that most talk took place during breaks and lunch time. This sort of 'chat' associated with peer group and family contexts was clearly differentiated from schoolwork. When 'chat' did take place in lessons, it had an illicit feel to it, as these comments by pupils indicate:

Yeah, it's good. It takes up most of the lessons. It's not really doing English. (School A)

Depends which subject you can't really concentrate on. (School A)

We can chat in art, he chats, he gets sidetracked very easily. (School B)

We do a lot of talking in graphics, in graphics we just mess around and talk a lot. (School B)

Unless you enjoy the lesson, you just sit there and talk. (School C)

In CDT [craft, design and technology] we make things, but it could get boring so we talk – not to do with the lesson. (School D)

'Chat' is thus often associated with time-out or off-task. Pupils perceive it as something to 'get away with' or 'sidetracking' and therefore not related to the subject. Unlike teacher talk, question-and-answer sessions and structured discussion, it is seen as subverting rather than contributing to learning. The problem facing themes is that the sort of talk that allows links to be made between subject discourses and everyday life challenges this strong boundary between legitimate school talk and illegitimate non-school talk. Themes can therefore create ambiguity about the status and permissibility of different types of talk – in the eyes of pupils as well as those of some teachers.

Furthermore, those very types of talk that attempt to forge connections between school talk and 'street talk', and which are therefore important to the effective teaching of themes, are valued differentially by different subjects. What counts as legitimate talk varies from subject to subject. Some pupils are able to differentiate subjects according to whether or not, and in what ways, oral work is legitimate. Our focus-group interviews with pupils asked them to differentiate the different types of talk that take place in subjects:

Don't get people to join in the conversation so much in science, they just write on the board and then talk about it. Then he just explains how the experiment works. Then in English he asks about the book you are reading. Not so much writing on the board. It's discussing.

In English you have more debates. (School G)

Right, what are you talking about in your biology lesson?
About the work we've done really to see if we've taken it all in.
Right, so it's very work-orientated talk rather than chat?
Yeah.
Is it like a debate?
No, it's either yes or no. (School B)

These pupils recognized in which subjects there was a place for their own views and ideas and in which subjects these were not validated. They were thus able to identify differences in framing between different subjects.

Where classroom discourse is tightly framed, teachers will be perceived by pupils to be in complete control of what is said. One example is when teachers limit pupils' contributions to answering closed questions. However, tight framing can have the effect of making recognition rules more explicit, because it makes the limits of common-sense understanding clear. Pupils will then be able to work out that answers based on common sense, rather than on subject principles, are not given credit. However, if the framing is too tight some pupils may not be able to connect subject principles with any of their own ideas and the subject principles may simply elude them.

If the discourse rules are much looser, a great deal of what pupils say may be accepted, but it will be more difficult for them to work out what the specialist area of knowledge is. However, in some cases, teachers themselves use loose framing to work out what lay theories pupils already hold in a subject area. Once they have worked out what lay theories pupils hold they can then use this, as scaffolding in Bruner's sense (Bruner and Haste, 1987), to introduce a subject principle. This can provide a 'relevant' context through which to illustrate a principle.

Teachers often like to use examples that they hope are familiar to pupils in order to provide contexts through which they can demonstrate subject principles. In many cases, though, these apparently 'real' examples are not drawn directly from pupils at all and are actually at some variance with pupils' experience of everyday life. Some pupils therefore find it difficult to make sense of either the principles or the examples (Keddie, 1971; Noss, 1990; Cooper, 1992). Another way to use pupils' understanding is to show how their common-sense theories conflict with the understanding required to grasp the subject principle. Indeed, Driver et al. (1985) suggest that unless teachers point out to pupils how their common-sense theories conflict with scientific theories, they may never acquire scientific principles.

However, if subjects are also to do the work implied by the permeation model of themes and help prepare pupils for life beyond school, yet another relationship between subject knowledge and common sense would be necessary. The subject principles would need to be related back to everyday life either by the pupils themselves, or with the help of teachers. In the lessons we observed, this rarely happened, because the dominant 'realization rules' in play were those of the subject. Furthermore, those pupils who had successfully learnt to differentiate subjects according to these rules were inhibited from making thematic links across subjects or beyond subjects to the world outside school.

During one Year 10 science lesson about teeth and tooth decay, in a school that had on paper a very clear permeation policy for cross-curricular themes, the interviewer asked a pupil:

Don't you need to say something about how you should brush your teeth?
I don't think we're supposed to do that.
Why?
It's not what we're doing.
Why are you doing this work then?
Because it's in the National Curriculum, I suppose. [laughs]
But the textbook has a picture of how you should brush your teeth.
I don't think that's really science. (School G)

For this pupil, even an illustration in the science textbook was not enough to legitimate a connection between the National Curriculum subject 'science' and everyday life. To him the science lesson was self-contained and self-referential. To have produced work inconsistent with what he perceived as the subject code would have indicated that, through inappropriate application of recognition and realization rules, he had failed to achieve the required scientific competence. The task was thus perceived as one associated purely with scientific knowledge rather than with personal behaviour.

While the particular example may seem trivial, it clearly has wider implications for a permeation approach to, say, drugs or HIV education. Even explicitly participatory approaches to health education in other contexts have experienced considerable difficulties in forging links between knowledge and behaviour. Health educators' initial concern that the National Curriculum would concentrate unduly on factual knowledge at the expense of process skills and participatory learning styles was allayed to some extent by the NCC Guidance for this theme (NCC, 1990b). Despite this, the classroom practice that we observed seemed to confirm their fear that quality in health education would be defined in relation to subject-specific attainment targets rather than the developmental needs of pupils or the responsibilities of adult life.

Ironically, the teacher of the particular science class reported here was a staunch advocate of cross-curricular themes and had a senior responsibility for the implementation of the whole-school curriculum policy. He had earlier told us of his fear that the National Curriculum might make it difficult to link science to pupils' experiences, and his own practice seemed now to provide evidence to support this thesis. Unfortunately, this was not an isolated instance. Furthermore, some science teachers, and particularly male science teachers, complained most strongly that teaching cross-curricular themes 'polluted' their subject. That explicit theme-related work is perceived as both residual and potentially threatening to the integrity of science as a subject is evident in this comment from one such teacher:

There are occasions in science where things will crop up, but probably not as often, but I mean we were doing some work on alcohol, for instance, this week in Year 11 ... things can come up, even though what you're doing tends to be very much more structured in some science lessons, there are issues that do *intrude* and *if there's time* we can discuss them. [our emphasis] (School C)

In a focus-group interview with teachers in another school discussing where themes are taught, a science teacher said of the themes:

Not in Key Stage Three, sorry, because you've got the National Curriculum document which you've got to wade through in a pre-set time and I mean the science department as a whole – I know Rob is responsible for economic awareness – we've done virtually nothing on that because if you're trying to get over a particular attainment target, and let's say you've allowed yourself one lesson or maybe two lessons to do that, then you want the *essential thread* to go through. Whereas, y'know, you've got to go off at a tangent sometimes to bring in economic awareness ... what you're doing then is *diluting the message*. [our emphasis] (School D)

In yet another school the science teacher in the focus-group interview stated about health education:

It's not our job at all. We do do it, but we shouldn't have to. Parents should do it. Our main aim is to get them through the exam. Social niceties are not really our ... we're not nappy changers ... nannies. (School E)

To some extent, then, the teacher who taught the lesson about tooth decay was the exception, at least in his stated commitment to teaching themes and his worry that the National Curriculum would squeeze them out. Yet his practice did not differ significantly from those teachers who believed it was important to protect the purity of their subject. Science teachers seem to keep a strong control over the message and guard their position as subject specialists very tightly. While their tight control over the discourse alienates some pupils, it also has the effect of producing a discourse which pupils perceive as having strong rules and procedures that in Bernstein's terms provide recognition rules.

At the same time, many of these same teachers felt that themes, as opposed to subjects, benefited from their 'invisibility'. A teacher talking about economic and industrial understanding told us:

It has to be seen as part of the whole pattern rather than something that's taken out and emphasized. It occurs in so many places ... you were talking about nineteenth-century history ... it occurs in history ... it occurs in literature; it's there in all of them, it's just there as the background, it's bound to be. I think we raise children's awareness, but I don't think it should be a structured ... should ... what's the word? ... I don't think we should throw it at them ... as

lumps that . . . what they need to know . . . it should be kept in perspective . . .
It doesn't kind of exist on its own. It permeates things. (School G)

But this means that all theme-related knowledge forms only the background to
subject principles. In Bernstein's sense, the themes are foregrounded by the
subjects, which are, in turn, strongly insulated from one another. If themes are
to be effective, pupils themselves have to be able to make connections between
any elements of the themes that they will have come across scattered around
different subjects and apply this knowledge to life outside school; a complex
set of cognitive and practical tasks.

Furthermore, Bernstein's work would suggest that some groups of pupils are
likely to be better placed to make the connections than others. It certainly
seems likely that relatively 'invisible' themes will only be put back together, or
subject knowledge recontextualized, by pupils who are able to recognize an
appropriate context for doing so and then apply yet another set of realization
and recognition rules that are different from those of individual subjects. This
context may be a PSE lesson in school or it may be in the home or peer group.
If the context is the home or is heavily home-determined, then the opportunities to make sense of theme-related knowledge are likely to be differentially
distributed according to social and cultural backgrounds.

During the fieldwork, questionnaires were administered to Year 8 and Year
10 pupils in some of the schools we visited. They asked if pupils had heard of
each of the cross-curricular themes and then, separately, if they had been taught
any of them. Initial analysis suggests that pupils do not 'see' a lot of what
curriculum managers identify as theme-related work. But they are in broad
agreement about which themes they have heard of and which they have been
taught. In general they agree that they are taught careers education and
guidance, health education and environmental education. Across the schools
from which we have relevant data, very few pupils had heard of the term
'economic and industrial understanding' or thought they were being taught
any. The findings were similar for education for citizenship except in one
school, which had a specific citizenship module as part of a PSE programme.

However, the broad agreements among pupils appeared to break down
when we asked them to explain briefly what they understood each of the
themes to be. In focus-group interviews, some pupils seemed to describe
themes according to the conventions of subject discourses, using abstract
principles, while others would describe them according to topic orientations
that tended to be in the form of concrete examples. For example, some said
that economic and industrial understanding was about 'how the economy
works' and others that it was about 'managing on your wages'.

We therefore investigated the reasons for the different ways in which pupils
talked about the themes. If the work of Holland (1981) were to be replicated

in this rather different context, we would expect middle-class children to prioritize abstract principles associated with subjects, with working-class children more likely to refer spontaneously to aspects of everyday life. We found that the extent to which there were actually significant differences between how pupils from different backgrounds described the themes varied from theme to theme. The most significant differences related to health education and economic and industrial understanding, where pupils from non-manual backgrounds were far more likely to discuss themes in context-independent language than those from manual backgrounds (Whitty et al., 1994b).

However, there were also some significant differences between schools in this respect. Not surprisingly, most of the pupils in a school that relied largely on teaching the themes through a highly academic subject-based curriculum described economic and industrial understanding in terms of concepts drawn from economics. Pupils in schools that adopted more varied approaches were more likely to characterize this theme in context-dependent terms and, in one school, there were no examples at all of context-independent language in relation to this theme.

Personal and Social Education (PSE)

Effective teaching of the themes requires movement between context-dependent and context-independent language. It is therefore important to find ways of enabling all pupils to make connections between the abstract knowledge associated with subjects and pupils' own experiences in everyday life. Some schools do try to offer pupils the possibility of learning about the themes elsewhere than in the core and other foundation subjects, though this is more true of some themes than others. Personal and social eduction (PSE) lessons or similar provision might constitute an important context for pupils to pull together all the subject-related knowledge associated with themes. Such provision could, in theory, help to counteract the differential social distribution of opportunities to do so outside school.

In fact, though, none of the PSE courses we observed during fieldwork even attempted to bring together theme-related subject knowledge in this way. Even the most highly organized schools did not attempt to relate PSE courses to other subject provision in a clear and coherent manner. Instead, if PSE was offered, the reason was to teach those aspects of themes that were not likely to be included in subjects. Such curriculum provision thereby took on the form of a 'subject' in its own right, strongly classified in relation to other subjects. However, if schools organize the teaching of themes in this way, it can no longer really be called 'cross-curricular' and the challenge of bringing together knowledge from different subject areas may be avoided rather than confronted.

PSE was as likely to suffer from its separation from other subjects as to benefit from it. Where, as often happens, PSE and similar lessons did not have clear recognition rules, there was a tendency for them not to be seen as 'proper' subjects and some pupils found it difficult to make sense of them. We asked pupils about PSE and other issues in the focus-group interviews:

> *Where do you discuss issues like moral issues?*
> We do that in PSE, but it's much more boring [than in RE]. In PSE no one takes it seriously . . . fall asleep.
> Depends on the teacher. Mr Y, they take the mick out of him. He talks and talks and never stops.
> PSE is a 'catch-all' lesson. It takes in everything.
> *What is the difference in talk between PSE and English?*
> In PSE, its always the practical things, how we . . . it's always, how we could do it in the tutor group. Why our tutor group is like this. What can we do about it. They talk about how to solve it. They tell you it's there. In PSE they tell you how to get rid of it. Which is the problem.
> *I see, it's a sort of practical thing?*
> Yeah.
> It's more down to earth.
> Whereas in a subject area . . . like English . . .
> It's more depth in a subject really, you go into it more. (School C)

For these pupils, PSE was perceived to be superficial and lacking a focus, and even its concern with practical issues was seen in negative terms. Thus, although little attention was paid to the themes within subject classrooms, the teaching of the themes in a separate PSE lesson often merely confirmed their lowly status.

Part of the difficulty lies in the fact that in PSE there are no agreed conventions about how to frame the discourse. Potentially anything can be said and many teachers expressed anxiety about how to limit the talk. They were aware of having moral positions that would not necessarily be those of pupils, and they were unsure about how much they could allow pupils to say in PSE lessons. Pupils themselves were aware of the rather arbitrary conventions governing PSE discussions, and therefore perceived the limitations of what could and could not be said in PSE as personal attributes of the teachers.

The recognition of a lack of a perceptible PSE 'voice' was articulated by Year 10 pupils in this extract from a focus-group interview:

> It's what they think personally. So, if they think it's really interesting then they want to talk about it. They really get into it, if not they'll probably just go quickly.

It's because the teachers have had to work it out, all the course work. It's because in every school, everyone's doing it in totally different ways. The teachers have just sat down and worked, written out sheets, or whatever they are working from. If, say, they were working from a textbook, say, and it's been developed over a period of time, I'm sure it would be better.

I don't like PSE, have to swap round different teachers. You never know where you are. They don't tell you what you are doing. (School A)

The recognition rules that create areas of specialist meaning which are subjects, such as textbooks, homework and examinations, were clearly not available in this context.

Even when PSE was assessed, the assessment criteria appeared to be independent of any identifiable public discourse:

If you sit there and look attentive, you'll get a good mark.

Say 'yeah' a lot.

If you put your hand up often and give an intelligent comment.

Get in the teacher's good books.

Yeah, I did that the other day. I had to have a report filled in. I put my hand up and answered a question. She gave me an 'A'. (School C)

Here pupils explained how they manipulated the teacher to get good marks. In mainstream subjects it is not this easy because what counts as 'correct' or 'an intelligent comment' is distinguishable from incorrect or unintelligent answers according to subject conventions, which are perceived to be more public or more formal, or at least they are thought to emanate from a source other than the individual teacher.

One reason for accepting control from teachers in other lessons, from the pupils' point of view, is because they lead to examination results, which in turn lead to jobs.

People would concentrate on PSE if there was an exam at the end. I don't want one, because that'd be another exam, but if people thought they had to work towards something they would concentrate.

There would be a reason to listen.

But we haven't got anything, we don't get a grade, or an exam that would help us, or anything. So there's nothing to work for. (School A)

If teachers ask pupils to discuss issues or themes in PSE time, which lacks all the main recognition rules available in all other curriculum areas, pupils often fail to see the point of it and it is hardly surprising that they tend to associate the range of legitimate meanings with the idiosyncrasies and moral preferences of individual teachers. Some pupils, especially those in academic groups, were quite cynical of teachers' motives for teaching PSE:

> It's so they can say, 'Oh they know it. We've told them. So, if they go away and abuse alcohol, it's their fault 'cos we've told them about how evil it is, so it's their fault. So, we've covered ourselves'. (School A)

A different conception of quality in PSE is clearly going to be needed if it is going to compensate for the deficiencies we have identified in the permeation approach to the teaching of themes, and provide opportunities for pupils of all social backgrounds to have access to the range of meanings needed for genuine empowerment in the world beyond school.

Assessing the Themes

Nevertheless, many people still expect the themes to fulfil the requirements of Section One of the Reform Act, with the implication that themes can affect the lives of pupils outside school in a way that subjects do not. There is therefore an urgent need to rethink what counts as quality in cross-curricular provision and to provide more appropriate recognition and realization rules.

Bernstein (1971) identifies evaluation (or assessment) as a third 'message system' operating in schools alongside – and often driving – curriculum and pedagogy. The evaluation message system in schools is provided mainly through the examination system, and the lack of a distinctive assessment system for the themes helps to explain their lack of visibility and status. So far, little attention seems to have been given to this in discussions about the themes. Where themes are delivered exclusively through subjects, the components are likely to be assessed in relationship to the attainment targets for particular subjects rather than in terms of their relationships to other subjects or to pupils' life outside schools. Yet, if subject discourses are aimed at transmitting abstract principles, then the forms of assessment used for subjects will not be entirely appropriate to themes.

Alternative modes of assessment could help to provide appropriate recognition and realization rules for the themes and/or for PSE. Ideally, this would demand that pupils pull together appropriate knowledge from a range of subjects, and the criteria for successful learning in relation to the themes would thus need to be based on the ability of pupils to integrate knowledge. Some may wish to go further and suggest that the assessment of such knowledge should be tied to social issues that are relevant to pupils' lives or even to social behaviour. In this case, the assessment procedures for themes would be most unlikely to involve standard paper and pencil testing. In our survey, though, 63 per cent of schools had no plans to assess themes separately from subjects. Of the 37 per cent of schools that stated that they did intend to assess the themes separately from subjects, a few felt it important to give themes status by formally examining them in some way, but most of these schools were referring to entries in pupils' Records of Achievement.

Towards the end of the project, we conducted a telephone survey followed by fieldwork in six schools that had tried to use such devices. This showed that the actual use of Records of Achievement for reporting achievements in relation to the cross-curricular themes was even more limited than our original survey had suggested. Nevertheless, the findings in those schools that were actually addressing this issue did reinforce the importance of having a message system to provide appropriate recognition and realization rules for work relating to the themes. Those schools that were using integrated humanities GCSE schemes to examine work in PSE seemed to have made the most progress in establishing an identifiable evaluation message system for the themes. This gave PSE a status that approximated to that associated with at least some of the National Curriculum subjects, but employed a more flexible approach to assessment. We were also impressed by the way in which one school was using the nationally recognized Youth Awards Scheme to enhance the visibility and status of theme-related work without translating it into a largely academic mode. Yet another school was trying to use the Duke of Edinburgh's award scheme in this way.

Without such alternative forms of assessing and recording work related to the themes, the burden of decontextualizing theme-related knowledge from subjects and recontextualizing it in everyday life will have to be shouldered largely by pupils themselves. The burden might be lightened, first, by theme-related knowledge being highlighted in some way for pupils in subjects and, second, if time is provided in the curriculum where pupils can be helped to recontextualize the appropriate aspects of subject knowledge. Such changes would be greatly facilitated by new approaches to assessment in social education to replace or supplement those employed in National Curriculum subjects or in PSE in most of our fieldwork schools. Even so, given the culture of secondary school teaching and the enduring tensions between subject knowledge and everyday life, it will not be easy to gain widespread acceptance of such devices.

Dearing and Beyond

The original idea of having cross-curricular themes threaded through subjects has not proved to be an effective way of dealing with curricular overload, the ambiguous status of PSE in many schools and the limitations of traditional school subjects as a basis for social education. Nevertheless, our national survey indicated that, in principle, there is still considerable support for the themes or, at least, a recognition that they were partly designed to meet an important educational need. In practice, though, the notion of theme-related cross-curricular provision through subjects as the main strategy for social education will clearly need to be rethought.

Unfortunately, the 1993/4 review of the National Curriculum and its assessment by Sir Ron Dearing failed to treat cross-curricular themes as an important issue, making only some passing references to careers and sex education (Dearing, 1993, 1994). Yet it seems clear that the core and foundation subjects, as defined in the National Curriculum orders, will continue to provide an inadequate basis for effective social education. The criteria of quality implied in Section One of the Education Reform Act are unlikely to be given priority in subject classrooms in terms of content, teaching style and assessment, even with the revised subject orders. The notions of good practice being sponsored by the pressure groups associated with the themes, which emphasize a need to relate school knowledge to the world beyond school, are likely to be submerged by the curriculum and pedagogic imperatives derived from the National Curriculum and its associated modes of assessment.

The main hope to be gleaned from the Dearing review in relation to the issues raised in this chapter lies in the promised overall reduction in curriculum content and assessment loads. As a result, schools may be able to provide new contexts and opportunities for bringing theme-related work together and exploring its relationship to everyday life. If there is also time and space for such work to be assessed in ways that are consistent with the aims of social education, then progress might be made. There is, however, a danger in Dearing that we could revert to a traditional model of social education through subjects for the academic elite, with the more explicit treatment of the themes effectively being confined to those pupils following the proposed vocational pathway.

The nature of the issues that still need to be confronted can be seen in debates over the future of GCSE integrated humanities, which our research suggested could provide a way of reconciling some of the conflicting pressures on schools in this field. After some initial hesitation, the three examination boards that offer GCSE syllabuses in integrated humanities were revising them for 1996 or 1997. Some schools which, prior to Dearing, had felt obliged to abandon their humanities programmes are now retaining them. They will have to reduce their coursework component to 25 per cent to conform to new requirements, possibly making the assessment less appropriate for examining work in relation to the themes, but the content and skills to be assessed will remain basically the same as those that have been used successfully by some schools for this purpose. Integrated humanities programmes may also enable schools to offer core courses flexible enough to span both GCSE and GNVQ accreditation at Key Stage Four – thus helping to avoid a rigid separation between academic and vocational pathways. Whether many schools will actually seize this opportunity to find new ways of defining and assessing quality in the social education of all pupils remains to be seen.

5

'Grammar', 'Language' and Classroom Practice

Christopher Brumfit, Rosamond Mitchell and Janet Hooper

Editor's Introduction

The next two chapters develop further our concern with the processes of teaching and learning, and how these are perceived by teachers and learners. Both chapters focus on teaching and learning in the early secondary years (Key Stage Three), and both look at issues that go beyond teaching and learning within individual subject areas. Thus the present chapter, by Christopher Brumfit, Rosamond Mitchell and Janet Hooper, is concerned with the role of 'Knowledge about Language' (KAL) in the teaching of English and foreign languages (FL). As the authors make clear, there are strongly competing views about the extent to which KAL should be explicitly taught – for example, in the formal teaching of grammar. At the same time, there is little evidence concerning actual practice in this area. In this chapter, Brumfit, Mitchell and Hooper describe observations made in English and foreign language classrooms in three contrasting secondary schools; they also report on interviews carried out with teachers and pupils. Their conclusion that 'pupils in secondary school receive largely unrelated messages in the KAL area from their English and FL classes' has important messages for practitioners and policy-makers, and these messages are spelt out at the end of the chapter.

Introduction

The teaching of English has been one of the most contentious areas in discussion of National Curriculum principles, and in successive revisions of the curriculum since the 1988 Education Reform Act. Within this discussion, the role of formal grammar teaching and its contribution to the improvement of pupils' practical language skills has been one of the key issues. But little is known about recent practice in the classroom in this area. What is the contribution of teachers to learners' understandings of what 'language' is? And how are such understandings drawn upon in practice, in the quest to improve children's practical language skills? In this chapter we address the issue of explicit 'Knowledge about Language' (KAL) in language education policy, and provide empirical evidence about the KAL-related understandings and practices of a selected group of teachers and their pupils.

The chapter begins by summarizing the evolution of policy in the late 1980s. We then provide an account of the place of KAL in a number of language classrooms during the year 1991–2, and examine critically the quality of current practice. We shall draw upon our understanding of the models of language provided by teachers, and those implicit (and sometimes explicit) in the responses of learners. Finally, we shall consider the relationship between current practice and policy development.

Implicit and Explicit Knowledge

Competent and fluent language users, whatever their level of education, have developed a certain kind of awareness of the nature of language and how it functions as a system, simply through the process of using it in practice. This has been demonstrated in a variety of contexts – both for illiterate, unschooled adults (e.g. by Scribner and Cole, 1981), and for children still in the process of acquiring their first language (an area reviewed by Bowey, 1988). But on the whole, without formal teaching, such awareness remains *implicit*. For example, the illiterates studied by Scribner and Cole had no problems identifying grammatically incorrect utterances, but could not say what was wrong with them. However, even basic formal education begins to add *explicit* knowledge to this pre-literate awareness. Thus literacy instruction promotes explicit understanding of how 'letters' in different combinations go to make up 'words', and of how 'sentences' are conventionally set out in written English.

Our project was concerned with the conscious efforts of teachers to move learners beyond implicit levels of language awareness, and to develop their explicit understanding of the nature of language. This explicit under- standing has been given a variety of labels, including the term 'Language Awareness', which gained some popularity in the 1980s (e.g. Donmall, 1985; James and Garrett, 1991). In this chapter, however, we shall be following the dominant usage in current British curriculum debates, and will refer to explicit, conscious and articulated understanding by the label 'Knowledge about Language' (KAL).

The Battle for a Rationale

Language teachers have traditionally seen some role for 'Knowledge about Language' in their teaching programme, whether their main concern was with mother tongue/standard language development, or with the teaching of second/foreign languages. Most obviously, the formal teaching of second/ foreign languages has historically centred around the study of grammar. The teaching of English as a standard language in the eighteenth and nineteenth centuries, to a newly literate mass public, was also preoccupied with notions of 'correctness', which led to a concern with sentence-level explicit grammatical analysis and instruction (Crowley, 1989).

The twentieth century has, however, seen the rise of experiential theories of language learning and development for both first and second/foreign languages: the view that we learn primarily by *using* language has achieved wide influence. Most obviously, teachers of English in England have adopted 'growth'-oriented philosophies and largely abandoned the formal teaching of grammar (Protherough, 1989). Teachers of foreign languages also, influenced by language-learning theories such as those of Krashen (1981), or by the communicative language-teaching movement (Brumfit and Johnson, 1979), have been encouraged to promote more meaning-oriented use of the foreign language within the classroom, and de-emphasize formal grammar instruction (Mitchell, 1988; Peck, 1988).

However, there are signs of some rethinking in recent discussions of language education policy, which have tended towards the reinstatement of 'Knowledge about Language' within the curriculum. As far as English is concerned, recent government initiatives have reflected concern at teachers' perceived lack of linguistic knowledge (DES, 1988c, ch. 6), and a major INSET (Inservice Training) programme was devised in the late 1980s to address this (the 'Language in the National Curriculum' (LINC) programme: Carter, 1990). The report of the 'Kingman Inquiry into the Teaching of English Language' proposed an extensive programme of systematic, explicit language study for schools (DES, 1988c, ch. 5), and a limited KAL element was incorporated in the National Curriculum for English legally adopted two years later (DES, 1990a), following recommendations of the Cox Report (DES, 1989a). In second/foreign language teaching, KAL has remained an issue of little concern in official British curriculum documents, though the National Curriculum for 'Modern Foreign Languages' briefly recognized the issue (DES, 1991c). More broadly, revived international debates on the role of 'instruction' in classroom foreign language learning (see reviews in, e.g., Ellis, 1990; Harley, 1993) have led to a revival of interest in the contribution of pedagogic grammar to learning, under new titles of 'consciousness-raising' or 'input enhancement' (e.g. Sharwood-Smith, 1993).

Rationales and Models

The recent revival of interest in 'Knowledge about Language' has been marked by controversy and disagreement, against a backdrop of public concerns about literacy standards. The English National Curriculum document adopted in 1990 came under attack from educational traditionalists almost immediately on a variety of grounds. In particular, it was argued vigorously that the perceived neglect of formal grammar teaching, and the emphasis of KAL-related work on social and dialectal variation in modern English, constituted threats to the teaching of Standard English. Through the early 1990s, a number of revisions to the English document were proposed by successive government curriculum bodies (though up to the Dearing review, none was actually adopted); all of these included the refocusing of KAL work on the grammar of Standard English. Similarly controversial were the materials produced by the LINC teacher-training project, at a cost of £23 million (Carter, 1992). Like the 1990 National Curriculum itself, these materials included sections stressing the variability of modern English (and its social meaning), and focused principally on the description and analysis of texts rather than sentence-level grammar. The materials aroused such a degree of ministerial hostility that publication was prohibited.

Essentially, these disagreements reflect different definitions of 'Knowledge about Language', and different rationales for its inclusion in the curriculum. Elsewhere we have summarized the range of possible rationales for KAL which have recently been argued for by different groups (Brumfit et al., 1992; Mitchell et al., 1994). The main traditional rationale has been the claim that explicit study of language helps learners to use the language system effectively. This argument is reasserted for English in the Kingman Report (DES, 1988c), and press debates about the English National Curriculum reflect continuing popular belief that explicit grammar teaching is essential to ensure accurate mastery of (written) Standard English (see Mitchell, 1993).

Alternative rationales more recently developed for KAL-focused activity include concerns to promote public understanding of multilingualism, as part of the appropriate educational response to increasing ethnic and cultural diversity (DES, 1985), and the 'critical language awareness' movement, which seeks to sensitize pupils to the social uses and misuses of language for social control (Fairclough, 1990). It is also argued that motivation for second/foreign language learning can be enhanced by the explicit study of language and language development.

Differing views on the purposes of talk about language in the classroom lead to concentration on varying aspects of language. Traditionally, KAL was interpreted largely as sentence-level grammar, and some English teachers still equate KAL with their childhood experiences of 'clause analysis' (Chandler, 1988). However, recent models of KAL are more ambitious in scope and show a range of influences from various branches of contemporary linguistics, including sociolinguistics and discourse analysis. Thus, for example, discussions of KAL for foreign language classrooms have been influenced by the concept of 'communicative competence', and especially the related notion of 'appropriacy', ideas clearly borrowed from sociolinguistics. Discussions of KAL among English teachers have also been influenced by sociolinguistic perspectives on language variation, while as we have seen, the LINC project reflected a move away from traditional sentence-level grammar and an increased emphasis on the structure and workings of larger language units (texts and genres).

A range of more or less formal 'models' for KAL has been proposed in the course of current debates, reflecting these differing rationales and theoretical orientations. The varying components of these models may be summarized as follows:

1   The forms of the English language (speech, writing, word forms, phrase structure and sentence structure, structure of texts)(Kingman; LINC).
2   Communication and comprehension (Kingman).
3   Acquisition and development (Kingman; LINC).
4   Historical and geographical variation (Kingman; Cox; LINC).
5   Language variation according to situation, purpose, mode, regional or social group, etc. (Cox; LINC).
6   Language in literature (a separate element in Cox).

The Southampton KAL Project

In our own research a similar checklist was used, consisting of five dimensions of 'Knowledge about Language', derived from our reading of these discussions of KAL and from the practices of teachers that we observed. Numbers 1 and 3 were straightforward, but the different dimensions of language variation needed teasing out more carefully, so our final categories were:

1   Language as System (as 1 above).
2   Language Learning and Development (3 above).
3   Styles and Genres of Language (part of 5).

4   Social and Regional Variation (the rest of 5).
5   Language Change through Time (4).

With these categories, we were able to address empirical questions about the role of KAL in teaching. Theoretical debates and popular discussions of rationales and models for KAL in the classroom have been informed by little empirical evidence regarding teachers' current beliefs and classroom practices in this area. There is also only scattered evidence on the nature and extent of the 'Knowledge about Language' that learners are able to articulate explicitly, and the uses that they may make of it in different forms of language activity. It was for these reasons that the study described in the rest of this chapter was undertaken.

The project was designed first of all to investigate how 'language' itself gets talked about, in contemporary English and foreign language classrooms. In addition, we wanted to explore the models of language available to both teachers and pupils, and their perceptions regarding the contribution of KAL to language development. The study focused on secondary schools, and more particularly on Year 9 (13–14-year-olds), where pupils are in contact with a range of language teachers with potentially varying models of language, and where they are old enough to be developing relatively sophisticated and stable understandings of their own, partly via 'folk' linguistics absorbed outside the classroom, and partly from classroom experience.

The aims of the project were primarily descriptive in the first instance, to inform the KAL debate with evidence about current practice. During 1991/2, Year 9 classes in three secondary schools were observed and audiorecorded through extended (eight-week) parallel sequences of English and foreign language lessons (these included French, German and Spanish lessons). In addition, pupils from these classes participated in a variety of special tasks and interviews designed to explore their understandings of the nature of language. Their teachers were also asked about their theories of language development, and their beliefs about the place of KAL in language education. Finally, both teachers and pupils were asked to comment on the possible contribution of KAL to specific pieces of pupils' work, oral and written, produced in the normal course of classroom activity.

In each of the two subject areas examined, despite variation in the styles of individual teachers, a distinctive subject-specific approach to KAL could be identified. KAL-related practice in foreign languages and in English will therefore be presented separately below.

Practice in the Foreign Language Classroom

There were a number of differences between the individual foreign language (FL) teachers in their overall teaching style, and also in their approach to KAL. Most obviously, the amount of time devoted to pre-planned KAL work varied considerably. So, for example, one teacher seemed to operate a regular pattern in which every third or fourth lesson had a major KAL focus; another included one or more planned KAL episodes in a majority of her lessons; another included brief planned episodes in just four lessons over seven weeks of observation. One included regular KAL episodes in her French lessons, but virtually none in her German lessons. One teacher, who spoke Spanish regularly as the normal means of classroom communication, also conducted KAL-related work through Spanish. For all the others, English was the normal language associated with KAL.

However, in important respects the approach to KAL of the FL teachers was similar. Most strikingly, for all four teachers, the KAL area that received much the most consistent attention was Area 1, 'Language as System'. Thus, out of 30 KAL episodes noted in the lessons of one teacher of French, 23 concerned Area 1. For another, out of 36 episodes, 21 concerned Area 1. For the other two teachers, Area 1 was even more dominant. The only other KAL areas receiving more than passing attention were Area 2, 'Language Learning and Development' (12 episodes in the lessons of one teacher and occasional references by another), and Area 3, 'Styles and Genres of Language' (four episodes in the lessons of one French teacher). Almost all of these explicit references to Area 3 were accounted for by reference to a single sociolinguistic issue, the use of polite and familiar ways of saying 'you' in French (*tu* and *vous*). Altogether there were only four explicit, broader comments on particular language genres (also Area 3), three of them on how to lay out a letter. Areas 4 (dialectal/multilingual issues) and 5 (language change) received only passing and incidental mentions.

So, the central KAL area addressed by the FL teachers was Area 1, 'Language as System'. But the target language system was handled very selectively; three out of the four teachers concentrated their attention on particular details of grammar and word formation. Thus one provided her French class with explicit accounts of sets of verb endings, and possessive and demonstrative adjectives; another devoted a whole French lesson to explaining the relative *qui*; another described the article system of Spanish, and how nouns are made singular or plural. In all three cases, this selection of detailed points followed closely the recommendations of the textbook they were using; the main principle underlying the selection seemed to be one of *contrast*, i.e. points where the French/Spanish/German system differs most strikingly from English grammar.

The fourth FL teacher was somewhat exceptional. She was not following a single textbook, and concentrated her KAL Area 1 work on sentence structure at a fairly abstract level, teaching explicitly the concepts 'Subject', 'Verb', 'Complement' through a variety of action games. This teacher also paid systematic attention to Area 2, 'Language Learning and Development'. She did this by regularly asking her pupils, at the end of the lesson, what new language (e.g. new vocabulary) they thought they had learnt that day, and by what means they had learnt it; she would then invite them to reflect explicitly on the usefulness of a range of conscious learning strategies. (Just one other teacher touched on this Area, but more briefly.)

In interview, several FL teachers argued for broader rationales for KAL than were apparent in the observations (e.g. that explicit discussion of language was interesting in its own right). However, the dominant rationale for explicit attention to KAL in the classroom, as far as the FL teachers were concerned, was the direct contribution they saw it making to the development of pupils' target language proficiency, and this was clearly reflected in the focus of their KAL work on 'Language as System'.

Practice in the English Classroom

While the KAL work observed in the FL classrooms converged substantially on Area 1, the work of the three English teachers participating in the study had a very different slant.

In response to perceived National Curriculum requirements for increased attention to KAL in the English classroom, teachers in two of the three schools reported that entire units of work on KAL were currently being planned and/ or implemented at various points across Years 7–9. (In the early 1990s this was common practice; another example is reported in chapter 6 by Cooper and McIntyre.) So, in one school, explicit KAL units were being planned on 'Child Language Acquisition' (relevant to our Area 2), on 'Accent and Dialect' (Area 4), and on 'Language Repertoires' (Area 3). In another, a unit on 'Language Change' (Area 5) had been taught in Year 8 (and several pupils recollected and commented on this, in discussions and interviews). However, as it happened, none of these units was currently being taught to Year 9 during the periods of observation in the different schools. Thus in all cases the KAL work actually observed by the Southampton researchers arose out of units of work with other focuses. (Some teachers argued in any case that this was a more desirable strategy for the teaching of KAL, in principle, than the development of free-standing KAL units.) This work will now be discussed, for each of the three English classrooms observed in our study.

In School 1, during the period of observation, the teacher was working mainly on a Shakespeare text (*Romeo and Juliet*: 12 observed lessons, including four devoted to reading aloud, and others involving the production of a related 'newspaper' by pupils working in small groups). Three further observed lessons were given over to the study of poetry.

For this teacher, the main KAL area receiving attention was Area 3 ('Styles and Genres of Language'). In over 20 episodes, pre-planned to a considerable extent, the main emphasis was either on the characteristics of newspaper reporting, or the stylistic devices of poetry. This teacher also paid incidental attention to Area 2, giving explicit advice on reading aloud. Area 1 ('Language as System') received planned attention on two occasions, when substantial episodes intended to provide remedial guidance on punctuation interrupted the Shakespeare lesson series; otherwise it received intermittent responsive attention when pupils asked for help with accuracy of written work.

The English teacher at School 2 was also reading a play with her class, in this case a modern children's play, during many of the observed lessons. A small number of poetry lessons were also seen. However, unlike the work seen at School 1, there was little explicit discussion of the stylistic/linguistic characteristics of these genres. Instead, most KAL-related talk arose around a project to develop pupils' interviewing skills (with videorecording), and a subsequent initiative to develop essay-writing skills. Both these sequences involved extensive teacher-led discussion of the characteristics of effective interviews and effective essays, and the development of criteria for evaluating both; thus these episodes related mostly to KAL Areas 2 and 3, identified 15 and seven times respectively.

In addition, of all the teachers in the sample, this teacher was the one who paid most attention to Area 4 ('Social and Regional Variation': seven episodes). She taught one substantial planned episode, on contrasts between 'slang' and Standard English (see chapter 6 for a further example of this), and referred in passing elsewhere to accent/dialect variation and associated language attitudes. She also referred intermittently in positive terms to the bilingualism of a proportion of the pupils in the school, with the aim of raising the profile and status of their mother tongue (Bengali). However, she paid very little attention to KAL Area 1, 'Language as System' (apart from brief comments of a responsive/corrective nature, occasionally to individuals, once to the whole class). Area 5 (language change) did not appear at all during this particular sequence of lessons.

The teacher of English in School 3 generated the fewest explicit KAL episodes. Though studying a 'class novel' during some of the observed lessons, this teacher was also very concerned to develop the creative potential of his pupils, and to enable them to see connections between activities in English lessons and 'real life', including events in the news, and their own personal and emotional development. He had a range of strategies to promote this, including close study of selected text extracts, contrasting journalism with literature, and brainstorming techniques to promote word associations and extend pupils' repertoire of vocabulary. Much of this work was presented in a 'deep end' experiential mode, with only intermittent commentary on the purposes underlying the various activities. However, such KAL episodes as there were typically arose from text study, and concerned for example the techniques used by Dickens to create a particular descriptive account, or the imagery of a poem; they thus fell into Area 3 ('Styles and Genres of Language': 15 episodes). All other areas of KAL were referred to rarely or not at all in his lessons. His preoccupation with creative processes might have been expected to result in more explicit attention to Area 2, but his prime aim seemed to be that pupils should experience creativity, rather than reflect explicitly on it.

The three English teachers, then, had certain things in common. Most obviously, their work was text focused, and in so far as they engaged with KAL, they shared a commitment to explicit talk about the characteristics of particular kinds of text, whether literary or non-literary. (This did not always happen, however; for example, the reading of plays did not necessarily lead to discussion of dramatic form.) Unsurprisingly, their comments were often concerned with features of whole texts, and rarely paid attention to the specific detail of sentence structure. Area 1, 'Language as System', was given strikingly little attention by any of the English teachers (apart from one teacher's 'blitz' on punctuation).

As for their rationales for KAL, two of the three English teachers (though not so obviously the third) seemed to believe that establishment of explicit criteria at a fairly high level of generality (e.g. for newspaper writing or interviewing) would feed through into more effective language performance by their pupils. It was felt that systematic and explicit study of technical details of literary genres would improve the quality of pupils' encounters with, and response to, literature; one teacher also aspired to foster pluralist language attitudes through classroom discussion. On the other hand, there was only one, isolated episode of punctuation teaching, to suggest any real belief on the part of these teachers that pupils' accuracy (never mind creativity) in English could be improved through explicit 'Language as System' instruction.

Pupils' Knowledge about Language

While classroom observation tells us much about teachers' models of language, their theories of language development, and their beliefs about the place of KAL in language education, it inevitably reveals much less about the beliefs and understandings of their pupils. Special complementary efforts were there- fore made throughout the periods of lesson observations, and also in a phase of special activities conducted in the summer of 1992, to explore pupils' knowledge and beliefs through a variety of tasks conducted in small groups outside 'normal' language lessons. These activities aimed to explore pupils' own understandings of the nature of language, the origins of pupils' KAL, and their beliefs about the relationship of such knowledge with language development.

In the following sections, we will seek to summarize the picture of pupils' 'Knowledge about Language', as revealed through these special activities. This will be done using the same five headings that were used when analysing classroom practice.

Pupils' KAL: 'Language as System'

Pupils' explicit knowledge of 'Language as System' was explored through group problem-solving tasks, plus individual discussions on texts the children had produced in class. Generally, these Year 9 pupils showed practical competence in such tasks as unscrambling jumbled texts, creating sentences from nonsense words, or correcting grammatically deviant language (such as baby talk). However, their ability to comment on and explain their decision-making in these tasks was very limited.

It was another task conducted individually, discussions about texts produced in class (such as pen pal letters written in French), that gave the fullest insights into pupils' explicit knowledge of sentence grammar. Most pupils knew the names of some parts of speech ('noun', 'verb', 'adjective'). However, when asked to explain the relevant concepts, they tended to offer rather one-sided definitions, referring to typical meanings, but ignoring matters of form. Thus, for example, a verb would most frequently be defined as a 'doing word', and only a small number of pupils could extend this to include other features such as characteristic word endings:

> Because 'dance' is a doing word . . . well, 'tennis' you could say is a doing word, but [it doesn't] have 'E-R' on the end. (School 1)

Pupils in upper-ability and mixed-ability FL sets could also talk about some other grammatical concepts ('tense', 'gender' and 'number'); they were aware that these mattered, for example in selecting correct word endings, though few had much grasp of detail. For example, one pupil could comment on a correction she had made:

> I just know that if you're saying something you did in the past, it's got to have an accent on it, but if it's just like 'listenING', it doesn't need it. (School 1)

Here we can see evidence of awareness of the *principle* of using special word endings to indicate verb tense marking, even if details are still fuzzy.

Pupils in a lower FL set, and some other pupils identified as 'weak' by their teachers, had little or no grasp of such concepts. Interestingly, however, a number of individual pupils in different schools identified an increased understanding of 'how sentences are put together' as their major achievement in FL learning in Year 9:

> Before I just used to sort of learn it as single words, now I can sort of write a sentence, because we've been learning things like how to write in sentences, we're learning different words, and which goes with which. (School 2)

Pupils' understanding of text structure above the level of the sentence remained generally unsophisticated. They could talk in general terms about the need for 'paragraphs' and appropriate spelling and punctuation in written texts, but did not have much else to say about the structuring of non-fictional writing; they typically evaluated their own writing mostly in terms of content and surface presentation. For example, a School 3 pupil commented in these terms on a letter he had written in French:

> I was pleased with it, I described myself a lot, said what hobbies I had and stuff like that. Well, there's a couple of mistakes probably on there. (School 3)

It was much more unusual to find comments on these French texts in terms of authenticity *as letters*, though one pupil did remark that hers was 'not the sort of thing I'd [really] write to a French pen friend . . . I wouldn't exactly be telling them where I lived, because they'd obviously know'.

The main exception was connected with creative writing, as seen, for example, in School 3, where pupils all talked with considerably more sophistication about the crafting of a poem they had recently written. Indeed, this ability could be linked quite directly with the kind of textual analysis seen in classroom discussions led by their teacher (and described in an earlier section).

Pupils' KAL: 'Language Learning and Development'

In a second cluster of specially devised tasks, which prompted pupils to reflect on their own classroom experience of studying both English and a foreign language, we explored pupils' understandings of the processes of language learning and development.

In both English and foreign language, pupils showed a general ability to reflect on the environment that would best promote effective learning. Most obviously, they attached great importance to their teachers' personal qualities. Thus the English groups commended their teachers most often for telling pupils what to do, for explaining and making sure pupils understood, and for making learning fun and interesting. A business-like attitude to work (keeping attention, keeping control, getting to the point) and insistence that pupils worked hard were also mentioned with some frequency.

The FL groups generally favoured the same generic qualities, but identified some subject-specific qualities in addition. One group commended their teacher's personal proficiency in French, and several commented on the kind of communication style that would be most helpful in an FL teacher. Such comments ranged from general suggestions such as 'speak more French to us, so we could learn to speak more fluently', or 'say phrases to us that we understand', to more analytic comments on the need for the teacher to speak slowly, or even to swap systematically between languages:

> I think the teacher should say it in French, and then if we don't understand it, she'll repeat it in English. (School 2)

Pupils generally assumed that experiences that they found personally interesting and involving would also be effective for learning. Thus, for example, pupils focusing on FL learning recommended role play, computer activities, games and puzzles, 'acting out' and watching TV as enjoyable and so more likely to lead to learning. (Similar beliefs also emerge from the work of Cooper and McIntyre in chapter 6.)

Pupils could also make some comments about the range of activities that they saw as likely to help develop particular language skills. Thus, for example, various pupils claimed that classroom conversation, reading aloud, grammar study, and/or visits abroad would help develop FL speaking skills. In English-focused discussions, interactions among the language skills were commonly referred to. So, reading in English was seen as a self-reinforcing skill, but also as a practice that builds vocabulary, and helps with spelling, with oral communication (through reading aloud) and with understanding variation in written language.

While able to recognize general connections between different broad types of classroom activity and the development of different language skills. it was, however, unusual for pupils to talk about how current classroom activities helped their learning in any very specific terms. The commonest ground for recommending an activity was that it 'helps you learn'/'helps you understand'. However, there were some striking exceptions to this; the FL-related discussions of two groups (all boys, as it happened) stood out prominently in terms of the variety and specificity of their comments. Both groups came from School 3, where (as described earlier) the French teacher had invested considerable effort in explicit discussion both of 'Language as System' and of language-learning strategies. These two groups, and other individuals from the same class, made consistent reference to these classroom activities while carrying out our discussion tasks considerably later in the school year. Some sample comments follow, to illustrate the lasting awareness that seemed to arise from this more analytic approach:

> The verbs helped us understand making sentences a lot better, so did the sentence-building.

> [Sentence-building] builds your confidence. Where before the teacher said to us, now try and write your sentence . . . we found that we could only write a couple of words in a sentence. Then she showed us how to use the sentence-building – we were writing really long sentences, about 20 words long. That was pretty good.

> Pupil A: [The teacher] asks people how they've remembered something, so we remember it.
> Pupil B: Yeah, and if you get it wrong then you seem to remember it a bit more.

These comments illustrate one of the strongest connections we were able to make between teachers' observed attempts in the classroom to introduce reflection on language itself, and pupils' personal 'Knowledge about Language'.

Pupils' KAL: 'Language Variation'

Our third KAL area, 'Styles and Genres of Language', covered explicit knowledge in the areas of style, register and genre (text types). On a problem-solving group task, pupils could identify different types of text, though they were generally unable to explain in any technical way what precise features of the selected texts were distinctive to the genre. In evaluating their own non-fiction writing, pupils were preoccupied with matters of content and self-expression rather than style or appropriacy (as we have seen above). It was only in the context of creative writing (poetry) that they were able or willing to articulate more technical and analytic comments on matters of style.

However, pupils showed much greater analytic ability in our Area 4, 'Social and Regional Variation'. The main data source was a group discussion task concerning speech styles in English. Across all three schools, pupils showed a lively awareness of social variation in spoken English, and could talk at some length about their own practices. Many pupils claimed personally to use a relatively neutral speech style, for which they offered informal definitions: 'not too slang, not too posh, just in between' (School 2). This neutral style was contrasted with 'high' and 'low' styles, which pupils perceived in others' speech. Pupils were aware of variation in their own speech according to situation and interlocutor. Talk about different speech styles was richly illustrated with mimicked examples, and some pupils could also identify some specific pronunciation features (e.g. glottal stops) and syntactic features (e.g. 'ain't') that they associated with particular styles. School 2, with the most working-class intake, showed keenest awareness of features of urban dialect and, in particular, of possible social stigmas attaching to them. (It was also in this school, of course, that we had observed regular references to accent/dialect issues in the English classroom.)

Despite this relatively high level of awareness, however, pupils generally lacked technical vocabulary for discussion of dialectal and social variation, and there was considerable confusion and overlap among the concepts employed. Generally their comments seemed to reflect folk-linguistic models current in the community, rather than classroom-derived knowledge.

As an extension to our research on 'Social and Regional Variation', we also informally interviewed a number of bilingual pupils in Schools 2 and 3 about their language skills and language-use patterns. These interviews revealed a rich diversity of multilingual knowledge and practices. The bilingual pupils could describe their own language abilities effectively, comparing proficiency in different languages, and discriminating between oral and written skills. They could explain where and when they spoke a particular language, and with whom; they could reflect on changes in such patterns over time.

However, it seemed that bilingual pupils' understandings came almost entirely from practical experience and non-school sources. When such pupils attempted to describe any more technical aspects of 'their' language, such as the script used, pronunciation features or dialectal variation, for example, they quickly ran out of terminology. One Punjabi-speaking boy referred to a TV programme as an information source (on the relationship between Punjabi, Hindi and Urdu); but it seemed that none of the KAL teaching offered in any of the schools had dealt systematically with bilingualism/multilingualism, world languages, or indeed any aspect of language variation beyond the world of English.

Pupils' KAL: 'Language Change'

Of all the KAL areas identified within the study, the issue of 'Language Change' attracted least discussion in the observed lessons. Consequently, the pupil tasks for this dimension were analysed only impressionistically. In one task, pupils showed some capacity to produce pastiche 'Shakespearean' dialogue, mainly through a display of 'archaic' lexis, address forms and exclamations. In another, they showed some awareness of the entry of 'new' words into the English language. But little awareness was shown of syntactic change, and nothing more than limited common-sense speculations were advanced as to why such changes might come about.

Conclusion: KAL in Curriculum Theory and in Classroom Practice

These limited case studies lead to tentative conclusions regarding current KAL classroom practices, and their relationship with curriculum proposals and debates.

1   Pupils in secondary school receive largely unrelated messages in the KAL area from their English and FL classes. In the FL classroom, attention is focused on 'Language as System' at the sentence level or below, while in the English classroom, attention is focused on the level of the whole text, and the distinctive characteristics of language genres, literary and non-literary. Neither group of teachers takes much interest in the KAL issues being addressed by the other. Evidence from pupils' discussion suggests that at least when doing written work in English or in an FL, they tend to concentrate their attention selectively on the issues highlighted by their different teachers (though they also have a more general concern with basic accuracy). As learners must move from sentence-level competence to discourse competence in their language development, whatever the language, this discontinuity is unhelpful. All teachers need to recognize pupils' concerns for low-level accuracy, and we believe that linking that concern to understanding of broader discourse issues will significantly help effective language use, in both English and foreign languages.

2   It seemed that teachers' classroom practice had been only partially influenced by recent curriculum debates on KAL, at least in these case-study schools. The FL teachers adhered to a fairly traditional view of the usefulness of selected grammatical information for enhancing classroom learning, and were systematically working to build up knowledge of this kind (with the exception of lower-ability sets). The English teachers were debating the introduction of a greater KAL emphasis in the form of identifiable units and modules of work; but meanwhile, their classroom activity reflected traditional preoccupations with literature, with personal and social growth, and with creativity. In the service of these aims, explicit introduction to genres and styles of both talk and writing was seen as useful at a general level; but detailed language analysis was not regularly undertaken, and systematic exposition of

sentence-level 'Language as System' was seen as irrelevant to learners beyond the initial stages of literacy development.

It is here that there may be the greatest mismatch between popular political (and media) views and current practice. We are sceptical that these tensions can (or should) ever be resolved fully, given the symbolic cultural meaning of English teaching in particular, and its inevitably ideological foundations. We are convinced that any attempt to impose traditional-style grammar teaching on the present teaching force via curriculum fiat would fail miserably (especially in the light of paragraphs 3 and 4 below). Our own views on how to achieve greater consistency (and developmental progression) in KAL work are set out in paragraph 6.

3   Despite recent investment in teacher training, via the LINC programme, teachers' own 'Knowledge about Language' remained patchy and idiosyncratic. (The LINC programme had not had a major impact locally and was referred to negatively by those teachers in these schools who had had contact with it.) The further development of teachers' knowledge in this area will be a long-term business, requiring substantial investment in in-service work (Brumfit, 1993).

4   Teachers see the point of KAL activity in the classroom, and undertake it most systematically, where they perceive it to be contributing to pupils' own language development. Though different in focus, the FL teachers' work on 'Language as System', and on learning strategies, and the English teachers' work on genre and style, were both driven largely by a belief that there would be a more or less direct payoff for pupils' improved performance. KAL work with other rationales (enhancement of motivation for language learning, multiculturalism, critical language awareness etc.) was much more intermittent and individual-dependent.

5   Pupils' KAL was also patchy, and generally lacking in control of technical details; much of it seemed to derive from life experience rather than from classroom information and discussion. However, there were examples of particular KAL topics where pupils' grasp of technical concepts and vocabulary, and ability to discuss fluently, were much more fully developed. In several cases these strong points of pupil knowledge could be traced back to particular teacher-led classroom episodes or KAL-focused units of work. Thus we found a number of very positive examples of ways in which KAL instruction can connect with pupils' understanding; what was lacking was a systematic developmental framework into which such episodes could fit.

6   Curriculum planners seeking to promote a more coherent approach to KAL work must confront both rigid subject boundaries and the limitations of

teachers' own knowledge base, over the long term. Most importantly, perhaps, the basis for teachers' beliefs about the positive role of certain kinds of KAL in classroom language development (and for the non-role of others, such as sentence-level work in English) requires reassessment in what would inevitably be a long-term research/development programme. Without such studies, as we have seen in the erratic U-turns of National Curriculum policy for language and the waste of LINC's developmental resources, coherent policy-making is itself at risk. The following points could guide a more theoretically defensible approach:

(a) bring together curriculum planning for English and for foreign languages as a single coherent strand;
(b) examine the bases for the role of explicit commentary and reflection on learning processes in language development, and in other subject areas;
(c) use the experience of other countries in offering language policies and teaching methods for KAL as part of their educational provision;
(d) locate curriculum development within a continuing programme of empirical work on current classroom practice, closely related to the needs for teacher updating and development.

Without such support, policy-making will flounder because it will be isolated from classroom practice, learners' experience and teachers' knowledge base. With such support, the basis for a substantial increase in learners' knowledge and skills will have been laid.

6

The Importance of Power-sharing in Classroom Learning

Paul Cooper and Donald McIntyre

Editor's Introduction

This chapter, by Paul Cooper and Donald McIntyre, continues our concern with teachers' and pupils' perceptions of teaching and learning. The authors pay particular attention to what teachers and pupils consider to be the most effective ways of achieving pupil learning, and the extent to which teachers and pupils agree on these issues. In this chapter, Cooper and McIntyre report on observations made in English and history lessons in Key Stage Three, and on subsequent interviews about those lessons carried out with teachers and pupils. The authors use their data to identify and describe two main teaching approaches – 'reactive teaching' and 'interactive teaching' – which are regarded as effective both by pupils and teachers. They conclude that 'teachers and pupils value learning situations in which control over the content and direction of lessons is shared in different ways'; at the same time, they suggest that some aspects of the current educational reforms are creating pressures on teachers that may make this harder to bring about in the classroom.

Introduction

This chapter is concerned with some of the ways in which teachers and pupils talk and think about effective classroom teaching and learning. We are particularly interested in what teachers and pupils are able to tell us about the ways they think about lessons, as well as how they think during lessons. The research we describe in this chapter is based on the idea that teachers and pupils are experts in their particular classroom roles. Like all experts they make what they do seem easy, and quite often they believe it to be easy, passing off their skilled behaviour as 'common sense'. What we show here is that skilled teaching is far from easy. Rather, it is based on highly specialized understandings and, therefore, uncommon sense. We suggest that by gaining access to teachers' and pupils' knowledge about how they go about achieving the goals of classroom teaching and learning (their 'craft knowledge') on a day-to-day basis, we are uncovering information that will be invaluable to all teachers, whether experienced, newly qualified or in training. There are many different ways in which such information will be helpful, including: as a source of models of practice to imitate and test in the classroom; as examples of practice that can be compared to readers' existing practice; and particularly, as a set of ideas to be debated and to act as a springboard to reflection on teachers' existing practice.

The substantive focus of this chapter is the way in which teacher and pupil thinking interacts in the classroom, and how this relates to the kinds of learning opportunities experienced by pupils. We argue, with reference to detailed interviews with teachers and Year 7 pupils in English and history lessons, that teachers and pupils have at times distinct agendas, and, therefore, sometimes differing perceptions of what makes an effective classroom experience. We also show, however, that when pupils and teachers focus on their perceptions of teaching that leads to effective learning, there is considerable overlap between the teacher and pupil agendas. The shared ingredients of these agendas are:

- a belief in the importance of the active involvement of pupils in the learning process;
- the teachers' willingness to make use of pupils' ideas and ways of thinking in their own thinking about how to make new knowledge accessible;
- an emphasis on encouraging pupils to construct and share their own understandings during lessons.

It will be shown that a key issue here is the extent to which teachers are willing to share with pupils control over lesson content and learning objectives, and that effective teaching (as defined by teachers and pupils in this study) often seems to depend on the form of power-sharing in these areas.

Issues

The main question that our project addresses is:

In what ways do teachers and pupils perceive effective classroom teaching and learning?

This is an important question because it is underpinned by a number of different principles that make up a distinctive and, we think, highly constructive approach to thinking about the quality of teaching and learning, and how improvements might be made in these areas. These principles can be expressed briefly in terms of the following propositions:

1   Teaching and learning are both highly skilled activities.
2   Like other skilled activities (e.g. the performance of crafts and sports), the bases for successful teaching and learning can be traced to certain underlying theories (e.g. the skills of carpentry can be closely related to understandings of the technical nature of wood).
3   While it is not necessary to understand the theories underlying the craft of teaching and learning in order to master the skills of teaching and learning, an understanding of such theories may lead to informed decision-making and facilitate speed of skill acquisition and skill development.
4   In order to gain access to the theories underpinning the skilled activities of teaching and learning, it is appropriate to make explicit the thinking of pupils and teachers when they engage in or reflect on these skilled activities.

It is important to stress, therefore, that in our research we did not set out to test one or more theories about what effective teaching and learning might be like; rather, our study was designed to gain access to the implicit theories that drive what teachers and pupils do in the classroom. We saw our task as researchers as helping teachers and pupils to articulate the complex thinking that we believe to underpin their skilled activity. This endeavour created its own set of distinctive methodological problems. We had to devise research methods that would enable us to feel confident that we were gaining access to teachers' and pupils' authentic perceptions of their classroom thinking, and their thinking about what goes on during teaching and learning. We will include a brief account of the methods we devised, first, because the validity of what we present depends to a large extent on our methods of data collection, and second, because we believe that our methodology will be of interest to teachers and others who might wish to engage in classroom research of this kind.

A further important issue, which is implicit in what we have so far written, is our respect for teachers as expert professionals, and our respect for pupils as autonomous, thinking beings. These are topical issues in England and Wales at the present time, and too complex for us to discuss in any detail in a short chapter such as this. However, suffice it to say that at a time when teachers are increasingly under pressure to be accountable in terms of extraneous and sometimes irrelevant 'efficiency' measures and performance indicators (e.g. examination league tables), and when their practice is subjected to the scrutiny and judgement of those who may or may not have a concern for the quality of teaching and learning as it is experienced by all children, this research gives a voice to teachers that we hope will be heard in the ongoing debate. Similarly, it seems appropriate to give voice to those who have recent and relevant experience of teaching methods: namely, the pupils.

On a positive note, we would argue that the outcomes of our research have a practical significance for teachers and teacher educators concerned with meeting the requirements of the National Curriculum. In particular, we would suggest that what we have to say here has important implications for the issue of differentiation in the curriculum. A central theme in the responses of pupils and teachers in this study was the need for learning situations to be structured so as to enable students to engage in ways that are best suited to their particular characteristics as learners. The focus of our study is precisely on the mechanisms by which the teachers and pupils believed they achieved effective learning through pedagogical (i.e. teaching) strategies as opposed to purely organizational strategies (e.g. student grouping) (Straddling and Saunders, 1993). In particular, the present study suggests that students may be able to contribute a great deal more to the differentiation process than is often thought possible, if they are given the kinds of opportunities for involvement discussed here.

The Study

The intention of the present study is to access and describe teachers' and pupils' ways of construing and facilitating effective classroom teaching and learning, and to explore the relationship between teacher and pupil perspectives. Within this context, particular attention is given to issues of: subject teaching and learning in English and history; teachers' ways of construing and taking account of individual differences among pupils; and teachers' responses to the newly introduced National Curriculum in these two subject areas.

Methodology

Research such as this, which attempts to give an 'insider's' view of a particular phenomenon, poses particular challenges for the researcher. In effect, we are claiming that our analysis is based on an accurate account by teachers and pupils of their thinking. In order to support this claim, it is necessary to say something briefly about how we obtained this data (for a more detailed discussion of methodology, see Cooper, 1993b). We believe such an account to be essential if the reader is to be persuaded of the validity of our claims. The two major challenges that faced us were:

1   To motivate teachers and pupils to reveal to us authentic accounts of their thinking that were not distorted by our method of inquiry, so that they were telling us what they really thought, and not simply telling us what we led them to believe we wanted to hear.

2   To motivate teachers and pupils to talk about their thinking in the context of actual teaching and learning events, rather than in generalized terms. The challenge here was to employ a method of data gathering that enabled us to claim that the thinking we accessed was firmly grounded in classroom activity.

While we accept that we can never be absolutely sure of accessing accurate recall of anyone's thoughts, we can take measures that will help to motivate people to give intentionally honest responses. This is what we mean by 'authenticity'.

The central aim of the research was to enable teachers and pupils to articulate their authentic understandings of their own effective teaching and learning. This aim required a method of data collection that would stimulate and motivate participants to explore and make explicit thoughts and feelings of a personal and possibly idiosyncratic nature, that are not necessarily the subject of routine conscious reflection.

The method we chose was based on one already successfully employed by Brown and McIntyre (1993) in their study of teachers' craft knowledge, combined with interview techniques developed by Cooper (1989, 1993a). This involved the use of an 'informant'-style interview (Powney and Watts, 1987) in conjunction with a programme of participant observation. Participants were interviewed as soon as possible after lessons that had been observed by the interviewer, and were asked to talk about any aspects of the lessons that they believed to have been particularly successful or otherwise notable. The interviewer's role was then to prompt the interviewee to elaborate and exemplify points made. The interview technique was developed with reference to cognitive theories that suggest that recall can be improved if interviewees are initially asked very open-ended questions that allow them to recall almost any aspect of a chosen situation. This idiosyncratic recall acts as a reference point from which the interviewee is then able to reconstruct other aspects of the situation that they first appear to have forgotten or to be unaware of (Baddeley, 1990; Roy, 1990; see Cooper, 1993b, for a more detailed account of the interview technique).

Participants

Eight English teachers, five history teachers and their respective Year 7 classes participated in the study. Eight of these teachers were studied over a four-hour unit of work on three separate occasions throughout the year. The remaining teachers were studied for a single five- to six-hour unit. A second phase of the project has so far extended the study into Year 9, and looked at the perceptions of four English teachers and their Year 9 pupils in two English departments. A 'unit' is defined as a series of consecutive lessons that have a clearly stated and coherent subject-related theme or series of connected themes. The content of units was decided by the teacher concerned.

Analysis

Interview transcripts were analysed using a form of comparative analysis developed by Brown and McIntyre (1993). This involves a process by which the unfolding descriptive theories that emerge from the data are constantly tested and refined to take account of all relevant data. The analysis takes the following form:

1 reading a random sample of transcripts;
2 identifying points of similarity and difference among these transcripts in relation to our research questions;
3 generating theories describing emergent answers to research questions;
4 testing theories against a new set of transcripts;
5 testing new theories against transcripts already dealt with;
6 carrying all existing theories forward to new transcripts;
7 repeating above processes until all data have been examined and all theories tested against all data.

Findings

This chapter is particularly concerned with the things that teachers and pupils have told us about their most effective ways of achieving pupil subject learning. Before going on to discuss this in detail, it is necessary to give an indication of how this particular concern with subject learning fits in with the wider range of teacher and pupil concerns.

The teachers' and pupils' ideas about effective teaching and learning can be divided into two broad categories: ideas related to *classroom process* and ideas related to *pupil learning outcomes*.

For teachers, there appear to be two different ways of construing 'effective teaching'. On the one hand, 'effectiveness' was determined by their success in devising a lesson that took appropriate account of particular *process* variables, including: the demands of the National Curriculum, the available time, the available resources, and their perceptions of individual differences among pupils. Some teachers were deeply concerned with a need to offer pupils a 'varied diet' in terms of lesson content and activity, therefore the nature of a particular lesson would, for these teachers, be influenced strongly by what had gone before. Teachers who felt that previous lessons had been, intellectually, particularly demanding for their pupils would sometimes select a lesson topic and style of working that they construed as having a recreational dimension. Although teachers often believed that, in taking account of conditions in these ways, they were contributing to pupils' learning, pupil learning was not the most important priority, and sometimes this was perceived as only an indirect consequence of their activities. Thus a significant part of teachers' thinking was consistently directed towards the creation of particular conditions in the classroom. Although these conditions were often seen by teachers to be conducive to effective learning, the creation of the conditions themselves was a sufficient basis for teacher satisfaction, sometimes with a deliberate disregard for evidence of pupil learning. For example, where teachers required pupils to work on a task in a particular manner, such as in collaborative groups, or individually, or through the use of research materials, they would often express satisfaction or otherwise with the lesson on the basis of the pupil behaviour they had observed. Examples of successful process outcomes would be:

- a successful group work lesson would often be one where pupils had been seen to engage in group discussion with a high participation level, and a low level of inappropriate behaviour (e.g. loud talking/shouting; boisterous behaviour etc.);
- a successful lesson involving individual work would be one where pupils were seen to be engaged in apparent silent study, with minimal inappropriate behaviour;
- a successful lesson involving pupil research would be marked by the range and quantity of materials apparently employed by pupils, with minimal inappropriate behaviour.

The second way that teachers had of construing effective teaching showed considerable overlap with pupil views. This saw effective teaching in terms of its direct relationship to *pupil learning*. This showed itself in a concern for the degree to which the teaching methods had succeeded in providing structures that enabled pupils to gain access to particular knowledge.

Pupils believed teaching methods to be effective when they resulted in pupil learning or extended pupil understanding in some way. Many different styles of teaching were associated with positive outcomes, including transmission (e.g. teacher-directed 'chalk and talk' lessons) and more interactive modes (e.g. where pupils participated more fully in lessons, through discussion or self-directed study). The critical issue for pupils appeared to be the degree to which the teaching created structures that fostered understanding, by enabling them

to perceive personally meaningful connections between their existing knowledge and new knowledge. Effective teaching, from the pupil perspective, was
most often associated with teaching methods and strategies that were enjoyable
and produced high levels of imaginative and practical pupil involvement in
lesson activity such as:

- story telling (by the teacher);
- drama and role play exercises;
- visual stimuli (e.g. photographs, drawings, diagrams, video);
- whole-group and small-group discussion;
- teacher-led question-and-answer sessions;
- opportunities for pupil collaboration in groups and pairs (e.g. on problem-
  solving tasks, joint/group production tasks, brainstorming).

Within the pupil group there were interesting differences in pupil perceptions
of effectiveness on certain occasions, of which teachers were unaware. Pupils
whom teachers perceived to be of particularly high ability sometimes complained that teachers overstructured learning situations, and in so doing
inhibited the pupils' use of their own learning and sense-making strategies.
These views often coincided with other pupils' and teachers' beliefs that the
structuring had been a necessary aid to pupil understanding. Pupils of perceived
low ability, on the other hand, sometimes had difficulty in deriving benefit
from teacher structures that were overly dependent on literacy skills, and
though teachers were often aware of this problem in general, they sometimes
failed to identify its occurrence in practice.

From Practice to Theory

Having briefly described some of the main findings of the study, it is now
necessary to develop a theoretical analysis of these findings. The analysis that is
presented below reveals to us important relationships between the everyday
thinking of the participants in our study and particular psychological theories
of how children learn. It must be emphasized that the theoretical models that
we draw upon in our analysis were chosen because they appeared to be highly
consonant with teachers' and pupils' common-sense thinking, as it was revealed
to us in interviews. We believe that this process of developing theory from
practice is a useful way of generating new theories and identifying existing
theories that are of practical value in the school context. The particular value
of such explanatory theories lies in the degree to which they can provide a
framework for enabling teachers to think about and further develop their
practical teaching skills. Such theories, when reached via the route of teachers'

practical craft knowledge, are also useful for the beginning teacher and others who wish to gain easy access to the knowledge that underlies successful teaching, helping to avoid the necessity to repeatedly 'reinvent the wheel'.

The Transactional Nature of Teaching and Learning

There is a strong sense in which both teachers and pupils see effective teaching and learning as 'transactional' processes (Bruner, 1987; see also Vygotsky, 1987). To a large extent their views of learning conform to a model proposed by Bruner and Haste (1987), which describes learning as a complex 'interweaving' of 'language, interaction and cognition'. The main contention of this view is that learners learn through a process of first being exposed to new knowledge, and then attempting to make sense of the new knowledge in terms of their existing knowledge. A simple illustration of this view of learning would be the situation where a child is able to define accurately the meaning of a foreign word on the basis of phonic or lexical similarities with other known words.

This sense-making cannot be done by the individual in isolation; it involves the learner in articulating his or her understandings and matching them with those that are presented by others (e.g. the teacher, a peer, the text of a book, the speaker of a foreign language). This enables us to see learning as an essentially social process. Through repeated matching and comparing of understandings the learner eventually comes to a point where he or she perceives there to be a shared understanding. This process of constant matching and comparison is known as 'calibration' (Bruner and Haste, 1987). The teacher's role in this transaction is to create circumstances that enable the learner 'to integrate her capacities and interpretations with those of significant others around her' (p. 5). This is achieved (1) through the provision of *grammars* and *scripts*, and (2) through the process of *scaffolding*.

Grammars and *scripts* define appropriate ways of behaving and using language in a given situation. They are the patterns of expression and behaviour that are used by the pupil for 'making sense' of learning situations. The teacher provides them either through direct instruction, or by legitimizing the pupil's 'own behaviours and utterances' (Bruner and Haste, 1987, p. 20). It is interesting to note that the phenomenon of the teacher dictating the form of classroom discourse has been widely acknowledged by psychologists, sociologists and anthropologists (see Cole, 1985, for a discussion of the ways in which these disciplines can be seen to converge in the work of the Russian psychologist Vygotsky on children's learning). In the present volume there is an example of a similar phenomenon being observed and discussed in terms of Bernstein's concepts of recognition and realization rules (see chapter 4 by Whitty, Aggleton and Rowe).

Scaffolding is the process whereby the teacher provides model structures that enable the pupil to apply existing skills in new ways in the appropriation of new knowledge. It is the extension to the child's capabilities afforded when the teacher instructs the pupil in procedures that enable him or her to employ existing skills in a new way in order to solve a problem. For example, scaffolding describes the process whereby a maths teacher provides a pupil with a formula for calculating the area of a particular triangle. The child already has knowledge of the characteristics of a triangle, of arithmetic and certain of the conventions of mathematical formulae; once given the formula he or she is able to apply it to all triangles of a similar type. In English an example might be the extension of a pupil's compositional skills through the presentation of a 'beginning, middle and end' essay structure. The child is already able to write continuous, imaginative prose; the provision of this structure enables the child to incorporate structural considerations in the planning of compositions and thus extend the range of literary devices already possessed. The important point here, however, is that for scaffolding to be effective, the structure that is supplied by the teacher must be selected on the basis of its goodness of fit with the pupil's existing knowledge and cognitive structures. The selection of the appropriate structure, therefore, depends on the teacher's knowledge of the pupil's learning characteristics, and the teacher's ability to match these characteristics with his or her expert subject knowledge. In this way, effective teaching and learning can be seen as a process in which the teacher and the student compare their individual understandings and adjust them on the basis of the comparison.

The emphasis on the importance of relations between people, in this transactional theory of learning, also leads us to consideration of a further area of concern that is common to the theories of learning that emerge from this study: that of *affect*. 'Affect' refers to the emotional and temperamental aspects of human functioning. If we accept (as the transactional model requires) that learning is dependent on effective communication and cooperation between teachers and pupils, it follows that a necessary condition for effective learning to take place is the creation of circumstances that facilitate effective communication and cooperation. Furthermore, it can be argued that the appropriate forms of interaction that this view of learning considers necessary, are dependent on the quality of the individual's self-image: his or her sense of self-worth, and the belief in one's ability to take on and contribute to the resolution of problems. This requires an emotionally supportive environment, in which the learner feels valued and respected by the significant others (i.e. teachers and fellow pupils) with whom he or she is expected to interact in the learning process.

The rest of this chapter is devoted to a more detailed explication of these processes as they relate to first-hand experiences of effective teaching and learning as they are described by teachers and pupils in our study. There are two major teaching patterns that we have identified on the basis of what they told us. These are:

1 reactive teaching;
2 interactive teaching.

It will be shown that these patterns are essentially transactional in nature, through reference to the theoretical position presented above.

Teaching that Leads to Learning

When teachers talk about effective teaching that leads directly to pupil learning, they often talk in terms of the ways in which their pedagogical decisions are informed by perceptions they have (i.e. 'knowledge') of their pupils. Success often seems to depend on the extent to which teachers effectively integrate their knowledge of pupils with other knowledge – such as knowledge of subject content, curriculum requirements and different possible ways of giving pupils access to this knowledge – into their overall teaching plans. The manner in which teachers manage this integration is best seen in terms of a continuum that involves, at one end, *interactive teaching*, and at the other, *reactive teaching*.

Interactive teaching sees the teacher integrating knowledge of pupils with pre-lesson plans, in a way that places the main emphasis on pre-set learning goals and the demands of the curriculum. Reactive teaching has the teacher evolve plans more directly from his or her knowledge of pupils. Reactive teaching is characterized by the teacher's willingness to adjust learning objectives in order to accommodate pupil concerns. Much of the time teachers seem to engage in teaching that is somewhere towards the mid-point of the continuum, such as when teachers consciously and deliberately react to pupils' concerns and interests at the pre-active stage in the formulation of lesson plans, or when teachers introduce minor modifications to lesson plans at the interactive stage in direct response to emergent pupil concerns or interests. Having said this, individual teachers employ reactive and interactive strategies along with other teaching strategies as and when they feel them to be appropriate.

It should be stressed that the interactive–reactive continuum represents merely a segment of the wider continuum of teacher strategies. At the extreme end of the continuum beyond interactive teaching we would find transmission strategies, while at the extreme beyond reactive teaching would be strategies designed to facilitate self-directed learning (figure 6.1). Placement on this continuum is determined by the degree to which teachers share with pupils

Figure 6.1   A continuum of teaching strategies.

control over the learning situation, and the degree to which certain areas of decision-making are left open to negotiation.

Interactive Teaching

The interactive end of the continuum can be illustrated with reference to the work of any of the teachers in this study. A particularly good example is provided by an English teacher who expresses a high degree of satisfaction with the learning outcomes he has observed from a unit concerned with 'Knowledge about Language' (KAL – see chapter 5). In his summing up of the unit, he indicates a consciously strong commitment to what we term 'interactive teaching':

> [I was] pleased with the motivation of all the kids, and the way in which they brought, very enthusiastically, their own knowledge, or their own interest to that [i.e. the lesson content]. And the way in which they sparked ideas off each other, and started talking about issues to do with language that I hadn't necessarily introduced. And they seemed to have got a good understanding of the key terms that I tried to convey to them, in that sense. And now they talk quite confidently about 'jargon' and 'slang' and 'Standard English' and 'dialect'. And all I wanted to do, really, was to foster an awareness of those basic terms, so when they go to new texts they might think about that more.

It is quite clear that this teacher plans his teaching in such a way as to foster a transactional pattern of teaching and learning. An important mechanism for achieving this is the initiation and reinforcement of certain pupil scripts (Bruner and Haste, 1987), which contain directions as to how pupils should contribute to lessons. One 'pupil contribution script' requires pupils to bring items into lessons that have some bearing on the already planned lesson content:

> I always work like that. I always think that if children bring things to lessons that are going to help you along in a particular way, then you ought to use them. I think you ought to use them for two reasons. First of all, because it gives a positive message to the kids that a lesson is not just a teacher giving and children receiving {*script reinforcement*}. And that it's a two-way process, and that teachers can learn from children, and that it's a sharing and facilitating . . . Particularly in English, I think, because you're exploring things rather than having great bodies of knowledge {*scaffolding*}. So it's a positive thing, and I think it motivates them. And I like it from that point of view. But secondly, if you don't do that [i.e. utilize pupil material] I think you may well fall into the trap of teacher expectation, whereby you are too fixed in your own path, and you are determined to guide the class down a certain path. And if they say, 'Hey! this is interesting. Can't we stop and look at this for a little bit?', to say 'no' to that is unthinkable, because the teacher's being too rigid in their planning, and forcing the class down certain particular roads. Now I know that you have to have those planned out in your planning, and you have to take children in certain directions, because you've got objectives to meet, but if the things they're bringing in are stimulating and helpful, then I think it's a good idea to do that [i.e. utilize them].

The teacher clearly sees the use of reinforcement as essential to the establishment of the 'pupil contribution script' as an important part of the classroom process. He is also describing here a form of 'scaffolding' in that he appears to be using this script to model a particular way of construing learning in English, as two-way and collaborative. This approach is distinctively interactive because, in this case, the teacher sees the proper use of pupil input as being only within the parameters set by his pre-active lesson plans:

> If they ask questions like, 'can we look at this?', if I can see a way of fitting it into the [pre-planned] structure, well then the answer is usually 'yes, we can'.

An example from the KAL unit of work illustrates the particular value for pupils of integrating pupil input into the lesson, and exemplifies more clearly the mechanism of 'calibration'. The same teacher has asked the class to explain the difference between 'Standard English' and 'dialect'. During the lesson debrief the teacher describes the intention to make clear to pupils the distinction between these two terms, as a central predetermined objective of the lesson. A pupil provides what the teacher believes to be a particularly striking and apposite answer to this question, in the form of an elaborate metaphor, which the teacher then incorporates into the lesson through a process of reinforcement. There is evidence that the reinforcement has important implications for pupils' learning, in that it acts as a scaffold from which pupils develop their own representations. The reinforcement also has the effect of legitimizing this form of pupil response.

The truly interactional nature of this episode is illustrated at several points as it develops. Jim, the originator of the much valued metaphor, describes its inception in terms of a response to teacher input. The teacher has previously given the class an explanation of the nature of, and differences between, Standard English and dialect:

> Mr H. told us, and I just got the idea off it.

He describes the mechanism by which the transformation takes place in terms that closely reflect Bruner and Haste's (1987) formulation of the concept of 'calibration':

> I'm taking it [i.e. the teacher's explanation] in and pushing it out again in a different way . . . People put different things in their own terms, and you just adapt it to your own way. Somebody else might say, 'it's like the sea and the waves rise out of the sea and each wave's like a different dialect'. Maybe.

The process involves the pupil adjusting his internal representation of the teacher's explanation, in terms of his own existing patterns of understanding. It is a process of matching subjective understandings. Jim describes the actual analogy he developed in the following terms:

> We all have language, and everybody just branches off from it. And if we didn't all speak one language – sort of just a main middle stalk or trunk, maybe – it would be like just a big wood, maybe. But we kept it down to just one tree, with the branches . . . There's just one stalk with the dialects branching off. And if they want to make a new word, they come back to the branch and out sprouts another twig. And maybe people get words off. Let's say Lancashire may say 'ain't', and Yorkshire got it off them, and said 'nain't', and maybe got it off them and said 'main't', and 'gain't', and it all goes back to the same thing, maybe.

The teacher describes his own in-lesson thinking and response to Jim's input in the following terms, highlighting once again the complex array of knowledge about the pupil, pupils in general, his aims as a teacher and the subject:

> I think Jim is a good example of that because normally I think he's perhaps very frustrated by his perceived levels of achievement, because, as we said before, he has problems with his writing . . . So just that one lesson where he came out

with that wonderful example that I told you about before [i.e. the tree analogy], when I took that out and said, 'Right! I'm going to use that now. That's so good! I'm going to use that in future because that's really sharpened my thinking'. And because I made a big fuss over that, and particularly stressed it in the lesson – kept going on about it, and I kept using it in front of the class – you know, I could visibly see him perk up and start to puff his chest out a bit and engage more in the lesson ... And all the way through the rest of the work his oral contribution was far more significant [than usual] because, I think, he felt a little bit more ownership. And I wrote it on the board, and some of them put it in their books ... And he could see his idea going down into people's books.

He is also describing his own experience of calibration, when he suggests that the pupil's analogy has 'sharpened my thinking', thus suggesting that the products of the pupil's initial calibration encapsulated the teacher's subjective intention even more precisely than the teacher's own original explanation. This illustrates well the continual and recursive nature of calibration.

The impact of these events on other pupils is illustrated by one pupil who, in his recollection of the lesson, shows how he has further transformed Jim's analogy into a form that is, presumably, more meaningful to him, though still recognizably linked to Jim's original formulation – thus further exemplifying the processes of scaffolding and calibration:

He [i.e. Jim] said Standard English is like a horizontal line that people can come back to. And it's got lines going off it with different dialects. Standard English is what people come back to, to communicate with someone else from somewhere else.

The conceptualization of the distinction between Standard English and dialect can be seen to have gone through two transformations, each of which represents an example of calibration, whereby individual pupils develop their personal ways of understanding this particular item of knowledge that has been introduced by the teacher. The process is clearly aided by the teacher's efforts to highlight Jim's input and, thereby, present Jim's behaviour as an appropriate script and the substance of his input (i.e. as a metaphorical visualization) as an appropriate way of interpreting the subject content. In this way the teacher's and Jim's efforts combine. Having had Jim's input highlighted and endorsed as appropriate, the pupil in this example uses Jim's input as a 'scaffold' to develop his own representation of the content in the form of a similar, personalized visual metaphor.

A further aspect of scaffolding and script endorsement, illustrated in this example, is the way in which the teacher facilitates learning and understanding through the use of pupil models. Pupils commonly report, in the current study, that pupil models are often preferred to teacher models because of the greater ease they have in reaching shared understandings. There are many examples, like the one cited above, of pupils finding their peers' transformations of teacher input facilitative of their own understanding and learning. This points to the particular value of the teacher actively employing pupil perceptions to mediate their learning objectives in the learning situation. This also underlines the socio-cultural aspect of calibration, as a mechanism that is facilitated by the extent to which interacting individuals share a field of reference. This suggests that the more successful the teacher is in focusing and facilitating effective pupil calibration, the more effective the teacher will be in facilitating effective pupil learning.

Reactive Teaching

Teachers' accounts suggest that purely reactive teaching occurs less commonly than the kind of interactive teaching described above. The major difference between the interactive and reactive strategies is to do with the sequencing of the teacher's thought processes. When in purely interactive mode, the teacher's first consideration is the range of learning objectives that he or she has developed prior to the lesson. In purely reactive mode the teacher's first consideration is his or her perceptions of pupil states or interests. Reactive teaching, therefore, describes the situation in which the teacher's choice of lesson objectives, lesson content and teaching strategy are determined by the teacher's perceptions of pupil concerns or interests. A key point of interest here is that in being reactive in this way, teachers sometimes create valuable learning situations that they have not foreseen and that they would have been unlikely to create had they started from the point of planned learning objectives.

A typical example of reactive teaching is provided by an English teacher who finds herself in circumstances in which she feels constrained to offer her Year 7 class a drama lesson, during a teaching module on story:

> They usually have drama on a Monday, and I thought they'd probably lynch me if they hadn't got drama. So what could I do that's drama related, that will relate to story work as well?

The teacher's chosen solution is to select a poem that she believes 'lends itself to drama work'. It becomes clear that it is during the course of wrestling with these, to her, disparate objectives that she finds a valuable teaching point. The drama exercise is thus transformed, in the view of the teacher, from a burdensome task into a learning experience that she regrets being unable to develop, owing to the lack of availability of the drama room:

Well, my first priority was to try and create a drama lesson – because they'd walked in yesterday and said, 'it's drama today, isn't it?' [thereby confirming the teacher's expectation] . . . That was the main thing. And then it was to think of ways of actually getting across the idea of story telling with drama. Which is why I went for somebody telling the story and the others forming a little tableau. And it was just basically . . . a different way of tackling the idea [of story telling] . . . Ideally, it would have been nice to have gone back to the drama room today and been able to take that a stage further. But the drama room was in use.

The valuable learning point that the teacher believes to have emerged from the exercise is:

That one medium can be translated to a different one for a different purpose.

There is a further emergent teaching point, which the teacher feels was not dealt with adequately. The teacher's description of the way in which the theme emerged in her thinking and the way in which it was ultimately, in her view, discarded, are also indicative of the reactive mode:

I walked into the drama room and thought, 'Oh gosh! this [poem] is [in the form of] a fairy tale, isn't it!' And I thought it might be interesting. The idea was there to get them to focus on what they thought a fairy tale was, and so to start off talking about a type of story. And then to get them to look at the poem, and then to say, 'how does this match with the idea [i.e. of a conventional fairy tale]?' But I could sense that they were so keen to be getting on with the drama, that I actually forgot to come back to that point.

In this example the teacher's thinking and actions are explicitly directed towards the achievement of a close match between lesson activity and pupil interest. In addition to this, she is striving to scaffold pupils' activities in such a way as to advance pupils' learning and understanding of English. Through this she illustrates the process of 'calibration'. The intricate and recursive nature of the calibration process is demonstrated when she introduces the fairy tale theme, and then relinquishes it in response to pupils' apparent keenness to 'get on with the drama'.

This example shows the way in which reactive teaching can sometimes lead to the development of teaching and learning opportunities that are unforeseen by the teacher. Confirmation of some of the teacher's perceptions of learning opportunities is provided in the post-lesson pupil interviews. The pupils interviewed were mostly concerned with their enjoyment of the dramatic activity, the complexities of transforming the poem into a performance, and the way in which the lesson had raised their awareness of the structural features of fairy tale form. This girl emphasizes the structural aspects of fairy tale:

> [The lesson was about] acting, thinking what a fairy tale was. Thinking what they're doing in the fairy tale . . . Usually they have a happy ending, occasionally they don't, but a lot of the time they do. There's usually nice characters and horrible characters . . . I think I knew about them [i.e. the characteristics of fairy tales], but I hadn't thought about them [before this lesson].

This boy describes the way in which his group generated a method of dramatic characterization by introducing events that were not in the original poem:

> We put at the beginning that she was doing all the work for the husband, like getting cups of tea, sewing and stuff like that.
> *That was what you introduced, was it?*
> Yeah.
> *What was in the original?*
> It just said [in the poem] that no one's on her side, and she couldn't stand anything that he did, so she ran away.
> *So you actually made that up, her being bossed around. Why was that?*
> To make out that the husband was horrible.

In stating that this group of pupils has managed to generate solutions to the problems of transferring a story from one medium to another, this pupil is indicating that the task has been successfully scaffolded by the teacher through her division of the pupils into groups and her efforts in setting up the task (i.e. instructions to pupils and choice of poem). As a result of this scaffolding, these pupils have engaged in the kind of thinking that the teacher believed the activities she set would engender.

It can be seen that there are important differences between the interactive and reactive modes of teaching, which can be related to differences in the form and use of scripts, scaffolding and calibration. In reactive mode, pupil influence is more dominant. Reactive pupil scripts give pupils influence over areas of teacher decision-making that in the interactive mode are the preserve of the teacher alone, such as the generation of lesson objectives. Scaffolding is more likely to involve pupil collaboration, which is not mediated by the teacher as in the interactive mode. In terms of calibration, it would seem that in the interactive mode the teacher defines the focus for pupil calibration and will filter out unwanted foci in order to meet objectives, while in reactive mode the teacher is dependent on gaining access to pupil subjectivity in order to generate appropriate objectives.

The Interactive–Reactive Continuum

The essential difference between reactive and interactive teaching centres on the extent to which teachers allow lesson activity to be determined by their perceptions of pupil states or interests and the manner in which they allow this to proceed. The evidence of teachers' and pupils' accounts, along with the evidence of classroom observation, suggests that for a great deal of the time teachers in the present study employed teaching approaches that combined interactive and reactive elements, with lessons being directed towards clear learning objectives but also containing spaces for pupils to develop their own lines of interest. Typically, therefore, reactive teaching existed within a broader interactive context.

There were various factors influencing the employment of interactive/reactive approaches. Some of these differences could be related to individual differences between teachers, while others were related to the teachers' perceptions of specific conditions in which they were teaching. Teachers who engaged in detailed pre-active planning tended to be less willing to depart from their planned lesson contents than those whose planning was less detailed. Similarly, where lesson content was perceived to require careful pre-planning, teaching tended to the interactive rather than the reactive.

This latter point is well illustrated by the history teachers in this study, who unanimously interpreted the Key Stage Three history curriculum as requiring the delivery of a high degree of factual content. This meant that these teachers found less opportunity for reactive teaching than some of them would have liked, because they felt constrained by the limited time available to them to maximize their coverage of curriculum content. As a result they often felt obliged to engage in a transmission style of teaching, which, generally, they believed to be weak in terms of its ability to advance pupil understanding or learning, but an efficient method for achieving maximal coverage of content. The following remarks by history teachers illustrate this point:

> If you think about the time frame we've got to do this in, we've got to do three history study units in a year, we've got five periods a week for half a year. So it's basically six weeks per study unit. That's 30 single periods. Most of them are taught by double periods. So it's going to be: boom, boom, boom, boom! Straight, y'know?

> I'm feeling under pressure about getting through it all ... I know that I can't afford to give more than this week to Thomas Becket, and in many ways that's too much, because we've only got two weeks, so I'm going to have to devise ways of dealing with Magna Carta and the Peasants' Revolt fairly speedily ... We're supposed to be doing the origins of Parliament, and Scotland and Wales,

and the legacy of the Middle Ages. I just, you know, how do I get all that done in such a short time?

The National Curriculum is going to force us into a situation where we have to cut corners in terms of time, by cutting corners in terms of the quality of work we want them to produce . . . What's going to be sacrificed? Can we make a big enough stand? Can we make a persuasive enough argument to say, when push comes to shove, we have to go for quality of work rather than coverage of the National Curriculum?

Where teachers were feeling under this sort of pressure it tended to be the case that only those pupils who were judged to be 'more able' and in need of extension tasks were given opportunities to develop areas of personal interest.

The influence of the formal curriculum was further emphasized in our study of English teachers and Year 9 pupils. This produced far fewer examples of reactive teaching and a tendency towards the interactive–transmission end of the continuum, in direct response to the perceived demands of the curriculum, and the need to prepare pupils for some form of terminal assessment. When teachers did employ reactive strategies with Year 9 classes, this tended to be dependent on their perceptions of their pupils' ability levels: the guiding principle here appearing to be that 'brighter' pupils could be trusted to make valuable use of the limited time in the pursuit of their own interests. This finding suggests possibly interesting applications of the analytical framework presented in this paper to existing research on teacher expectancy effects (e.g. Brophy and Good, 1986; Keddie, 1971).

Conclusion

This chapter has described aspects of a study of teachers' and pupils' perceptions of effective teaching and learning that indicate support for a transactional theory of teaching and learning. The present study shows that learning opportunities are felt by pupils and teachers to be heightened when teaching strategies are transactional, that is, when they involve the integration of pupil and teacher concerns and interests. In short, it would seem that teachers and pupils value learning situations in which control over the content and direction of lessons is shared in different ways. It is also suggested that opportunities for such transactional teaching may be limited by the presence of certain conditions, such as the requirement to prepare pupils for terminal examinations, particularly for those pupils who are perceived by their teachers to be of less than high ability. It is hoped that ongoing research by the present authors will shed further light on these concerns.

Another important practical message from this study concerns the inappropriateness of thinking about teaching strategies in terms of dichotomies. Individual teachers in the present study employed a wide range of teaching strategies, drawing on interactive and reactive as well as transmission strategies, depending on their perceptions of the conditions in which they had to teach and the demands imposed by the National Curriculum. Similarly, the diversity of the teaching strategies shown above to be preferred by pupils, along with individual differences in learning style, show the practical value of a varied repertoire of teaching strategies. This point is further emphasized when we consider the ways in which teachers responded to the National Curriculum. While English teachers tended to interpret National Curriculum orders in ways that enabled them to incorporate pupils' concerns and interests, history teachers often complained that the history orders did not give them sufficient time to do this. Consequently, history teachers tended to make greater use of transmission methods of teaching than they claimed to prefer. This emphasizes the context-dependent nature of teaching strategies and the practical value of a wide repertoire to enable teachers to respond to a corresponding diversity of contexts.

Finally, in relation to some of the broader themes introduced at the beginning of this chapter, it seems fair to say that this work also illustrates something of the complexity that underpins skilled teaching, as well as the wealth of insight that can be gained from exploring teacher and pupil perspectives.

7

Teaching and Learning in the Preschool Period

Penny Munn and Rudolph Schaffer

Editor's Introduction

Chapter 7, by Penny Munn and Rudolph Schaffer, differs in two distinct ways from the other chapters in the book. First, the chapter is concerned with children in the preschool period – a period that is formally excluded from the current reforms, although, as we shall see, it is not unaffected by them. Second, the authors draw on data collected in Scotland, where the reforms have taken a somewhat different direction from England and Wales. Despite these differences, the contents of this chapter are highly relevant to issues discussed elsewhere in the book. Thus Munn and Schaffer continue the concern of the preceding chapters in the processes of teaching and learning; as with chapter 6, the authors' perspective is strongly influenced by interactional theories of learning, and they clearly demonstrate the value of this approach in understanding preschool learning. In addition, Munn and Schaffer share with subsequent chapters a concern with progression in children's learning – in their case, in the areas of preschool literacy and numeracy – and they show for the first time how these two areas might be linked. The chapter has clear implications both for preschool educators and for primary teachers wishing to understand more about the knowledge that children bring with them to school.

Introduction

This chapter is about the teaching and learning that occur prior to school entry, which, we submit, are highly relevant to experiences in school. To understand how children can profit from school experiences one must take into account what they bring with them from previous learning encounters, for these will have provided them not only with specific skills and items of knowledge, but also with more general strategies of learning and sense-making that will affect their approach to schooling. A developmental orientation that goes back to the early years is therefore a useful one to adopt in attempts to understand teaching and learning at any stage. We are especially concerned with the early emergence of literacy and numeracy, and with the way in which young children begin to understand the cultural practices of reading, writing and counting. We shall make the point that this involves not only specific skills and items of knowledge, but also, the approaches adopted by children to these activities and their understanding of what they activities mean to others.

Of all 'basic' skills, literacy and numeracy are the most basic, and are the focus of recurrent anxiety about standards. This anxiety is understandable; not only is it desirable to have high levels of basic literacy and numeracy throughout the population, but also many educational practices assume a degree of basic literacy and numeracy (see chapters 6 and 8, among others, for illustrations of the role of basic literacy and numeracy at later stages of the curriculum). Entry to the school system at age 5 (or, in England and Wales, at age 4) does not necessarily entail a smooth entry to the cultural systems of reading and number. Britain is unique among European countries for its early age of school entry. Some European countries have experienced a progressive lowering of the age of school entry from around 6 or 7 – a move that has provoked heated debate among teachers on the question of when to teach reading and of how to introduce academic subjects at such an early age. These debates have given rise to innovative approaches that involve either teaching at a metacognitive level (Pramling, 1990) or contextualizing academic teaching in novel ways. In Britain, however, other kinds of changes to the primary curriculum have raised the issue of how preschool learning is linked to the school curriculum.

There are many educational gains that are related in a simple way to the content of what is taught, but early developments in literacy and numeracy skills are not like this. These developments are dependent on a prior understanding of the nature of symbol systems and abstract representation that is not explicitly taught, but that is taken for granted by teachers as part of the cultural heritage that children bring with them to school. School learning is fundamentally text based, and therefore school entry is associated with children's entry to a separate world of text that is extremely powerful and yet transparent to the literate. How well equipped are children of 5 (or even 4) to enter this world? Part of the rationale for this project was to provide material for baseline assessment methods that would be appropriate for such young children.

In order to align a new emphasis on 'the basics' with the traditional preschool curriculum it is necessary to review what we know about early transitions into literacy and numeracy – with particular reference to children's experiences in nursery schools and the views that nursery teachers themselves hold about children's entry to school. The rationale for our current study arose from the implications that recent changes in educational policy have for preschool practice and curriculum. Although these changes do not explicitly affect preschools, there are many indications of future directions for preschools implicit in the current reforms. One major implication of the National Curriculum is that there will be an increased emphasis on the knowledge that children bring to school. Primary teachers will thus need to pay more attention to baseline assessment because rapid and capable delivery of the National Curriculum in the first year of school will require an efficient diagnostic assessment that will directly inform the teacher's practice. It is with this consideration that we offer some findings from our current research to illustrate the nature of learning in the preschool years and discuss their implications, with particular reference to the issue of diagnostic assessment.

In this chapter we describe two aspects of preschool learning. The first of these is the social context of learning on which very young children are dependent for intellectual progression. In the earliest years this social context consists of adults who directly support the child's efforts at learning. The second of these is the individual learning in the area of literacy and numeracy that develops in children in the year before their entry to school. This individual learning is based on children's increasing powers of abstraction and in particular on the experiences they have had with systems of representation. By describing these two aspects we aim to give a picture of early literacy and numeracy that is both contextualized and individualized. At the end of the chapter we return to our first theme of the social context of learning by describing some aspects of the teacher philosophies that structure preschools and support children's progress towards literacy and numeracy.

The Social Context of Early Learning

Any attempt to understand children's learning must take into account the fact that this is a lifelong process that starts at birth, not on entry to school. Learning, that is, takes place in a developmental framework, and what goes on at one stage is influenced by what went on at the previous stage. Thus our research on preschool learning is based on the premise that it is not only important in its own right, but that it also has relevance to subsequent school-based learning. Similarly, a child's learning experiences at the preschool level have continuity with the nature of learning that took place at home in the earliest years; that continuity, as well as the discontinuities that arise whenever children move from one setting to another, needs consideration, particularly in view of the frequent neglect in discussions of school-based learning of the developmental antecedents of children's acquisition of knowledge and skills.

The most important conclusion that arises from studies of learning in the early years is that this is essentially a social interactional process. As Vygotsky (1978) in his influential writings put it, adult teaching and child learning take place in the context of social exchanges. To understand how children acquire certain competencies as a result of adult instruction it is therefore necessary to think of one integrated teaching–learning process (it is indeed no coincidence that the single Russian word Vygotsky used in this connection combines the two aspects of teaching and learning into one activity). Thus initially complex tasks must be tackled by a problem-solving dyad, with the adult assuming the directive and organizing functions and the child merely enacting specific behaviours assigned to him or her by the adult. Only gradually will the child take over more and more of the goal-oriented, planning aspects of the task from the adult and assume responsibility for the guidance of his or her own behaviour. As Vygotsky put it, problem-solving then moves from an interpersonal to an intrapersonal plane.

To accomplish this successfully, however, the adult needs to be sensitive to the child's existing level of competence and pitch tutorial efforts accordingly. As we saw in chapter 6, the process whereby the necessary help and guidance are provided, to be gradually withdrawn as the child becomes more capable of independent performance, has been referred to as *scaffolding*. As Wood (1988) has put it, 'built well, such scaffolds help children to learn to achieve heights that they cannot scale alone'. The term is, of course, only a metaphor and not an explanation as to how the tuition process works; it is perhaps also slightly misleading in that it seems to imply a somewhat rigid structure, or one that does not actively involve the child. Nevertheless, a model of teaching efficiency, at least at early stages of development, can be derived from this approach, that is, one that regards high-quality tuition as the process whereby the adult sensitively allows himself or herself to be paced by the child, offers help when required at a level appropriate to the child's accomplishments so far, and is able to step back whenever the child succeeds in order to make room for initiative. It is essentially an interactive process; to watch only the adult or only the child provides one with little insight as to what is going on. An eye needs to be kept on both partners simultaneously in that social communication is the base on which the integrated process of teaching–learning takes place.

Acquiring Literacy and Numeracy

Our research interests concern primarily the earliest stages of developing literacy and numeracy, and for that purpose we have found the above theoretical framework a most useful one. Such basic 'educational' experiences first become meaningful in contexts of social interaction, that is, through the scaffolding efforts of parents and preschool staff involved in informal play with the child.

Take literacy: the most common occasion of first introducing children to the nature and conventions of literacy is through joint picture book reading. As various studies (e.g. DeLoache and DeMendoza, 1987) have shown, conveying to children that pictures and text are meaningful provides them with the earliest experiences of representational media and decontextualized information. Moreover, through the presentation of age-appropriate material children's interest and motivation are aroused by such books. Joint story reading enables children to experience the conventions of reading, such as the need to hold books upright and turn pages in sequence, stimulates children's interest in the adult activity of reading and ultimately helps children to understand that stories are read from text – an understanding that is quite crucial for children's progress in reading. However, all this learning can only occur through participation with a sensitive facilitating adult who will provide the child with chunks of information and tuition appropriate to the child's level of comprehension, and in the context of the child's interest in picture and story.

A similar situation prevails with respect to the emergence of numeracy. This, too, initially requires a social interactive context in which the notion of number is first introduced and made meaningful to the young child, usually through the playful efforts of a parent. As research by Saxe et al. (1987) has shown, most parents engage in a great variety of games, songs, rhymes and social activities involving number, the nature of which vary in complexity according to the child's age. Again, the concept of scaffolding is applicable here, as Saxe and his co-workers noted when observing mothers' efforts to teach their children tasks assigned to them (a counting game and a quantity reproduction activity). The mothers mostly recognized the type of difficulty the children experienced and responded with instructions tailored to that difficulty. When the children made errors in counting or correspondence, mothers shifted the way they organized the task to a more elementary level. When the children were successful, on the other hand, the mothers shifted to a more complex level of instruction. Tuition was thus a joint effort accomplished in the one-to-one interaction of adult and child; contexts were created by the mothers in which the children were able to solve problems that they could not manage on their own. In due course, however, as a result of the particular kind of help given, the children did become increasingly independent in acquiring these early educational skills.

From Home to Preschool

The transition from home to nursery school inevitably involves a number of sharp discontinuities in children's experiences. These include the physical environment, the identity of caregivers and the type of relationship established with them, the routines regulating the child's daily life and also the fact that children are now part of a group of similarly aged children and that one-to-one interactions with an adult are no longer the norm as they were at home.

Yet the role of social interaction as a context for learning remains an important one. This became apparent to us in the course of an earlier study in which we looked at the literacy and numeracy experiences encountered by 2- and 3-year-old children in day nurseries (Munn and Schaffer, 1993). The environments in these nurseries were full of aspects related to literacy and numeracy: letters and numbers appeared in plenty on the posters, notices, books, labels, pictures, containers and other such objects and materials surrounding the children. The issue was not whether such items were available, but rather how much and how effectively the staff conveyed to the children an appreciation of their significance and thus gradually drew them into meaningful use of the material. Very few literacy and numeracy incidents were observed when the children were not in the company of an adult; contact with material outside social interactions produced only infrequent and fleeting experience. Adult–child interaction routines were thus of fundamental importance in giving these young children experience of literacy and numeracy. In those nurseries where large group size and lack of continuity in relationships put pressure on adult–child interaction, children had relatively few experiences of literacy and numeracy. In all cases, however, it required interactions of a high quality to promote early learning – that is, interactions where children were able to contribute to the activity and where adults sensitively responded to these contributions, offering help to compensate for children's deficiencies and support to keep them on task.

Teaching–Learning in Preschool Settings

Whereas very young children are wholly dependent on the cultural skills of their families, schooling opens out many more aspects of the wider culture. In our current project we have therefore looked at a number of nursery schools in order to examine the ways in which preschool children begin using representational systems and the views that nursery teachers have on their learning. It is a central tenet of the social-developmental approach pioneered by Vygotsky that the cultural technologies of literacy and numeracy function to alter cognitive processes in a fundamental way (Vygotsky and Luria, 1930; 1993). It is the changes associated with the emergence of literacy and numeracy that we now seek to describe in order to have a better understanding of what children bring with them on entry to primary school.

Our project involved 56 children in their final preschool year, drawn from eight nurseries in Glasgow. The mean age of the children was 46 months at the start of the study and 55 months when they were seen at the end of their preschool year. We saw the children in each term of that year in order to assess the ways in which their emerging literacy and numeracy functioned. At each of these timepoints we interviewed the children about reading and number, using storybooks and games to produce situations in which the children could by their actions demonstrate concepts that they were not able to talk about. We were interested not so much in how the children performed on tasks related to literacy and numeracy as in how the children themselves saw activities that are central to literacy and numeracy; in other words, what frames of reference they were using to make sense of their learning experiences. For this reason the visits were not conducted as assessments, but as informal interviews (see Munn, 1994a, for a detailed description of these interviews).

In this chapter we shall focus on the children's responses in the interviews that took place in June, just before they started school. At these visits seven of the children were absent from school, so our sample totals 49. The child interviews at this timepoint provide information on the ideas about literacy and numeracy that the children were taking to school with them. Around this time we also interviewed the nursery teachers who directed the schools about the children's entry to school and how the preschool curriculum had prepared them for this. These interviews provide insights into the understanding with which the teachers structured the nursery environment to maximize the children's learning. We shall first of all describe the children's understanding of number and reading and then describe the teachers' thoughts on the children's learning.

Children's Ideas about Numeracy

Children's ideas about counting were investigated by means of questions that probed as to whether the children thought they could count, whether they counted in other contexts and why they counted. The children's conversations about counting showed quite a poor understanding of the adult purpose of counting. Only one of the children justified counting as an activity that allowed them to know 'how many'; the reasons that children generally gave for counting were that they liked doing it or that it helped them learn their numbers. During the interview the children were asked to demonstrate their counting with a number of small blocks. Further questions involving the requests 'how many?' and 'give me . . .' elicited situations in which the children demonstrated their understanding of the cardinality principle (the understanding that a number word refers to an abstract quantity – see Munn and Stephen, 1993, for a discussion of the development of this understanding). A variable that was of central theoretical interest was whether children actually counted blocks out (either silently or to themselves) when giving the interviewer a particular quantity, or whether they used a 'grabbing' strategy based on visual apprehension of quantity. The shift in strategy from 'grabbing' to 'counting' has been documented on experimental samples as occurring before age 4 (Wynn, 1990), so it was notable that over a third of our sample had not progressed to using the counting strategy by the final nursery visit.

The children also played a game based on Hughes (1986), in which small quantities of blocks were hidden in tins. The children were asked to write down on each tin 'how many there are', and later to find the tin to which an extra block had been secretly added. This game provided considerable insights into the children's use of symbols for recording quantity – both the nature of the written symbols used and the way in which the children referred to them (or not) in solving the secret addition. If the children used the written record they had previously made to infer the site of the secret addition, then their recording strategies were deemed to be 'functional' – in other words, they not only knew how to record small quantities, but they could also read back the records they had made, thus using them as a memory aid.

The strategies that the children used to record quantity were very varied, and figure 7.1 shows examples of these. The children's recording strategies tended to be either iconic (i.e., pictographic records that directly embodied the one-to-one correspondences used in counting) or conventionally numeric. Nine of the children at some stage used conventional numerals in an iconic manner – a strategy that was a transitional stage in the adoption of the conventional use of numerals (Munn, 1994a). Some of the children used neither iconic nor symbolic strategy, remaining at the 'pretend writing' stage.

We saw two distinct transitions in around half of the children before they went to school. The first was a shift from a 'grabbing' to a 'counting' strategy when giving a specific quantity of items. The second transition was a shift from iconic, self-invented recording strategies to the use of numerals to record quantities. These were transitions into two separate cultural practices – counting and numeral use. How did they relate to one another?

Table 7.1 shows the numbers of children at the third visit who used these strategies for recording quantity according to whether they had used a 'counting' or a 'grabbing' strategy when asked to give the interviewer specified quantities of blocks. Remember that these categorizations related to the children's strategies rather than their abilities – to the way their skills functioned

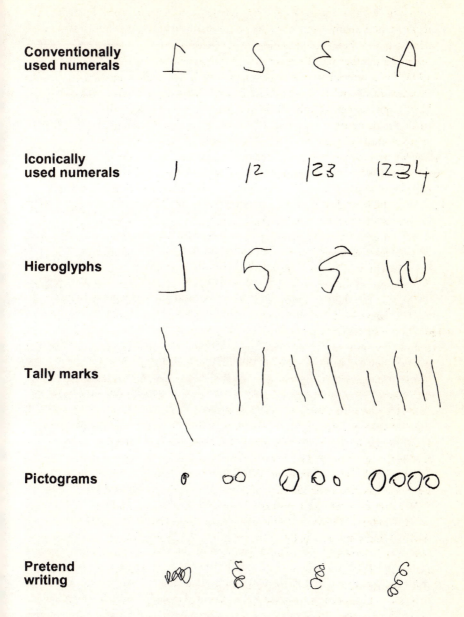

Figure 7.1 Examples of methods of recording quantity.

Table 7.1 Number of children in each category of quantification and recording method at term 3[a]

Recording method	15 Grabbers		31 Counters	
	Functional	Non-functional	Functional	Non-functional
Pretend writing	0	0	1	0
Hieroglyphs	0	4	1	1
Pictograms/tally marks	1	8	3	4
Iconically used numerals	0	0	1	2
Conventionally used numerals	2	0	17	1
Total	3	12	23	8

[a] 3 children were uncodeable

rather than to a catalogue of these skills. All the children knew how to count, but some of them used this knowledge strategically when carrying out a request. Similarly, all the children had a concept of 'two' and a way of recording this quantity, but some of them used their record strategically in solving the secret addition – that is, some of the children had literate strategies with regard to their recordings of quantity.

The association shown in table 7.1 demonstrates that children's strategic use of counting was strongly associated with a literate strategy towards the written recording. 'Grabbers' tended to use non-functional strategies (mostly non-numerals), whereas 'counters' tended to use conventional numerals and to read these back to themselves in order to solve the problem. The dichotomy in function between numeric and iconic strategies suggests that some sort of privilege accrued to the children who were able to use numerals. Those children who used self-invented methods of recording – what Vygotsky and Luria (1930; 1993) called 'primitive' methods – tended not to use these records functionally, as an aid to their problem-solving. By contrast, all but one of the children who used the conventional symbols (numerals) used these in a functional way, with the symbol standing for their mental representation of the quantity in question.

It was notable that a sizeable proportion of the children in this sample were reaching school age with self-invented rather than conventional strategies for recording quantity; that these children tended not to read back the records they had written using their own self-invented system; and that there was an association between using the verbal number system and writing conventional numerals. In other words, those children who had had a great deal of practice with the verbal and written conventions tended to be able to make a simple deduction based on the logical principles that govern our number system.

Children's Ideas about Literacy

Children's ideas about reading were investigated via a storybook interview. As in the number interview, we were less concerned with children's performance than with the way in which their reading functioned in their everyday actions and thinking. Each child was invited to read from a beginning reader that contained a clear story in the pictures on the right-hand page, the full text of the story on the left-hand page, and a shortened version of the story beneath the picture. Some of the children refused at this stage, often giving justifications such as 'I can't do the words', which bracketed them with Sulzby's (1988) 'principled refusers'. Other children read the book silently and some 'read' the story from the pictures. After the interviewer had read the story (which was very simple and contained just one major event) the child was asked to read the story again. The children's responses to this second request were just as varied as to the first, with some children adopting a narrative strategy and 'reading' the pictures once they had heard the story, and some sticking to their principled refusal. However, this distinction in their response was not necessarily dependent on their awareness of the functions of text, as the next part of the interview showed.

Each child was asked to point to where the story had been read from, and to point to the words. What was of interest here was whether the children pointed to the picture or to the words. A number of children were not aware of text at all; they thought the story was read from the pictures and that this was where the words were as well. Some children who pointed to the picture as the source of the story were quite capable of pointing out a word, but they had not made the connection between the notion of 'a word' and the story that had been read to them. A proportion of the children, however, were clearly well aware of text; they knew not only that the story was read from the text, but that the technical term 'word' was also related to the text (even if they did confuse the notions 'word' and 'letter' when asked to count the words).

During the storybook interview, if the issue had not already been raised, the children were asked whether they could read or when they would learn to read. Some of the children sincerely believed that they were able to read and demonstrated no qualms or ambivalence about this. Other children showed conflicts in their beliefs about their own reading ability; they would say 'I can read', and then qualify this by saying 'But only some books', or 'But only when you read first'. Yet a third group of children were quite clear that they could not read, and they had a variety of opinions about when and how they would learn to read. Those children in this last group who refused to read on the grounds that they could not read the words (the principled refusers) were quite clear in their understanding that reading was text related. Their references to being able to read were references to text-decoding skills rather than to memorization or picture interpretation. They also made a clear distinction between 'reading' and 'telling stories' when talking about their own abilities.

We saw two transitions in the majority of the children before they went to school. The first was the development of understanding that the story was read from the text. The second was a shift from saying that they could read to stating quite explicitly that they could not read. These transitions amounted to a necessary preparation for becoming a beginning reader (see Munn, 1994b). However, there was no simple association between awareness of text and a belief that they could not read – in some of the children, an awareness of text was combined with a strategy of retelling the story from memory or 'reading' from the pictures. The important point about the changes that did occur was that the children were using a variety of strategies to maintain their identities as readers.

The Link between Numeracy and Literacy

Literacy and numeracy are not often studied together; aside from the fact that there are far more studies of literacy than of numeracy, the two 'skills' of reading and mathematics are more likely to be contrasted with each other than examined for their similarities. And yet if they are considered developmentally, there are more similarities than there are differences between the two areas. Both are cultural practices that have extensive implications for the way in which cognition and society are organized; in this sense they are both technologies. Both literacy and numeracy as cultural practices therefore influence the very earliest cognitive development to be seen in young children. From the point of view of the cognitive resources required to take part in these practices, both require the capacity to deal in written symbols – symbols for language in the case of literacy, and symbols for quantity and numerical operations in the case of numeracy. Both literacy and numeracy emerge in interactions with others well before the capacity to deal in written symbols is present. Before being able to deal in these symbols, children need to develop a high level of proficiency in using the systems that they represent.

We know that a fairly well-developed metalinguistic ability is required for adequate development in literacy. That is, those children who develop the ability to think about and play with language itself, particularly with the sounds of language, tend to show good progress in reading (Bryant et al., 1989). However, we do not know precisely which preschool abilities are needed for the adequate development of school mathematical skills, since the development of early numerical understanding has been less thoroughly studied than the

Table 7.2 Number of children in each category of record use and story-text awareness at term 3[a]

	Non-functional recording	*Functional recording*
Little or no awareness of function of text	11	8
Aware of function of text	7	18
Total	18	26

[a] 4 children were uncodeable

development of linguistic knowledge. For both areas – literacy and numeracy – the demands of school on previously acquired understanding are high. Implicit assumptions about the role of symbols are embedded in the teaching of these areas and are rapidly expected to become common knowledge between teacher and child. An understanding of how arbitrary written symbols relate to what they signify is implicit in school-based literacy and numeracy.

The most relevant aspects of the children's understanding of the function of written symbols were their indications that the story was 'read from' the text and their use of numerals (or, rarely, iconic symbols) to remember particular quantities. The relation between these two variables is therefore of considerable interest. How many of the children who were text aware in the storybook context also used numerals (or even pictograms) functionally? Table 7.2 shows the numbers of children who fell into each category. As can be seen, there was a significant tendency for those children who pointed to the text as the source of the story also to show functional use of written numerical records. In other words, an awareness of the function of text in a story coexisted to a significant degree with the strategy of using a written record of quantity as a problem-solving aid.

This association raises the question of whether there was a causal link between the children's use of written records of quantity and their awareness of the functions of text in relation to a story, and also of the direction of this causality. It could be argued that the children's understanding of the functions of text led to their strategy in regard to recording quantity – the idea leading to the practice. However, it is just as likely (if not more so) that the causal connection is in the other direction – the practice leading to the idea. In this case, the children's use of numerals (which are logographs, and thus far simpler to understand and use than letters) would actually lead them to an understanding of the functions of text. Such questions about the nature and direction of development cannot, of course, be answered from the present data, but demonstrate how a brief examination of linkages between early developments in literacy and numeracy can raise questions of both practical and theoretical importance.

Summary of Findings from the Children

Several aspects of children's learning about numeracy and literacy become clear from the child interview data. Some of the children had already made an entry into the world of symbols, in the sense of using written numerals to represent quantity and understanding that text conveyed story, while others counted and 'read' storybooks without very much insight into the potential uses that symbols might have. The children had not been taught explicitly about symbols in the nursery school; their understanding would have grown from their experiences of the cultural practices of reading and counting. These practices, as we have seen, are routinely 'scaffolded' by adults, thus inducting children into a 'common knowledge' about such practices.

The learning that went on in these children was complex and it took a long time to develop. For instance, the children's understanding of cardinality did not develop as an understanding of a set of rules that were subsequently applied to all number words, but developed as a function of experiences with particular number words. In similar fashion, children may appear to 'know the rules' of counting before school, yet they rarely apply the results of their counting in practical situations (Frydman and Bryant, 1988). Such mismatches between children's theoretical capacity and their actual behaviour have puzzled many psychologists – however, the key to solving the puzzle may lie in challenging our unquestioned assumption that children first develop ideas and that these new ideas are then responsible for changes in their behaviour. It is quite plausible that children begin their development by doing things without any idea of what they are doing, totally dependent on whatever scaffolding is available. Through this scaffolded activity they then acquire the adult function of the activity and only afterwards become conscious of the ideas and logical relations central to the activity.

We have seen how this is so for reading; after lengthy experience with the practice of joint storybook reading, children begin to understand vaguely the functions of text – a mere step on the long journey to becoming a reader and writer. The evidence on counting from these children suggests that what happens before school is that children first acquire the practices of counting and numeral use without a complete understanding of their function. It is only with sustained practice over a long timescale that children begin to use counting and numerals in ways that are similar to adults. On entry to school, however, familiarity with these practices will be crucial for the further development of their numerical skills, since they will be expected to share a common cultural knowledge about the function of symbols. Our data suggest that for many children this knowledge develops prior to school entry, and that its growth is rather slow.

The Nursery Teachers' Views

The teachers we interviewed were well aware of the implications of the Education Reform Act, although they varied in the extent to which they had followed the progress of the educational reforms. Some had participated in the consultation process, others had read widely, others had kept up with events by reading various documents and articles in the national press. While around half of the teachers approved of the current educational reforms, half of them had reservations about the changes – typically, concerns about the loss of breadth in the curriculum and fears that early years teaching would become content-led – although these reservations were often expressed along with cautious approval of the new accountability of teachers and the positive effect that this could have on poorer-achieving children. The overall perception of the new curriculum was that it had the capacity to nullify the traditional early years emphasis on the whole child. Many of the comments on the amount of time that now had to be spent on more formal aspects of teaching were related to worries about the effect on standards of teacher–child interaction.

> All establishments are very strongly oriented towards social and personal devel-
> opment of the children. We get to know children as children before we know
> them as learners. (Regional Curriculum Development Officer)

This perception of the importance of social and emotional development was in no way a diminution of preschool cognitive development, but was rather an acknowledgement of the strong affective component to early learning and the importance of presenting new things in the context of familiar and well-loved contexts. One of the teachers highlighted the significance of this approach for literacy in her description of the rationale behind her school-entry programme, which was focused on giving parents information about how best to teach their children about letters:

> It's very, very hard to undo what a parent has taught. (Headteacher, nursery 6)

The teachers' broad aims were to use their knowledge and expertise to create continuity for the children between home and school, and the professional context of their work was a powerful enabling force in this regard. In this particular education authority the potential 'downward spiral' of the new curriculum had been explicitly countered by the introduction of an official '0 to 5' curriculum, which emphasized the processes rather than the content of learning. The existence of this document served to demystify preschool practice to some extent, as well as to draw attention to the learning that was taking place before school.

Most of the nursery teachers were conscious of the new primary curriculum affecting their own practice by influencing the way that they planned learning experiences for the children in nursery. This planning was typically done in conjunction with nursery staff who were not teacher trained. Two of the teachers reported deliberately using the new guidelines as a lever in persuading nursery staff of the importance of particular aspects of education, while a further two pointed out the significance of having a written curriculum where educational planning includes staff who have no experience of school:

> I think it's taking away a bit of the mystique of what did happen in schools. It's making what happens a bit more visible. (Headteacher, nursery 5)

> We looked at maths and language to see what children were doing in Primary 1, 2 and 3. In that way I suppose it has affected our practice, because we never looked at primary work in such detail before. There wasn't anything to look at. They only had to take my word for it. (Headteacher, nursery 3)

The teachers all saw the curriculum changes as influencing the extent to which primary schools paid attention to children's experiences in the nursery. As one teacher put it:

> I've been knocking on the door of that primary school for over ten years now – and finally I get them coming to me asking 'How do you assess children this young?' (Headteacher, nursery 4)

All the nursery teachers were conscious of increased attempts to provide across-sector continuity in the form of programmes that linked primary and nursery schools. The teachers did not see their role as one of preparing the children for decontextualized academic study or for the conventions of school. One teacher's initial statement was explicit:

> We're not here to prepare children for school. We're not here to sit them round tables and get them used to doing worksheets. (Nursery teacher, nursery 1)

Others indicated similar views in passing:

Reading and counting and things like that we're not really worried about; they'll be taught all those things when they go to school. (Headteacher, nursery 3)

The teachers we interviewed laid very little stress on reading, writing and number work in the nursery since they regarded decontextualized teaching as premature for children of 4 and 5. This did not mean that they were complacent about the educational development of the preschool children in their care. They did see themselves as responsible for preparing the children for learning in general, and for the school curriculum in particular. However, many of them took issue with what they saw as the narrow, content-based description of learning implicit in the new curriculum. They tended to take a developmental view of specifically academic developments rather than attempt to provide training in isolated sub-skills. In order to encourage development in literacy they encouraged the entire activity of reading. In order to encourage numeracy, they encouraged contextualized number activity. The teachers made little attempt to isolate and identify the sub-processes of reading and counting – they regarded such an analytical approach as inconsistent with a professional stance of working with the whole child. In many cases the nursery teachers had a doubly privileged position as both the head of establishment and the sole source of information about primary schools and the primary curriculum – the nursery school ethos therefore usually reflected the educational philosophy of the nursery teacher responsible for managing the curriculum.

In some ways the teachers' views of the children's learning were in accordance with the kinds of transitions that we actually found the children making. The children's progress in understanding text and number was slow; it was dependent on the contexts that they routinely created for themselves with adults, and on their understanding of the goals of particular tasks. The finding that children's awareness of the purpose of the activity often lagged considerably behind their apparent competence lends weight to the teachers' stance of polite disbelief in supposed academic abilities before school. However, there were other aspects of the changes in the children that were arguably relevant to the preschool curriculum. If the teachers were aware that the children's understanding of text and number was changing in such a dramatic and complex manner, this awareness was not reflected in what they said was important about going to school. This raises the question of the role of teacher perceptions in children's learning. Did the teachers miss these changes because of their lack of emphasis on literacy and numeracy, or did they notice the changes but just not feel very convinced of their significance in the preschool? The comment 'They'll teach them all they need to know about reading and writing and that in Primary 1' may signify a lack of understanding of the role of teaching in early literacy and numeracy, or it may signify a particular use of the word 'teaching' – i.e., as a specific reference to didactic teaching. This issue of what teachers see as important before school relates to the quite central topic of assessment and the form that assessment should take at this age.

Our data suggest that the most important transitions in children's use of symbol-systems arise from scaffolded activity. Initially, the meaning of such activity for a child arises from the social context – from a desire to emulate a powerful adult. The importance of this contextual aspect of preschool learning cannot be overestimated. If children's early transitions in literacy and numeracy were routinely put into the context of a feeling child living in a social world, nursery teachers might be more willing to use their knowledge of specific transitions to inform an analytical, diagnostic style of teacher thinking around preschool literacy and numeracy. At present, there is considerable resistance in education to 'stage' accounts of development that militate against such diagnostic thinking. This suggests that current psychological accounts of development are difficult for teachers to translate into action in the context of individual children. However, an account of children's learning transitions that is not dependent on discrete stages and that emphasizes the context of their learning could be used both to develop a contextualized baseline assessment and to guide the design of specific literacy and numeracy activities in the preschool.

Conclusions and Implications

The work reported here has a number of implications for the way that teachers assess children's knowledge on entry to school, given the current context of reform. Our study of the knowledge that children bring to school had a specific theoretical basis, which saw teaching–learning as an active and interactive process. Before school, and without the benefit of a specific curriculum that includes explicit teaching of reading and number, children acquire knowledge about the literate and numerate practices of their culture through their own activity and through interactions with others. The findings that we summarized above show that when children enter school they often have a considerable history of dealing with written symbols and a relatively coherent knowledge of literacy and numeracy that has been developed as a result of scaffolded activity. However, there were quite striking differences between the children in their strategies, and it would surely help teachers to facilitate children's use of written symbols if they were to take account of these differences.

First, attention needs to be paid to how children have acquired knowledge, not only to what that knowledge is. In particular, consideration needs to be given to the extent to which any given child still requires support in individualized learning situations, or whether the child has developed strategies for independent learning. For teachers' purposes, knowing about the strategies children have used to learn about literacy and numeracy may be more relevant than knowing about what the children know about such areas (in the sense of a 'checklist' of items of knowledge acquired). A 'checklist' approach to baseline assessment would be misleading in that it would give teachers very little information about the way in which children's knowledge actually functions in their everyday life. A 'strategy' assessment, however, would emphasize the functions of children's abilities and the relation of these abilities to the child's life outside the school. This would help teachers to understand the extent to which children have had an active involvement with reading, writing and number before school. Our data indicate that those children who used text before school were the ones who progressed in their understanding of the communicative function of symbols. Clearly, children who have not had extensive experiences with literacy and numeracy before school will require considerable support in joint activity with adults before they can acquire a grasp of the communicative function of text and other symbols.

Second, our data illustrate the slowness of change in children's understanding of numerical and symbolic processes at this early stage. Although change was evident, it did not take place in all the children and was not the result of specific teaching. The timescale of preschool conceptual development contrasts starkly with the assumptions underlying the primary curriculum. On entry to school, children are believed (sometimes preferred) to have little knowledge of text and number. By the end of the first term at school they may be expected to have grasped (among other things) the cardinality principle, the letter–sound correspondence principle, and an understanding of the function of numerals. Children who arrive at school with considerable prior experience of scaffolded literate and numerate activities may not find these things a problem, but some children will not have had the experiences necessary to develop these concepts before school entry. Directions in curriculum development should take account of the considerable amount of learning that takes place prior to school entry, the slow pace of this learning, the variation that there is likely to be between children even at school entry, and the type of understanding of literacy and numeracy that young children are likely to have acquired. In particular, those children who arrive at school with little understanding of the functions of literacy and numeracy, and few strategies for accessing the meaning of teacher-led activities around reading, writing and counting, are unlikely to profit from teaching that merely emphasizes learning content.

Third, our data suggest that there is considerable coherence in preschool between children's understanding of numeracy and their understanding of literacy. If it is the case that children's knowledge in these two areas interacts in complex ways during the early years of schooling, then it may be important for teachers to consider children's understanding of number at school entry in the light of their level of literacy. If early curriculum development is to be child-oriented (rather than subject-oriented), then teachers need to build up a systematic body of knowledge concerning the functions of literacy and numeracy that children have when they come to school. A systematic programme of diagnostic assessment by teachers will thus directly inform the delivery of a standardized basic curriculum.

Finally, our interviews with nursery teachers suggest that they would offer strong resistance to downward pressure on the nursery curriculum that resulted in nursery teaching becoming more content-oriented. However, these same teachers saw it as their professional responsibility to prepare children for school-based learning, and they were enthusiastic to do this in the context of a process-led preschool curriculum. The weight that nursery teachers give to contextual factors in preschool learning could still be given ample respect within a system that links preschool learning to the primary curriculum by considering the *process* of learning.

8

Progression in Learning – Issues and Evidence in Mathematics and Science

Paul Black Margaret Brown, Shirley Simon and Ezra Blondel

Editor's Introduction

The final three chapters in the book continue the interest in children's learning that was raised in the previous chapter. Each of these three chapters looks in detail at the underlying progression in pupils' understanding as they move through a particular domain of learning. Thus chapter 8, by Paul Black, Margaret Brown, Shirley Simon and Ezra Blondel, focuses specifically on understanding in two areas of science and mathematics – forces and measures. The chapter reports on a study in which pupils from Years 2, 4, 6 and 8 were presented with a range of tasks aimed at eliciting their understanding in these two areas. While the areas are superficially different, the authors report some important similarities. For example, pupils' difficulties in both areas appear to arise from a lack of understanding of certain key concepts: these are the places, they argue, where teaching should be directed. At the same time, the authors show there is considerable variation in children's understanding at each age; there are some 7-year-olds who are at least as advanced as many 13- or 14-year-olds. Such findings present major practical problems both for curriculum designers and for teachers.

Introduction

Any curriculum, such as the National Curriculum, which attempts to cover the whole age-range of compulsory schooling must make some assumptions, whether explicit or implicit, about the sequence in which learning should best be articulated. Of course, this is not a new requirement – teachers have always had to choose learning sequences for the tasks they present to pupils. The new feature introduced by the Education Reform Act of 1988 is that such specifications have to be proposed and used on a uniform national basis. This has the advantage that it should ensure improved coherence in the teaching that pupils meet from one school year to the next and as they move between primary, middle and secondary schools. However, it also means that those drawing up the curriculum specifications have to choose and apply their models of progression in learning with great care because their decisions will guide fundamental changes in teaching in our schools.

While it is almost trite to say that schoolwork involves progress in learning by each child, it is hard to decide how progress is best achieved. Several features would seem to be involved, as follows:

1   Ways in which the structure of knowledge might suggest or logically require certain sequences – e.g. addition before multiplication.
2   The sequence in which material is presented or taught, inside or outside the classroom.
3   The sequence in which any particular child might be able to learn at any particular age.

Teachers' choices for classroom work (2) should be influenced by their perceptions of the nature of the knowledge and skills to be taught (1). These choices should also reflect both their general knowledge about children's learning and the results of their own formative assessment of each child's current thinking (3). As the National Curriculum and its implementation are developed, there is clearly a need to explore the above issues in order to improve the basis on which teachers may plan and monitor the learning of their pupils, both at an individual and a class level (Black and Simon, 1992).

The work described in this chapter is an attempt to explore the ways in which children's understanding of two topics changes across the age-range 6 to 12. The topics chosen were a science topic, 'Equilibrium of Forces', and a mathematics topic, 'Measures'. The forces topic was chosen for several reasons. The explanations of motion and of rest in terms of the actions of forces lie at the conceptual core of physics, yet the topic of equilibrium of forces is frequently misrepresented in teaching. The description and explanation of phenomena in terms of perceived forces is one of the first steps young pupils must make in building their understanding, and they can make progress in learning through their capacity to see, feel and reflect about actions of various types of forces on everyday events. Thus the ideas are fundamental, must start with thinking at primary school level, and are accessible through direct experience.

The topic of measures was chosen partly because it, too, is of fundamental importance in both science and mathematics, yet it has not been the subject of much research. Work to develop the ideas underlying measurement can and should start in the primary school. The fact that in successive versions of the National Curriculum it has changed location between different Attainment Targets is evidence of uncertainty about how best to handle it, partly because it requires pupils to deploy and develop basic thinking both about number and about spatial relationships. Thus it calls for the determination of actions on the basis of relevant concepts, rather than, as in the case of the forces topic, the formulation of concepts in reflection on experiences and actions. The aim of linking with science usage was emphasized in the present work by including weight as one of the two quantities that children were asked to measure.

Data were collected by individual interviews with 48 pupils — six from each of two multi-ethnic schools at each of the ages 6, 8, 10 and 12. Every interview involved the same set of practical tasks. Each pupil was interviewed on two occasions several months apart, and information about relevant teaching experienced during this interval was also collected.

This chapter is presented in two main sections, on the forces and on the measures topics, respectively.

Forces

Suitable tasks?

For the tasks to be used in interviewing pupils, examples had to be found in which phenomena that might attract children's attention would be directly relevant to the scientific concepts involved in understanding equilibrium. This led to the use of the following three tasks.

For the first (see figure 8.1a), pupils were asked to push a 1 kg mass across three different surfaces — a table top, wood and sandpaper. They were asked to describe the differences between the surfaces, to consider what was happening both when the push made the mass move and when it could not, and to attempt to explain why the surfaces were different. It was hoped that the underlying notion of a friction force at the contact surface might be more evident with three different surfaces. The problem with this task was that the weight of the mass was a distraction, as it is only indirectly involved in the horizontal forces (because it affects the size of the friction).

For the second task (figure 8.1b), children were given a heavy box, which could be lifted by pulling the upper ends of one elastic band, or two bands, or a loop of string, with the lower end in each case attached to the box. The

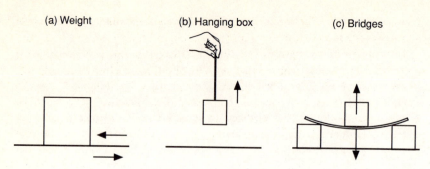

Figure 8.1   The three tasks used to explore equilibrium of forces.

children were asked to describe and explain what they observed, and to predict what would happen with the next event – i.e., when either the elastic bands or the weight were altered. The elastic could be seen to stretch as it was pulled upwards until it lifted the box off the table. The box would then be in equilibrium, between its weight pulling downward and the upward force due to the stretched elastic. With two bands a smaller stretch was needed to lift the box. The string would be a much more difficult example, because it gives rise to sufficient stretching force when it has been stretched by an unobservably small amount.

For the bridge task (figure 8.1c), two bricks and a piece of thick card were used to build a 'bridge' to support a box containing a 400 g weight. Other bridges were built using a thinner card and a box containing a 600 g weight. This latter box made the thin card bridge collapse. As before, pupils were asked to describe and explain what they saw, and to predict the effects of changes that they could subsequently observe. This task involved equilibrium between the downward, gravity force on the box, and an upward force arising from the distortion of the card. The association of a force with the bending of a card is not obvious and the everyday notion that things are just 'supported' without need to invoke upward forces would be more of an obstacle than for the hanging box. It was intended that the bending with different thicknesses of card would raise discussion, and that the collapse with the heaviest weight would suggest that the upward force might not always be big enough for equilibrium.

Previous research has suggested that children find it hard to think about equilibrium situations – nothing is happening, so there is nothing to explain (Pfundt and Duit, 1991). The tasks were framed to challenge this notion by showing equilibrium being attained through changes that children would have to predict, observe and explain. The tasks were also chosen to expose some of the main forces accessible to young children – i.e., pushes and pulls involving their own senses directly, weight, friction, and forces arising when materials are stretched or bent. The forces involved in floating and sinking were judged unsuitable, the source of the upward force being impossibly difficult to explain or to relate to other experiences (it is astonishing that this phenomenon has been so widely used in primary science). The purpose of having three tasks was to help explore the consistency in pupils' thinking across different situations. There was no intention in this work to introduce Newton's Third Law and the idea of pairing of action and reaction forces – this is a quite unnecessary complication for a first understanding of equilibrium.

An example

The following example will serve to illustrate the flavour of the interviews. The pupil, Hitesh (our pseudonym), a 12-year-old who was one of the most able in his group, was interviewed in May of Year 7. For the hanging box, he was asked to predict what would happen when one tried to lift it using one elastic band. He predicted that the band would stretch and suggested it might snap. When asked what made the elastic stretch he said that the weight in the box was pulling it down because of gravity: 'it's the stuff that makes things fall, it pulls everything down'. His notion of gravity was consistently applied across contexts within the interview.

When asked why the box was not falling Hitesh showed that he saw the system as a whole: 'cos gravity isn't strong enough . . . and then this is holding it up . . . if that snapped it would go down . . . there's not enough weight in the box'. He said that the elastic was pulling up on the box because 'the fibres inside get closer together', but with the piece of string, which did not appear to stretch, in place of the elastic, he did not think that its fibres were pulling together.

When asked about the relative sizes of 'pulls' (up and down) he first said that the downward pull was greater; then, after a pause, he said 'no, equal actually, if the pull down was greater it would fall'. With the string he said the pull up was greater because it was 'suspended on your finger'.

As he had not introduced the word force up to this point, he was then asked whether he had heard of forces. He said 'forces as in what? . . . I don't get it', but then he thought about it and said 'gravity's a force', showing he knew the word in this context. He identified gravity and 'the elastic band pulling it up'. So, for the hanging box, he had some notion of distortion force and forces in equilibrium, but not for both of the contexts (elastic and string).

The second interview was in the autumn, after some teaching about forces in June and July of Year 7. Although some of this work, on Hooke's law, gave opportunities for explaining forces in equilibrium, these were not exploited. Hitesh learned a simple definition of the word force and about the relationship between force and weight: 'Weight is how much gravity pulls on something . . . cos if there was no gravity nothing would weigh anything'.

Hitesh again predicted that the elastic would stretch because of the downward pull of gravity, with the pulling up of the elastic 'so it can move, go back to its normal shape'. When asked about the biggest pull, up or down, he said 'down, no actually up, because if it was down the whole thing would fall down'. He was asked if it could be the same and he said 'Yeah. My finger's holding it up and it's, there's not enough weight in here to pull it all the way down so I think it could be the same'.

In both pre- and post-interviews he had a firm notion of holding (support) and did not associate this with a pull/push or force. He therefore denied there was an upward pull by the hand supporting the top of the elastic. When asked what he knew about force in the post-test he said 'force is, er, it's something that pulls, pushes, um, twists and does things like that'. However, when asked then to identify forces he gave the same answers as previously (gravity, and elastic pulling up).

For the hanging box, when asked which was the biggest force, he said gravity: 'it keeps us on the ground and it's stretching the rubber band'. So, even though he had reasoned out equilibrium when talking about pulls, his limited notion of force and his strong notion of gravity dominated his reasoning later.

With the bridge task, Hitesh considered the whole system (weight, distance between cards, strength of card), but did not perceive an upward force. When asked if the bridge supports were doing anything, he said they were just holding that thing up, and strengthening the card. These features were common to both pre- and post-interviews.

Findings – predictions and observations

The responses have been analysed according to four main dimensions. The first of these concerns the predictions and observations that children offer (for a more detailed account, see Simon et al., 1994b). The predictions were classified into four main types. For the first, a few, mainly in Year 2, were reluctant to predict anything. Those in the second type focused only on the behaviour of the weight. In the third type, there was a focus only on the behaviour of the distorted material – the elastic or string, and the bridge cards. Finally, the fourth type included the few who brought in both the weight and changes in the material.

The main overall shift with age was from the second to the third of the above categories, i.e., away from concentration on the weight towards concentration on the distorted material. Few pupils brought in both at any age.

In general, pupils were not consistent in this dimension, either between the pre- and the post-interviews or between the bridge and the hanging box cases.

Findings – the nature of children's explanations

In this second dimension, the findings follow directly from the way children responded to 'why' questions, such as ' Why does the elastic stretch?', or 'Why is the card bending?', or 'Why doesn't the box fall?' Apart from the children who could not offer any explanation, there were five main types. The first included all such statements as 'this is the way things are' – the box does not fall because it is staying up. The second, more advanced type embraced explanations that merely identified an agent that was holding things up, for example the elastic, or the bridge supports. These two types might be classified as 'naive' or 'non-scientific', by contrast with the next three (Bliss et al.,1989; Hayes, 1979). A third type was similar to the second in identifying a single feature, but focused on the lightness or heaviness of the weight, i.e., on the downward force rather than on the support function. The fourth type was a more sophisticated version of the second in that, while still identifying only the support element, it referred to the properties of the materials involved, implying a possible link of that property with a force. The fifth type differed markedly from the others in that pupils included both downward and upward forces; such explanations embody an essential step towards the understanding of equilibrium.

Thus Hitesh's explanations for the hanging box were in the fifth category, as he explained in terms of both gravity and the pull of the elastic. However, in the case of the bridge, while he did mention both the effects of the weight and the distortion of the card, his explanation was in the third type, since he did not invoke any upward push or force.

While there were positive changes overall in the explanations between the older and the younger children, these were not striking. What was striking was the wide range within any one year group. Thus we found that between 15 per cent and 25 per cent – depending on the question – of the children in Year 2 could give explanations that were of better quality than those of 70 per cent of the children in Year 7/8.

Children were not generally consistent across the three tasks in the types of explanation they offered. However, there was a difference between the hanging box and the bridge tasks in the responses given to explain why the weight did not fall. In the former, only about 15 per cent gave 'scientific' explanations in both the pre- and post-tests, while for the bridge almost 60 per cent did so in the pre-test and 75 per cent in the post-test. It seems that the action of their hand in the hanging box task led to a fixation by children on the notion of 'holding' as an explanation, whereas for the bridge, more impersonal and abstract ideas could be entertained.

Findings – identifying relevant aspects

This third dimension focused on pupils' identification of pushes, pulls, force, friction, gravity, stretching and bending – relevant aspects that children must pick out if they are to explain what is happening. Hitesh was advanced in being able to identify all of these except the stretching of the string and the upward push of the card.

In this dimension, about half of the Year 2 children would not identify a force in any particular task, whereas about 90 per cent could do so by Year 8. In the case of the hanging box, responses could be classified in terms of those who identified a downward force, those who saw an upward force, and those who identified forces in both directions. For Years 2 and 4 overall, 20 per cent could identify both, whereas for Years 6 and 8 overall 55 per cent could do so. Identification of two forces is crucial, because thinking about equilibrium in scientific terms can only start when the existence of at least two forces in opposite directions is appreciated.

Those children who could identify two forces were asked whether or not they were equal. Their responses showed many ideas and perceptions that must be obstacles to arriving at an abstract scientific view. Some thought that because movement had been achieved, as in lifting the box, the forces could not be equal – after all, human effort only succeeds when one can force the object that is 'stuck' into motion. Some thought that where an object was distorted, this meant that forces must be unequal – after all, the 'normal' equilibrium is when a weight (say) is supported without evident distortion. Thus it is the concept of equilibrium itself that needs careful presentation. Finally, the particular case of weight can be seen both as the first and easiest force to recognize, but also problematic, for some children clearly thought of the gravity force as an extra feature, independent from the weight effect.

Identification of forces was the only aspect in which a significant number of children were consistent across the hanging box and bridge tasks in the same interview, and less frequently between pre- and post-test. Of course, this dimension does focus more directly on the abstract scientific features, and the tasks were constructed to have these in common while being different in other respects.

Findings – use of language

The fourth dimension is about pupils' use of language in the interviews when they try to convey their meanings and understandings. Primary children have little experience of scientific terms, but they do have experience of explaining in cause and effect terms, so they might produce answers that can only be appreciated if the language is analysed with care. Likewise, older pupils might use scientific terms but show little understanding in the way that they deploy them. The key words that seemed to need careful attention were:

rough, smooth, heavy, light, strong, weak, hold, stretch, bend, weight, balance, force, friction, gravity

Hitesh was able to use several of these. Each of them can raise difficulty. An underlying development may be reflected in changes in the implications of a word when pupils use it. When describing the friction surfaces, some – mainly younger – pupils used merely descriptive words such as sandy or sparkly, while older pupils tended to use words associated with the frictional effect, such as bumpy, or sticky, or (even) grips. It is not clear what, possibly different, meanings the terms 'rough' or 'smooth', used by most of these pupils, expressed for them. It seems very likely that their associations and implications changed markedly as the descriptive terms quoted above were observed to change.

For several of the terms, pupils used them in different ways, which could be classified as changing from few – vague – associations to more precise ones. 'Friction' carried no meaning for many of the youngest pupils, but its associations seemed to change for many of the older ones, from a general association with moving things, to a more focused awareness that it occurs between two surfaces when one of them is rough. 'Force' was a notable example here, being associated with human compulsion for the youngest pupils, with moving bodies and with pushes and pulls for others, and at the most mature level with abstract entities such as gravity and weight. Such change is not without complications: for some, pushes and pulls are associated with personal effort only, and the term force becomes an overarching one to include both personal effort and impersonal forces.

A different feature was brought out by examination of the uses of the terms 'heavy' and 'weight'. These seemed to start as properties (only) of objects, later to denote causes for bending and breaking, and later still to be used with distinctions between them, speaking of weight as a cause and of heaviness as an effect. Similarly, the same term 'stretching' seems to start simply as a description that something has changed in length, with the idea that this will usually mean that there is a force there coming only later.

Apart from the problems associated with the changing meanings and implications, additional points arise when there is no word in common usage to express a relevant scientific concept. For example, children do not have a clear concept of equilibrium and so do not associate or express it with a particular word. The word 'balance' will not do because it might mislead; for some it indicates level or horizontal, so the bridge is not in balance when it is bent by a load. (A very similar point, about the importance of the development of new vocabulary, is made in the concluding section of chapter 9.)

Implications

Teaching about forces at secondary level usually begins with assumptions about pupils' thinking that cannot, according to the results above, be justified. Younger children focus on isolated aspects of a situation, and do not appear either to observe or to think in terms of the system as a whole. They do not readily identify forces, and where they do, it is experienced effort and weight that appear to be salient, while distortion forces are not recognized. Thus the conditions for starting to consider the concept of equilibrium do not exist for many pupils. For the few who do get this far, the idea of equality or balance often seems to be associated with absence of changes or distortions, so that the notion that (say) a distortion of a material is needed to achieve equilibrium is contradictory.

The results show features to which teaching must be directed. Thus teachers should encourage children to look at situations as a whole, focusing on their several interacting features. Attention to these features and to the language used might suggest points at which the teacher should help children both to explore the situation, and to talk and think about it more comprehensively.

The use of the term 'force' should expand from situations where personal effort is the touchstone to those where observed effects are used as evidence of forces. Gravity, friction and distortion forces all need attention, moving from examples where (say) distortion and perceived force are clearly related (e.g. in compressing a spring), through those where the link is less obvious (e.g. a weight on a piece of foam rubber), to everyday cases where such features have to be inferred (Clement et al., 1989).

Children need particular help to spot the features common to phenomena that they see as unique. The unique and often distracting differences between phenomena are frequently evident and overwhelming to a child, while being almost invisible to the expert adult.

Our findings suggest a possible scheme for progression in children's understanding. A tentative outline could be as follows:

First stage: No relevant feature predicted or observed; explanations tauto-logous or naive; no forces identified. *Scientific terms not used.*

Second stage: Focus only on weight in prediction and observation; expla-nation in terms only of heaviness; weight identified as the only force. *Scientific terms limited to weight and force as weight.*

Third stage: Focus on distortions; distortion forces the only ones identified. *Scientific terms relevant to these used in conjunction with force.*

Fourth stage: Both weight and distortion effects noticed and used to predict; both features used in explanations; opposition of the two identified in explaining why things don't fall. *Wide range of scientific terms used appropriately.*

Fifth stage: Equality of the opposing effects seen as the distinctive feature of equilibrium; existence of distortion forces inferred where distortion not visibly evident; ideas used over a range of phenomena. *Able to give explanations of the scientific terms used.*

The points in italics about scientific terms can usefully be introduced and learnt as the thinking in each stage develops, but their use could develop in isolation from the other features. The scheme is set out as the basis for a teaching strategy, not as a description of how children will learn in the absence of relevant teaching. While it is tentative, it should make clear that a simple criterion, that children should 'get the explanation correct', is, on its own, of no use in guiding the learning of a child in the earlier stages. By way of caution, it must be added that the scheme does not imply either that any particular child can learn only in this sequence, or that all features of one stage will be learnt together before any of the next are acquired. Abilities for a stage that are exhibited in one context may not be shown in another context – indeed, the extension of the stage features across contexts adds another dimension to any such scheme of progression.

In the National Curriculum Order for Science (DES, 1991d), there was no statement that anything at rest must be acted on by at least two equal and opposing forces and no reference to the forces that materials exert when distorted (although there is reference to the converse – that forces distort materials). The problem that young children have in identifying distortion forces and in recognizing that equilibrium is a phenomenon to be explained was thus not addressed (Black, 1993). It was hardly surprising, therefore, that in the teaching observed during our research, the work did not seem to be informed by a clear understanding of our concepts of equilibrium of forces. It may or may not be difficult to improve pupils' understanding – beyond the levels observed in our work – with a suitable teaching approach. Our tasks, and the rationale underlying them as explained above, could provide a basis for an approach that might at least meet some of the conditions necessary for success (Simon et al., 1994a). The current version of the Science National Curriculum (DFE, 1995b) includes in the Programme of Study for Key Stage Two explicit reference to the forces exerted by springs and elastic bands, and to the notion that forces counterbalance.

Measures

Suitable tasks?

To explore understanding of measures, two practical situations were offered to each pupil. In one, concerned with length measurement, two 'towers' (actually cardboard boxes) were used, of almost the same height of about 25 cm and initially placed just over a metre apart. Pupils were asked which they thought was taller, and then invited to find out, using first a piece of string, then using plastic *duplo* blocks (as a non-standard unit). They were finally given a ruler and asked to use that to measure both the tower heights and the distance between the towers, which was greater than the length of the ruler (30 cm); they were asked about accuracy, about the units of their result, and about different sub-divisions on different ruler scales. In each case they were asked to estimate, then to measure and to say how accurate they thought their result was.

The second task involved a pair of heavy boxes. Pupils were asked which they thought was the heavier, and to estimate the weight of one of them. They were then asked to find out the weight of one using a balance, in terms of ball bearings and, later, in relation to gram weights. In each case they were asked about the accuracy of their result. Two kitchen scales were then introduced, one with conventional scales using imperial and metric units, and one with a digital readout. These led to questions about different units, about accuracy and so about the approximate nature of any measurement.

Although it would have been interesting to explore the differences between measures of several different types in this study, to do so would have introduced too many variables and made the assessment too difficult for the younger pupils. Thus it was decided to focus only on physical properties with ratio scales, taking one property with and one without a visual (extensive) quality. Length was selected as being familiar to young children and having a unique position with regard to the nature of scales, and weight because of the contrasting tactile perception, relative familiarity and link with ideas of force.

The ideas of units, number, continuity and scale formed the basic framework both for constructing the tasks and for analysing the pupils' responses. The various ideas involved under these four headings are set out in table 8.1. Although these aspects have been listed separately, they were in fact closely integrated in children's performance in carrying out the various measuring tasks and answering questions about them. The enquiry thus went beyond a test of specific skills of measurement, which children might learn without understanding the underlying concepts.

Table 8.1   A framework of the concepts involved in measurement

Units	Number	Continuity	Linear scale
intermediary	cardinal principle	infinite subdivision	linearity
arbitrariness	whole number	approximation	zero
reference point	addition	exactness	representation of units as
unity	subtraction		intervals
repeatedness	ratio		interpretation of
non-standard	place value		subdivisions of intervals
standard	fraction		
sub-units	decimal		
conversions			

Some examples

Most children made little progress between the first interview and the second, which took place about three months later after a period of teaching about measurement. However, one Year 2 boy, Rajesh, made considerable gains over this period. In the first interview he had no trouble with non-standard units provided that there were repeated objects available (bricks, ball bearings), but could not manage to measure a length using one duplo brick only. Similarly, he could not use a ruler to measure a distance greater than its length, although he could use his memory of a metre stick to estimate that the total distance was just over 1 metre. In the second interview Rajesh repeated both the brick and the ruler without any difficulty.

In the first interview, when a length was not an exact number of bricks, Rajesh was asked whether his result of 13 was exact: he answered 'Yeah, you just need a little bit of one up here'. Other answers given as whole numbers were said to be exact, even if they clearly were not. However, in the second interview, Rajesh twice referred to 'a half', once when estimating the large distance as 'over one and a half metre sticks', and once in the context of using a ruler: 'it's ten and a half centimetres'. The combination of a number with a unit in this phrase was also a new development, and occurred in more than one context, although not universally, in the second interview. For example, instead of 'a little bit' of a brick quoted above, he talked about 'around two centimetres'. The use of a word such as 'around', denoting an awareness of inexactness, was itself a departure that occurred only in the second interview, although in the context of both length and weight. In contrast to many Year 2 children, Rajesh demonstrated some familiarity in both interviews with the commonly used standard units, volunteering at some stage the unit names 'centimetre', 'metre' and 'gram', and, in the second interview, 'kilogram', although he clearly had little conception of the size of the units of weight.

A further major change that took place between the two interviews was the way that Rajesh used a scale. He started by using a ruler as a counting rod, ignoring the numbers on it. For example, when measuring the height of one of the towers, he put the ruler the wrong way up; this meant that instead of the zero, the 300 mm mark was aligned with the bottom of the tower and the zero was well above the top of the tower. He then proceeded to count the centimetre marks, starting from 'one' at the top of the tower opposite the number 40 (mm) on the scale, and ending at the bottom saying 'twenty-two' (approximately the correct answer), although the scale now said 300. In contrast, in the second interview he did not count but simply read the appropriate number off the scale. In fact he started with the scale the same way up as before, but now read fairly accurately the number aligned with the top of the tower using the inches scale, which did have its zero at the base of the tower, saying: 'I think it's ten; I think ten and a half centimetres'. When asked what side he was using he said 'metre side?', but when asked if he could use the other side he turned the ruler round so that the zero on that side was level with the base of the tower and read off the answer to the nearest labelled mark as 'two hundred and fifty'. Thus, between the two interviews Rajesh progressed from a performance that was just a little better than that typical of the weaker Year 2 pupils to one that was among the best for Year 2, and in advance of that shown by many of the older pupils.

To get a significantly more sophisticated understanding it is necessary to move to one of the 12-year-old pupils, Hitesh (the same pupil quoted earlier in the forces section). This boy showed himself able to 'think on his feet', using his reasoning to arrive at conclusions by spontaneously relating different features and resolving inconsistencies. However, he appeared to have less background knowledge than might have been expected of such a pupil. For example, he estimated the height of the tower fairly accurately at 25 cm, explaining that a 30 cm ruler would be 'a little bit bigger'. When reading the height of the tower he gave answers of both 'twenty-six' (although the ruler was calibrated in millimetres) and 'two hundred and fifty-seven and a half millimetres' in quick succession. When asked if these were the same he was able, after some hesitation, to explain that 250 millimetres was equal to 25 centimetres. In the later interview he gave the answer straight away as 25.7 centimetres, although the nearest calibration on the ruler was 250 mm.

Hitesh found it difficult to read a kitchen scale labelled at 250 g intervals with the intermediate markings representing 25 g, but eventually managed it by working out the value of the intervals by trial and error. Interestingly, he had again progressed by the second interview, immediately calculating the value of the scale subdivisions directly, saying 'Cos there's ten lines, so I divided 250 by ten'.

When Hitesh was weighing one of the packages using a digital kitchen scale that was set to read in ounces, he first said that the result of 8.8 ounces meant 'eight ounces and an eighth of an ounce'. However, he correctly responded that his answer was nearer 9 than 8, and indeed nearer 9 than 8.55. When asked about the accuracy of this result in comparison to that obtained using other scales, he said it was accurate because 'it gives you the exact . . . points'. The interview continued:

> *Points. But it only gives you one point, is that accurate?*
> No, not really accurate, but it's accurate enough.
> *Accurate enough. Do you think you can ever get it to be accurate?*
> Not really.
> *Why not?*
> Numbers just keep on going.

Hitesh was the only pupil in the study explicitly to refer to the notion of the infinite density of rational numbers.

Findings

Within each interview there was a surprising degree of consistency between children's performance on the different contexts related to different ways of measuring length and weight. This is not to say that pupils always displayed the same features, but that the variations were often explicable in relation to the demands made. For example, differences in success at reading a scale related to both the complexity of the scale and the familiarity and 'visualizability' of the units. Where pupils seemed on the verge of acquiring a new idea, this not surprisingly appeared on some occasions, perhaps where it was most obviously prompted by the context, but not on others.

The analysis performed so far suggests that it may be possible to model pupils' progress in measures using a number of stages, each of which is characterized in terms of performance in each year group using aspects of the four conceptual areas referred to earlier: units, number, continuity and scale. The characterization of these stages, shown in table 8.2, is empirically derived, yet, like the National Curriculum levels, is 'ideal' in that there may not actually be any pupils whose performance exactly matches to the last detail any particular stage. Nevertheless, they are proving useful as a framework for evaluating the specific attainment of each child. For example Rajesh, quoted in the previous section, seemed to make considerable progress between his two interviews to take him from an initial position only a little further on than the

Table 8.2 A possible model for measures stages

	Units	Number	Continuity	Scale
Almost all Year 2s (age 7)	Sensory comparison; uses multiple concrete non-standard units for measurement	Reads whole numbers to 100		Reads off number near end of object
Most Year 2s	Physically repeats a single concrete non-standard unit; appreciates less of larger units	Counts consistently; reads numbers to 1,000 (e.g. 250)		
Most Year 4s (age 9)	Estimates with non-standard units; sometimes volunteers name of length unit; familiar with names of cm, g, mm, (m?); uses knowledge of size of cm	Uses halves for non-standard units	One or more finite points between wholes, e.g. halves	
Most Year 6s (age 11)	Sometimes volunteers name of weight unit; usually volunteers cm; familiar with name of kg, uses knowledge of size of mm		Acknowledges inexactness of estimates	Selects the appropriate scale of direction
Most Year 8s (age 13)	Volunteers g, familiar with names of imperial units; selects g as correct unit; uses knowledge of size of m	Reads and interprets decimals with 1 place; uses place value to 1,000 in adding mentally	Aggregates on long distances and for weights; some sense of inexactness in results; some regard for consistency	Takes account of zero on ruler
Some Year 8s	Uses knowledge of size of mm, in, g, kg, oz, lb; accurate estimation		Recognizes inexactness of instruments	
A few Year 8s	Refers flexibly to several units in single context; converts readily between metric units; understanding of separate metric and imperial unit systems	Uses ratio in conversion and in calculation of subdivisions; uses equivalences of decimals, and fractions	Understanding of infinite density of number line, and therefore the inherent approximation of measurement	Calculates size of subdivision on scale; conversion between different scales

first stage to well into the third stage, with some aspects of the fourth. Similarly, Hitesh was initially well on the way to the final stage, and achieved additional aspects of it in his second interview.

In addition to this description of stages in terms of measurement concepts shown in table 8.2, it was noticeable that there was a strong correlation of performance with more general attributes. In particular a developing regard for consistency and accuracy, which led to further reflection and learning in the interview itself, seemed to relate strongly to progression in measurement ideas. Indeed, many features of the above stages relate to characterizations of progression used by researchers such as Piaget and Inhelder (1958), Biggs and Collis (1982) and Case (1985).

One aspect in which the performances of Rajesh and Hitesh are untypical is that there is in each case significant progress between the two interviews. For many pupils there were a few gains, sometimes balanced by one or two losses on the frontiers of their achievement. Such gains were generally not easy to relate to the teaching that took place in the interval; indeed, they seemed often to relate more closely to the learning triggered by the earlier interview.

As with forces there were considerable differences in the performances of pupils of the same age. Our results showed that some pupils perform consistently better than most of their peers, and some worse, and that at least some of these performances are common across the mathematics and science tasks. As with the results for forces, some Year 2 pupils consistently performed better than most Year 7/8 pupils, and the performance of two 12-year-olds was indistinguishable from that of several Year 2 pupils.

Implications

Unfortunately, it seems common in school mathematics to teach the specific skills of measurement of such quantities as length, area, volume, angle, weight and temperature with little emphasis on the underlying common concepts. For example, if pupils were asked to devise a measuring system for length, time or temperature that they could use if shipwrecked on a desert island, or to devise a measure of how good a memory they have, it is not clear that they would know what was required, let alone how to proceed. While expertise at measurement in the various domains is clearly very important, generalization and abstraction across domains will both help retention of more specific knowledge, and demonstrate these processes that characterize the subject of mathematics.

The examples given here illustrate how an approach focused on general measurement concepts might be adopted with pupils in relation to simple, but carefully constructed, measurement tasks. The results also begin to suggest the patterns of progression that pupils might show. The fact that the spread within age groups is large in relation to the changes with age is a challenge for whole-class teaching. However, both this feature and any of the results about progress with age must be seen in the light of our general finding, that the teaching experienced by these pupils had not attempted to do more than teach measurements as specific and unrelated routines.

The 1991 National Curriculum Mathematics Order (DES, 1991b) unscrambled the attainment target dedicated to measurement in the 1989 Order (DES, 1989b) and divided it between Number (Ma2) and Shape and Space (Ma4). This might have had some advantages in that the strong relationship of measurement to number concepts could have been made clear, but equally any notion of progression within measurement was obscured. In the 1994 Order (DFE, 1995a), measurement is once again unified, but this time is combined with Shape and Space. The statements of attainment in the 1989 Order, retained in the 1991 Programme of Study, show some connections with the stages described in table 8.2, although there are some inconsistencies. The statements of attainment in the 1991 Order are not interpretable on their own; they are extremely vague and do not easily relate to identifiable strategies used by pupils. Changes made as a result of the Dearing Review in 1994, while retaining some vagueness, have improved the fit to our empirical results, not surprisingly because some of these were communicated in an early form to SCAA officers. However, some of the higher levels to the 1994 Order still appear optimistic.

Conclusion

The two topics explored in this work are superficially very different. The one, forces, concerns abstract conceptual models of everyday situations; the other, measures, is concerned with procedures needed to produce practical results. This difference is reflected in the tasks used: for forces, the main data derived from the way pupils described and explained what they could see, while for measurement, the results depended on observation of what they did and of the results they obtained, although in many cases these were accompanied by verbal justifications.

Because of these differences, and because of the need to avoid imposing any a priori structure on the analysis, the two topics were analysed separately, and so the two sets of results appear to be of a different character. Despite the differences, there have turned out to be deeper similarities and some of these are explored below. In addition to comparing the two sets of results overall, it would be useful to explore the correlations between the responses of individual pupils, since all of those involved worked on both topics. However, this analysis at individual level has yet to be carried out.

Children's difficulties with some tasks have been shown, in this work as in previous research, to arise from a lack of understanding of significant underlying concepts. Thus an important part of the work, in both topics, has been to develop a clear rationale for describing the conceptual targets to be addressed in the teaching. With hindsight, it seems surprising that this has not been properly done before, and unfortunate that in both cases the National Curriculum Orders do not appear to be sufficiently based on this, or any comparably clear, rationale. The results obtained in both topics about the lack of marked change after teaching emphasize the need for a revised approach for such teaching. Basing National Curriculum Orders on such conceptual targets that represent significant steps in learning would not only help to focus teaching, but would also help to focus teacher assessment. (It might not, however, be easy to design short written items to assess reliably such conceptual steps.)

The perceived progress of some pupils that took place following reflection within the interviews themselves illustrates the importance of presenting pupils with a variety of new and challenging contexts and continually paying attention to the quality of justifications and reasoning rather than more simplistic 'right answers'. It is likely that, if they are exposed only to a limited set of rather singular contexts – such as 'floating and sinking', non-standard units of measurement in Key Stage One, or measuring lines in a workbook that always appear to be a whole number of centimetres long – pupils are unlikely to achieve the progress that is possible, and are more likely to be helpless when a new type of context is encountered. In view of the comparability of performance of some 6/7-year-olds with some 12-year-olds, it is especially important not to set too constricting limits on the range of conceptual targets, either at the upper or the lower end, and thus on the variety and degree of challenge of the contexts for any age group.

The use of different contexts in the interviews demonstrated apparent inconsistencies in pupils' thinking. However, these could in some cases be explained by differences in the nature of the tasks. For example, pupils' performance in weight tasks was inferior to that in length since they were clearly less familiar with units of weight than those of length; moreover, units of length had the advantage of being visual rather than tactile. In measures, although to a lesser extent in forces, pupils' performances were actually surprisingly consistent once the nature of the differing demands of the various contexts was better understood.

On the basis of our work, therefore, it is possible to pick out aspects of children's understanding that give important guidance for the teaching in these topics, mainly because the detailed data expose unsuspected conceptual steps to which attention has to be paid if children are not to be blocked by problems, the nature of which is not readily apparent to their teachers. It will not, however, be possible to say how well pupils might progress in teaching based on the sequences proposed above until they have been tried out. What seems clear is that it is not possible to set norms for targets for the learning of children at different ages in the areas we have explored until we have sustained programmes for learning that are more carefully developed than those that most pupils experience at present.

Overall, it must be profoundly disappointing that ideas that bright pupils can work out for themselves at age 6 or 7 when faced with more sophisticated contexts are still not understood by older pupils who have been in school for six more years. It remains to be seen whether this outcome can be altered by more focused teaching and assessment.

9

Evidence in Science Education

*Sandra Duggan, Richard Gott,
Fred Lubben and Robin Millar*

Editor's Introduction

The issues raised in chapter 8 about pupils' understanding in science are developed further in chapter 9. This chapter, by Sandra Duggan, Richard Gott, Fred Lubben and Robin Millar, is concerned not so much with the content of science (conceptual understanding) as with the processes of science (procedural understanding). In particular, the chapter focuses on the notion of 'concepts of evidence', and how these concepts develop between Years 4 and 9. The authors present findings from a study in which pupils in this age-range attempt a scientific investigation involving forces, and they look in particular at the ways in which pupils use the data they have collected. The chapter shows clearly how pupils frequently misunderstand the nature and purpose of scientific evidence, and argues that the ideas which underpin the understanding of evidence should be the subject of explicit teaching. In the final section of their chapter, Duggan, Gott, Lubben and Millar provide some practical suggestions as to how this might be done.

Introduction

The ability to interpret data as evidence to support or refute a statement, or as the basis for an engineering design, is fundamental to pure and applied science. It follows that an understanding of the role and significance of evidence should be an important part of science education. However, as we shall argue in this chapter, it is one that has often been neglected.

Science involves two kinds of knowledge and understanding: understanding the content of science (conceptual understanding) and understanding the methodology (the so-called 'processes') of science which leads to the collection of valid evidence based on reliable data (procedural understanding). In practice, these two kinds of understanding are interwoven; nevertheless, the distinction is a useful means of unravelling the way science functions in schools. While teaching can focus on either aspect of science, the majority of science teaching and assessment has traditionally focused on the conceptual content of science. We do not, of course, wish to deny the importance of conceptual understanding, but we put forward the view that an understanding of scientific evidence, and how the data that form the basis of that evidence are collected, interpreted and validated, is also important. Our findings will show that the use of data as evidence is not at present well understood by pupils.

A report by the Royal Society in 1985 suggested that, in the public at large, there was little understanding of the nature of scientific evidence. In summing up evidence from individuals and organizations professionally involved with science, the authors write:

> There was said to be much less understanding of the nature of scientific activity than knowledge of scientific facts. Neither the principles nor the limitations of scientific method were thought to be familiar to the general public. There was little understanding of basic concepts such as causality and probability . . . (Royal Society, 1985)

The implication is that these 'basic concepts' are an important element in the public understanding of science, and are essential if science education is to empower individuals to contribute to the decision-making processes of a democracy.

An understanding of scientific evidence must also be important to those for whom science is part of their work. A report by the Council of Science and Technology Institute (1993) attempted to map occupations where science, technology and maths were used. Out of an estimated 3 million who work in occupations which involve these subjects in some way, the report found that only 18 per cent are employed in occupations where science, technology or maths describes their main function, within which only a few per cent are 'pure scientists'. The remaining 82 per cent are employed in occupations where an understanding of science, technology and maths is critical to their jobs (such as medical practitioners, nurses and engineers), or where these subjects are regarded by them as enhancing their work. Occupations such as hairdressers, draughtspersons and farm workers were allocated to the latter category.

What sort of science is used in these occupations? The same report developed a description of what scientists, technologists and mathematicians do. They defined the key purpose as being:

To explore, establish, apply, manage and administer safe and ethical practices and procedures of science, technology and mathematics to generate new knowledge, and exploit this knowledge to serve the economy, the environment and society.

To achieve this purpose three 'skills' or abilities were identified: (1) a central core of skills concerned with the doing of science; (2) communication skills; and (3) management skills. The first of these, the 'central core of skills', is common to a wide range of occupations where science is used, and is defined in more detail in the report as the ability to:

- Generate own ideas, hypotheses and theoretical models and/or utilize those postulated by others.
- Design investigations, experiments, trials, texts, simulations and operations.
- Conduct investigations, experiments, trials, tests and operations.
- Evaluate data and results from the processes and outcomes of investigations, experiments, trials, tests and operations.

This definition shows that notions surrounding evidence such as the testing of ideas and evaluation play a major role in the central core of skills.

We have argued that, while appropriate conceptual understanding is essential, an understanding of evidence is also central, not only to the public understanding of science, but also for the requirements of employment in occupations where science (as well as maths and technology) are a significant part of the job. How, then, does the National Curriculum provide pupils with a grounding in evidence or in this central core of skills? We shall restrict our discussion to the first of the four attainment targets in science, Sc1 (scientific investigations), because it is here that pupils are given the opportunity to collect their own evidence and interpret and evaluate it. In passing we should note that Sc1 is often regarded as the most innovative part of the National Curriculum, formalizing as it does the position of investigative work in the primary and secondary curriculum and making it mandatory for teachers to include investigative work in their science teaching. The overall aims of Sc1 include the following statement:

The activities should develop the ability to plan and carry out investigations in which pupils:
(i)   ask questions, predict and hypothesise
(ii)   observe, measure and manipulate variables
(iii) interpret their results and *evaluate scientific evidence*. (DES, 1991d, authors' emphasis)

We can see that the match between Sc1 and the central core of skills defined above is remarkably close. However, both descriptions are too general for the teacher to know exactly what to teach in the classroom or laboratory. A worthy set of intentions is of little value unless those intentions can be pinned down to a set of more precise aims that can be translated into classroom activities. Teachers have, not surprisingly, found difficulty both in teaching and in assessing Sc1.

In this chapter, we shall try to define the common core of skills in more detail, focusing particularly on the idea of evidence and pupils' ability to interpret evidence that they have collected themselves. We shall then suggest how these ideas might help the practising teacher. We will begin by setting the scene with an example of how evidence is used by pupils in investigations.

Evidence in School Science – An Illustrative Example

The example presented here and the research data used in the rest of the chapter are drawn from our Procedural and Conceptual Knowledge in Science (PACKS) project. In the course of the main phase of this project, we visited schools and observed groups of pupils as they undertook investigations, one of which is described below. A more detailed account of the methodology can be found in Millar et al. (1994). The same paper discusses a model that considers the influence of substantive concepts on investigative performance. We intend to restrict our focus in this chapter to procedural aspects using the following task as an example. In this task, the pupils were asked to:

> find out how the height of the slope affects the amount of pull needed to move the brick up the slope.

A range of equipment was made available:

- half-bricks with a hook attached to one end;
- planks approximately 1 metre long;
- forcemeters;
- metre rules.

Both the height of the ramp and the force or pull can be identified quantitatively in that both variables can be measured. Alternatively, the height and pull can be judged or assessed in a qualitative way; for example low, medium and high heights or 'little' and 'big' pulls. An additional part of this investigation set a 'competition', which was presented to the participating groups at the outset:

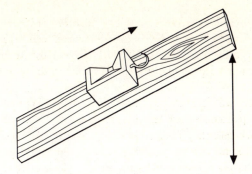

Figure 9.1 Equipment used in the 'forces' investigation.

After you have completed your investigation, we shall give you a height and ask you to predict how much pull or force is needed to move the brick up a slope of that height.

The competition was intended to encourage pupils to collect quantitative data and to give them a reason for doing so by requiring interpolation from the data. A group of two Year 9 pupils (Yvonne and Katie) predicted that:

> it will take more pull to get the brick uphill because the higher up the wood is, the harder it is to pull.

The girls used the same brick for each of the three heights they measured, propping the plank up on furniture around the laboratory and pulling the brick up the plank in the same way each time. They had therefore controlled the necessary variables – the brick, the plank and the method of pulling – thereby constructing a 'fair test'. Yvonne pulled the brick each time and measured the force carefully, identifying both variables quantitatively. The basic design of the investigation, so far, was good. The girls took only three readings using reasonably equal intervals, but these readings were spread over a limited range. Katie recorded the results in a table:

Height (cm)	Pull (N)
27	7.5
45	10
60	10

They did not repeat any readings and their results also suggest that accuracy in measuring the force may have been questionable. After they had taken their measurements, both girls carefully drew and coloured a bar chart using their results, which they said also served as the conclusion. We should note here that, for continuous or quantitative data, the choice of a line graph is preferable as it can illustrate the pattern in data in a way that a bar chart cannot.

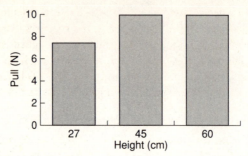

In the competition, where the group was asked to predict the force needed if the plank was at a height of 90 cm, Yvonne and Katie predicted that their brick would need a pull of 20–25 Newtons to move the brick up the plank. They may have reasoned that the force needed at a height of 90 cm would be twice that at 45 cm. Clearly, they had not taken the pattern in the bar chart into consideration, because this would suggest that the force remains at a constant 10 Newtons for heights of 45 cm and above. When the group was questioned, they said that they would not change anything if they did the investigation again, seemingly unaware of the inadequacies of their data in terms of range, number of readings or accuracy.

This example, which is typical of the Year 9 (13-year-olds) sample, shows that children can make considerable progress in the performance of investigations, but that the stage where they then have to represent their data and go on to interpret and evaluate the pattern in their data is often a point of difficulty. The idea of a continuous variable and the use of a line graph to represent the way in which a continuous variable behaves is not understood by many children. The competition used in this investigation highlights this difficulty, together with the fact that once the data have been collected and represented, much of this data may be ignored. In Yvonne and Katie's investigation, they ignored the pattern which, although incorrect, was clear in the bar chart. They did not use the data as a whole, preferring instead to use the data selectively. It is almost as if the drawing of charts or graphs was appended as a 'ritual' which 'you do in science'.

Concepts of Evidence

This example has demonstrated some of the difficulties that children experience in understanding evidence. But where do we begin in teaching the value of data as evidence? What is needed, we suggest, is a clearer understanding of the 'content' of procedural understanding, of which, as we argued earlier, evidence is a central part. In an attempt to define this content, we have developed the notion of 'concepts of evidence' (Gott and Duggan, 1994; Coles and Gott, 1993). These are the set of understandings that underpin the design of investigations (indeed, any experiment) and that guide the choice of design, measurement strategies, and data representation and validation. They are not the manipulative skills, which are, of course, necessary in practical science, but the concepts that allow the appropriate use of these skills in a particular task. For example, in a task about growth, it is not the ability to measure height with a ruler to which we refer, but the understanding needed to know what to measure, how often, over what range and with what accuracy.

Figure 9.2 shows how these concepts of evidence can be structured under four main headings: namely, those concepts associated with the *design* of the task, *measurement*, *data handling* and finally, but crucially, the *evaluation* of the complete task in terms of the reliability and validity of the ensuing evidence. Reliability can be defined as the understanding of the implications of the measurement strategy for the data – can the data be believed? Validity refers to understanding the implications of the design for the resulting data or an overall view of the task to check that it can answer the original question. The evaluation of the task therefore requires an understanding and consideration of the design, measurement and data handling in any particular task. Similarly, the

Concepts of evidence

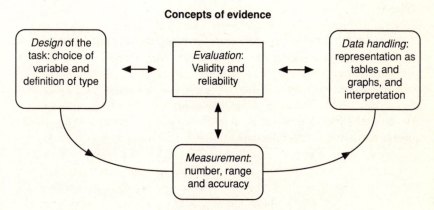

Figure 9.2 Concepts of evidence in an investigation.

understanding of evaluation – of validity and reliability – should ideally determine how the task is designed, how measurements are taken and how the data is handled. These last two points are depicted by the double arrows in figure 9.2.

Concepts of evidence are defined in more detail in table 9.1. The notion of concepts of evidence was derived from tasks that can be defined by their variable structure. While we acknowledge the limitations of such an approach, omitting as it does other parts of science, we regard it as a key starting point in defining the content of procedural understanding. The term 'variable' refers to any quantity that can take different values, such as material type, temperature, length or speed. Variables can be classified in terms of their role and function in the structure of the activity as 'independent', 'dependent' or 'control' variables. The values for the independent variable are chosen and manipulated by the investigator, who then measures the resulting value of the dependent variable for each change in value of the independent variable. Control variables are those that must be kept constant while the independent variable is changed to make the test 'fair'. This structure applies to many, but not all, investigations.

If we reconsider the case study described earlier in the light of table 9.1, we can say that the group demonstrated some understanding of the concepts of evidence associated with design, together with a somewhat poorer understanding of concepts of measurement. But they experienced difficulty with the concepts associated with data handling, and in particular, with the link between the data they had collected and the physical phenomenon they were investigating.

Having established a framework for discussing procedural understanding or 'the central core of skills', we will turn to some of the data from the PACKS project, which will help to shed light on pupils' understanding of the concepts of evidence associated with data handling.

Pupils' Understanding of Concepts of Evidence – Some Data from the PACKS Project

Previous research (Foulds et al., 1992) has shown that pupils' ability to interpret data and evaluate evidence as a whole is poor. The same study found that in the course of an investigation, there are two points which pupils find particularly difficult. The first is the point at which pupils decide on how to identify the type of variable – are they going to identify a particular variable in a quantitative or a qualitative way? This may not, of course, be a positive choice since pupils may not be able to measure, or simply not see the need to measure. This has repercussions for subsequent performance which are discussed more fully by Millar et al. (1994). The other point of difficulty is that at

Table 9.1 Concepts of evidence

	Concepts of evidence	Definition
R E L I A B I L I T Y A N D V A L I D I T Y	Associated with design — *Variable identifications*	Understanding the idea of a variable and identifying the relevant variable to change (the independent variable) and to measure or assess if qualitative (the dependent variable).
	Fair test	Understanding the structure of the fair test in terms of controlling the necessary variables and the importance that the control of variables has in relation to the validity of any resulting evidence.
	Sample size	Understanding the significance of an appropriate sample size to allow, for instance, for biological variation.
	Variable types	Understanding the distinction between categoric, discreet, continuous and derived variables and how they link to different graph types. For example a categoric independent variable such as type of surface cannot be displayed sensibly in a line graph. The behaviour of a continuous variable, on the other hand, is best shown in a line graph.
	Associated with measurement — *Relative scale*	Understanding the need to choose sensible values for qualities so that resulting measurements of the dependent variable will be meaningful. For instance, a large quantity of chemical in a small quantity of water causing saturation will lead to difficulty in differentiating the dissolving times of different chemicals.
	Range and interval	Understanding the need to select a sensible range of values of the variables within the task so that the resulting line graph consists of values that are spread sufficiently widely and reasonably spaced out so that the 'whole' pattern can be seen. A suitable number of readings is therefore also subsumed in this concept.
	Choice of instrument	Understanding the relationship between the choice of instrument and the required range, interval and accuracy.
	Repeatability	Understanding that the inherent variability in any physical measurement requires a consideration of the need for repeats.
	Accuracy	Understanding the appropriate degree of accuracy that is required to provide reliable data which will allow a meaningful interpretation.
	Associated with date handling — *Tables*	Understanding that tables are more than ways of presenting data after it has been collected. They can be used as ways of organizing the design and subsequent data collection and analysis in advance of the whole experiment.
	Graph types	Understanding that there is a close link between graphical representations and the type of variable they are to represent.
	Patterns	Understanding that patterns represent the behaviour of variables which can be uncovered from the patterns in tables and graphs.
	Multivariate data	Understanding the nature of multivariate date and how particular variables within those data can be held constant to discover the effect of one variable on another.

Source: Based on Gott and Duggan (1994). Reprinted by permission of Open University Press.

Table 9.2   Interpolating in the competition

Year	Interpolated correctly in the competition
Y4 (n = 16 groups)	8
Y6 (n = 17 groups)	7
Y9 (n = 14 groups)	7

which pupils have to represent and interpret patterns in the data. These two are linked – if a pupil does not understand the idea of patterns in the data then the drawing of a graph can be little more than a ritual. We shall focus primarily on representation and interpretation here and then briefly consider the way in which pupils identify variables.

The interpretation of patterns

The simplest way to see ·if pupils use the pattern in their data is to examine their conclusions to see, first of all, if their conclusions are based on the data. If the prediction, data and conclusion are all consistent, however, then it is usually not possible to say whether the pupils have used their data in their interpretation and conclusion unless there are obvious indicators to the contrary. For example, they may ignore anomalies or articulate a conclusion indicating that they are unclear what the data mean. In this particular investigation in the PACKS project, in which the prediction was almost always confirmed by the data, a better indicator of the pupils' use and understanding of pattern in data was exemplified in the competition, where pupils were asked to predict using their own data. The competition involves an understanding of the idea of interpolation, which in turn depends on an understanding that a table or graph represents a picture of the relationship between the two variables. The results in table 9.2 are from pupils in Years 4, 6 and 9 (ages approximately 8, 10 and 13) in primary and secondary schools in the North East of England.

It can be seen that about half the groups at each age could interpolate correctly from their investigation in the competition. Did these pupils use their data in tables or graphs to help them interpolate, or simply predict on the basis of what they had seen happen? Table 9.3 shows that approximately half the groups of younger children interpolated correctly from an investigation which included only a table or list of results. We might expect graphical representation to make interpolation easier, but it can be seen that although 12 out of the 14 groups of Y9 children drew a graph or bar chart, only six groups interpolated from it successfully in the competition. It appears that, in this investigation,

Table 9.3 Data handling in the investigation and performance in the the competition

Year	Recorded data in table or list only	Drew bar chart or line graph	Interpolated successfully from table in competition	Interpolated successfully from bar chart or line graph in competition
Y4 (n = 16 groups)	14	2	7	1
Y6 (n = 17 groups)	15	2	7	0
Y9 (n = 14 groups)	2	12	1	6

successful interpolation does not depend on the method of representation, but neither does it improve with age despite the increased use of graphs, whose intended purpose is to illustrate the pattern more clearly and hence facilitate interpolation.

After the investigation, the pupils were interviewed and presented with other, 'second-hand' data from the same investigation. The interview questions were aimed at determining whether or not pupils *could* use tables and graphs (in contrast to the investigation situation, where there is no way of knowing whether a failure to interpolate correctly reflects an inability to read from tables or graphs, or a failure to apply that understanding to the reality represented by their own data). In the interview the pupils were asked, amongst other things, to complete the gaps in a table:

Here are Louise and Anna's results:

Height of the ramp (cm)	Pull/Force (Newtons)
0	
10	12
20	14
40	
60	23
80	

Louise and Anna realized that they had forgotten to write down three readings.
Can you predict roughly what they might be?
Put your answer in the gaps in the table.
Explain how you worked each one out.

Table 9.4   Results of the interview about data in the forces tasks

Year	Interpolated correctly from table	Interpolated and extrapolated correctly from graph/chart
Y4 (n = 16 groups)	3	5
Y6 (n = 17 groups)	9	10
Y9 (n = 14 groups)	11	13

Table 9.4 shows that the number of pupils who completed the table correctly rose from three out of 16 at Year 4 to 11 out of 14 at Year 9. The same pattern was apparent when pupils were asked to interpolate from data on a preconstructed graph or bar chart.

Comparing tables 9.3 and 9.4, we see that the same number of Year 4 children, in this admittedly small sample, could interpolate from the data they had collected themselves in their own investigation, and from other data. Older children, however, find the data in tables, graphs and charts presented at the interview easier to handle than their own data. One possible explanation for this can be seen when we look more closely at the way pupils represent their data. The most useful way to represent data of the kind collected in this investigation, where both variables can easily be measured and are continuous, is to use a line graph. Only three groups (all in Year 9) constructed a line graph. Bar charts are less appropriate but can be used for approximate interpolation. In the PACKS sample, however, bar charts were often constructed which did not start from zero on the x-axis and took no account of the interval between readings. An example is shown below:

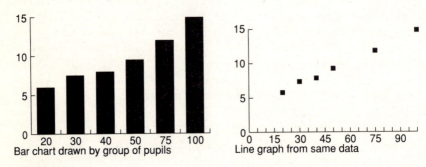

Bar chart drawn by group of pupils   Line graph from same data

The problem with such a construction is that the shape of the graph is not merely obscured but distorted: the line graph drawn from the same data reveals a straight line relationship as opposed to the curve in the bar chart. Clearly, the

Table 9.5 Number of groups adopting each type of identification variable

		Y4	Y6	Y9
Qualitive	Label	1		
	Order	6	2	
Quantitative	Label	3	1	
	Order	5	4	9
	Continuous	1	10	5

details of the relationship between variables are lost and accurate interpretation and interpolation becomes less likely.

Overall, it appears that while half of the Year 4 groups in the sample were able to interpolate successfully in the competition, this proportion does not improve with age. Older children (Year 9) made more attempts to construct graphs and charts from their own data, but they often drew these graphs and charts incorrectly. This suggests that the underlying understanding of the purpose of graphs (to recognize and use patterns) is lacking, and with it the understanding of the relationship between the graph and the behaviour of the physical phenomena under study. Pupils appear to be sidetracked by the ritual of graph drawing. While these findings are from a small sample and at this stage of our analysis from one investigation only, we can tentatively suggest that the lack of understanding of the purpose and use of different graph types may be a contributory factor in the difficulty that older children demonstrate in understanding evidence as a whole.

This specific example has to be seen in relation to the other concepts of evidence. It is closely linked, for example, to the understanding of different types of variables, which, as we mentioned at the beginning of this section, is the other key point of difficulty. Table 9.5 reports data showing the ways in which pupils treated the independent variable in this same investigation.

The groups are first categorized as to whether they define the independent variable qualitatively (judging) or quantitatively (measuring). The term 'label' is used to indicate pupils who see 'high' and 'low', in the qualitative case, or a pair of values such as 50 cm and 100 cm, in the quantitative case, as *descriptive* categories only. These pupils showed by, for example, constructing an unordered bar chart or table that they did not understand the numerical relationship between the data or the pattern within it.

If pupils demonstrated an understanding of the order of the data, then they were assigned to the 'order' group. Yvonne and Katie's investigation (described earlier) is an example of an order group. Their bar chart showed by its construction that the pupils had an idea of order, but that they did not understand the numerical relationship between the variables since the height was treated almost as if it were a descriptive category. The 'continuous' group was reserved for pupils who treated the variables as continuous quantities and who recognized and were able to use and apply the pattern in the data. It should be noted, however, that not all the groups who interpolated successfully are in the continuous category. This is because some groups were able to interpolate in the competition in a mathematical way by matching numbers, but did not demonstrate in their conclusion that they had understood the pattern in the data or the way in which the pattern related to the reality of the variables in the investigation. For instance, one group of Year 4 pupils recorded their data as follows:

Height (cm)	71	73	10	37	63	90	86	46	35	31
Pull (N)	11	13	5	7	10	12	11	9	7	6

and concluded:

the higher the board, the higher the pull.

If they had ordered their data as follows:

Height (cm)	10	31	35	37	46	63	71	73	86	90
Pull (N)	5	6	7	7	9	10	11	13	11	12

the levelling-off pattern in their data would have become apparent. In the competition, they were asked for the force at a height of 50 cm, which they recorded as 9 Newtons. So although successful at the competition, the group was put into the quantitative–label category, as they had taken numerical measurements but had not ordered their data.

Table 9.5 shows that Year 4 pupils have little idea about the continuous nature of variables, preferring to treat their data as a set of labels, which they might order, but which were not identified with the physical quantities in the one-to-one correspondence that we would hope them to achieve. Year 6 pupils treat the variables as continuous to a much greater extent, but there seems to be a regression towards the use of quantitative data in the 'order' category in Year 9. These categories are explored more fully in Millar et al. (1994).

In an investigation involving continuous variables, the ability to interpret patterns, or rather the understanding of the potential use of patterns, relies in turn on an understanding that:

- the variables are continuous;
- they represent the behaviour of some physical phenomenon and cannot be manipulated in defiance of that phenomenon;
- appropriate measurements should therefore be taken to allow that pattern to be uncovered;
- a line graph is the best way to illustrate the pattern;
- interpolation can then be made from the 'line of best fit'.

It is possible that younger pupils use the evidence of their eyes as well as, or even instead of, the data they collect. But as pupils are introduced to the idea of quantitative measurement and its associated panoply of tables, bar charts and line graphs in secondary school, there may well be a period when the sheer complexity of the ideas behind them forces pupils to become embroiled in what may appear, at first, to be nothing more than a ritual associated with science. The danger is that many might never emerge from this period of ritual, which may be a necessary precursor to meaningful learning, but which is clearly not meaningful in itself. There are echoes here of the U-shaped growth in understanding found by other researchers in looking at the development of a range of concepts (Strauss and Stavy, 1982; Archenhold et al., 1991).

Implications for Teaching and Learning in Science

We have discussed how evidence and its underlying concepts have an important role to play, not only in the public understanding of science, but also because they equate closely with the central core of skills that are seen by many as crucial to occupations involving science, maths and technology. This central core has been defined in more detail as consisting of skills and concepts of evidence that can be used as a basis for teaching.

The data presented here suggest that the ritual nature of writing up school science work, with its frequent rote use of tables and graphs, often given to pupils to 'fill in', has a particular effect on pupils in the early years of secondary education. Their understanding of the tasks is obstructed by the difficulties associated with the 'skills' of graphical construction which, we might surmise, are seen by many as the end of the investigation rather than a means to describe patterns in data and their link to reality.

Much has been written over the last few years about children's misconceptions and how they might be addressed. The effectiveness of the latter is not, as yet, convincing. The literature suggests that this may be due to a fundamental flaw in the structure of the material that is to be taught, whereby key links in the conceptual chain are simply omitted from the teaching altogether. For instance, in relation to chemistry, Johnson (1993) writes

> a failure to distinguish between substance and object (and to teach that distinction), reduces the chances of a pupil developing a meaningful concept of a substance. This in turn causes problems in developing ideas of particles, elements and compounds.

The results from chapter 8 (by Black, Brown, Simon and Blondel) suggested similar gaps in the area of forces. It could be that pupils' failure to understand ideas in science may be caused, in a more widespread way than has been recognized hitherto, by gaps in their understanding caused by similar gaps in the teaching schemes.

What we wish to draw attention to here is a huge gap in the teaching of the content of procedural understanding. It has been assumed, explicitly or implicitly, that such understanding will arise largely by a process of 'osmosis' or through practice. Some may believe that practical work exists in school science primarily to illustrate or allow pupils to enquire into a substantive concept, and hence that some basic skills are all that is required. As we have seen above, the consequence at the early secondary stage is confusion: caused, possibly, by the teaching of skills (of graph drawing and the use of instruments, for instance), but with perhaps less attention given to the associated concepts of evidence which turn those skills to meaningful use rather than meaningless ritual.

The 'concepts of evidence' described here are a first attempt to define a 'content' for procedural understanding that can begin to fill that gap. Once defined, we can begin to see ways in which these concepts can be taught using a variety of investigations, written work and straightforward teaching, and move away from the unhelpful idea that investigations are ways of discovering concepts.

The practical implications of our research lie in the integration of these concepts of evidence into a scheme of work where pupil activities are differentiated in such a way as to target particular concepts of evidence in the most efficient manner. It has been suggested (Gott and Duggan, 1994) that they can be taught in two possible ways. One approach is to focus the investigation on a particular concept of evidence. Repeatability, for instance, can be targeted by using any investigation in which variability is a prominent feature. In a task based on the bounciness of balls, for instance, the need for repeats is essential if the evidence is to be reliable *and* accurate enough to uncover the trend in the results. The role of the teacher here is crucial in guiding group and/or class discussion at strategic points throughout the investigation so that the aim of the lesson – to learn about repeatability – is clear to all. Alternatively, the teacher may prefer to question groups while they are collecting their data in order to encourage them to consider the impact of lack of repeats on the reliability of their measurements.

The importance of evidence as a whole can be introduced to pupils by carrying out investigations where there is a target audience, perhaps others in the class. If groups are doing different tasks, each group can see the need for convincing other groups who have not 'seen' and therefore are not in a position to 'believe'. Choice of task here is less important, although one in which there is not a self-evidently correct answer is likely to be more fruitful. Techniques such as asking groups of pupils to defend their results against cross-examination by an advocate from another group, or the class, can be of use here. Such techniques require careful introduction and a sense of theatre to drive home the importance of the audience, which has to be convinced by the 'objective' evidence of the scientist. Gradually, pupils begin to realize that the nature of scientific evidence is not straightforward. Ideas of this sort are also discussed by Millar (1989).

The second approach is to use follow-up exercises to reinforce or teach a particular concept of evidence that was, for instance, diagnosed as being weak in an investigation. Understanding the reasoning that underlies the choice of graph type, with its link to the type of variable, can be approached using 'second-hand' data, as in the example in figure 9.3 (see p. 166).

Developing the understanding of *patterns* in data is, as was noted in the results reported above, one of the more difficult concepts of evidence. Sketch graphs may have a part to play here. Asking pupils to say which graph 'feels' like the stretching of a rubber band, for example, seems to help in establishing that link with reality that is so often missing. Some examples for follow-up activities are given in figure 9.4 (see p. 167). After pupils have become familiar with the idea of sketch graphs, the teacher could ask pupils to predict before doing an investigation what the shape or pattern of the resulting graph might be. Such approaches demonstrate that the value of evidence and its underlying concepts can indeed be taught, although these ideas are, as yet, in their infancy. Much work remains to be done, for example, on how such ideas can best be incorporated into schemes of work.

Conclusions

The integration of concepts of evidence into schemes of work means that schemes will have to progress not only in terms of conceptual understanding, but also in terms of procedural understanding. Once it is appreciated that there is a 'content' to procedural understanding, and a content that can be clearly defined, it will enable schemes of work to target specific learning outcomes.

Susan, Vicky and Leanne had made model cars using margarine tubs. To 'launch' the cars, they used elastic bands stretched across stools. They each measured how far the cars travelled. They put their results in a table. They each drew a graph to show their results.

Amount elastic pulled back	Distance travelled
2 cm	35 cm
4 cm	55 cm
6 cm	70 cm
8 cm	87 cm
10 cm	101 cm

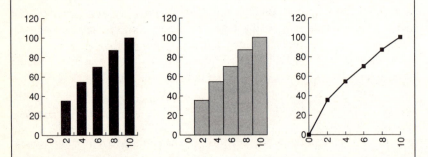

There was going to be a competition to see who could land their car closest to a line drawn on the floor.

They could measure how far it was from the elastic band to the line before they started.

1 The graphs all show the same results in different ways. Which graph do you think is best? Explain why you chose this one.

2 Discuss with your friends which graphs *they* think are best. When you have agreed which is the best, draw it onto a full sheet of paper. Remember that the labels are important.

Figure 9.3   An activity concerning the choice of type of graph.

Source: Gott and Duggan 1994. Reprinted by permission of Open University Press.

Try drawing sketch graphs for each of these:

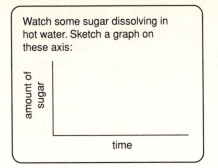

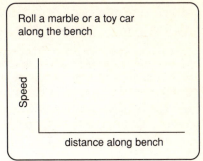

Then choose your own axes for these:

Your height as you got older

Force needed to push a lorry at a steady speed as it is loaded with bricks

Figure 9.4 Examples of a line graph exercise which can be used to teach the relationship between the behaviour of a variable and a graphical pattern.

Source: Gott and Duggan 1994. Reprinted by permission of Open University Press.

This approach is far less problematic than the present situation, where investigations do not have clearly defined learning outcomes.

One important element of this 'content' of procedural understanding concerns the language involved. There is no agreed set of definitions for what we have called concepts of evidence. If we are teaching 'force', then there is general agreement as to what the associated words mean – for example push, pull, gravity and friction – even if (as the authors of chapter 8 point out) these terms are not without problems, particularly with younger children. However, terms such as scale and range, or validity and reliability, while possibly sharing a language amongst teachers and scientists (though even that is doubtful), are not at present part of pupils' language. For example, the term 'control' variable(s), which refers to the factor(s) kept the same, is often confused with the independent variable, which is the variable that is changed by the investigator (and so under the investigator's 'control'). The issue of language is an important one not just for the common vocabulary itself, but for the way in which an agreed terminology makes the 'content' real and capable of manipulation.

As a final point, we suggest that the definition of a content of procedural understanding, and a range of ways in which that content might be taught and learnt, will enhance the quality of classroom interaction. Not least, this will occur because everyone will know the purpose of the investigation or activity and appreciate its importance as a means to a particular end, rather than as an inefficient way of learning traditional science concepts that could be better taught in other ways. But it will also allow teachers to harness the undoubted motivation that comes from investigative work, owing to the transfer of control to the pupil and the humanizing effect both of that transfer and of the types of task that can be constructed. The failure to do so at present can be traced, we believe at least in part, to teachers' understandable reluctance to adopt an investigative approach that has been portrayed as a teaching tool rather than an important area of science 'content' in its own right.

10

'There were no facts in those days': Children's Ideas about Historical Explanation

Peter Lee, Alaric Dickinson and Rosalyn Ashby

Nothing puzzles me. This is because they are not as clever and only go on what they are told, as there were no facts in those days.

(Year 9 pupil discussing Saxon trial by ordeal)

Editor's Introduction

Our concern with progression in pupils' understanding continues into the final chapter of the book, written by Peter Lee, Alaric Dickinson and Rosalyn Ashby. Here, the focus is on a different subject area, that of history, but there are still some interesting parallels with the findings emerging in other areas. As with the previous chapter, the authors' concern is not so much with pupils' understanding of historical knowledge and facts as with their understanding of the processes that historians use in creating their subject. The chapter describes how pupils' ideas about historical understanding develop between Years 3 and 10. Lee, Dickinson and Ashby focus in particular on two specific aspects of historical understanding — pupils' ideas about rational understanding in history, and pupils' concepts of causal explanation. Although the project is still at a relatively early stage, the initial findings fit closely with those emerging from the previous two chapters. Thus they reveal particular types of misunderstanding that could become the focus of specific teaching approaches; at the same time, they show yet again the large variation in understanding at each age level.

Introduction

The present chapter considers aspects of children's ideas about historical explanation. This introduction sets the context of the research, and gives a very brief outline of the project's aims and methods. The main body of the chapter is divided into three sections. The first section offers a brief sketch of some general issues involved in trying to understand children's ideas about the discipline of history. The second discusses children's ideas of rational under-standing, where the project is testing and refining our existing account of progression in children's ideas. The last part of the chapter reports some first steps towards giving an account of the development of children's ideas about causal explanation.

The public debates about history in the National Curriculum have treated school history as if it were an arena where contending political ideologies were locked in a fierce struggle. This was a gross distortion of what had been happening in schools, where the debate was much more concerned with strengthening history as a school subject. Since the late 1960s history teaching had undergone important changes. Teachers sought ways of making school history more rigorous, so that it required thinking as well as memory. There were arguments about content, some of which carried political implications, but the most far-reaching changes were not concerned with content, but with developing children's understanding of history as a discipline, rather than simply as a body of knowledge. Some teachers pressed these changes too far, treating substantive content as a mere vehicle for handing on concepts and (so-called) skills. Nevertheless, in general, by the late 1980s a balance seemed to be emerging, in which understanding of the discipline was seen as essential for genuine historical knowledge, and historical knowledge – properly understood – was seen as the *raison d'être* for understanding the discipline.

The National Curriculum Order (DES, 1991a) set out the basic content for school history, leaving teachers to turn the statutory programmes of study into schemes of work for classroom teaching. It also established three attainment targets for history: *knowledge and understanding of history, interpretations of history* and *the use of historical sources*, couched, not in terms of content, but in terms of second-order understandings (as their titles suggest). Each of these was broken down into ten sets of statements of attainment, or levels. This system reflected the changes in history teaching during the previous 15 years, and the even more rapid developments in assessing history since the mid 1980s. Examinations which for many years had rewarded discrete items of content, and allowed one or two marks out of 20 for historical understanding, were replaced by an assessment system in which candidates had to demonstrate their historical understanding, and in so doing show an appropriate knowledge of content.

(Whereas with the earlier examinations the danger lay in virtually omitting understanding, the fear was expressed in some quarters that too little knowledge would be required in the newer system. Experience will show whether a reliable balance is quickly achieved for the great majority of history examinations.)

As a result of these developments perhaps a third or more of teachers – it is difficult to be precise about the proportion – had to reassess their approach to history teaching. In primary schools where, with a few notable exceptions, there was little tradition of teaching history as a separate subject, the changes demanded by the National Curriculum were much more dramatic than in the secondary schools. The work of Ian Plewis and Marijcke Veltman (see chapter 1 of this volume) suggests that the National Curriculum has had an impact on primary school history – at least in ensuring its presence in some form for 5- to 7-year-olds – but OFSTED reports suggest that the rate of change varies considerably between different primary schools.

The changes introduced by the National Curriculum were partly a reflection of new teaching approaches, and partly a consequence of psychological research on children's understanding (some of it in history), and these changes in their turn helped stimulate further work. If teaching history meant helping children to see how assertions in history are related to evidence, it was important to find out what notions of evidence children were bringing to history lessons. And if children were to be helped to give better historical explanations, teachers needed to know how their ideas about explanation were likely to develop. It was clearly especially important for the National Curriculum assessment arrangements to have some understanding of children's ideas – it is difficult to justify a particular set of levels of attainment without some understanding of how children's ideas develop. And teaching is likely to be less than maximally effective if it attempts to change ideas that children do not in fact hold.

The Project

The work of the CHATA Project (Concepts of History and Teaching Approaches at Key Stages 2 and 3) fits into this context of a new National Curriculum, and changing teaching and research into children's ideas about history. The project is divided into three phases: investigation of the progression of children's ideas of *historical enquiry* and *historical explanation* between the ages of 7 and 14 years; the development of instruments for investigating teaching approaches in history and for categorizing the way in which history is seen in relation to the wider curriculum; and finally, exploration of the relationship between pupils' concepts of enquiry and explanation, curriculum contexts and differences in teaching approach. Data collection for the first phase is complete, and analysis is now under way.

Phase One of the project set out to test and refine provisional accounts of the development of children's understandings derived from earlier work, and to develop new accounts where no adequate existing accounts were available. In order to do this we investigated a number of possible sub-strands in the concepts of *enquiry* and *explanation*: in particular *evidence, accounts, rational understanding, cause* and *explanatory adequacy*. It is possible that we may also be able to say something about other ideas, for example *objectivity*; ultimately we hope to give a more general account of the development of children's wider overarching concepts of historical enquiry and explanation.

Three sets of tasks were designed to investigate children's ideas. In the trials of the first phase we employed video and interview methods, together with pencil-and-paper tests (approximately 600 written responses were collected). In the main investigation in Phase One, pencil-and-paper responses have been collected from 320 children between the ages of 7 and 14, across three sets of tasks (on three separate occasions). Of this main sample, 122 pupils have been interviewed on all three task-sets; 55 of these pupils are 7-year-olds, 31 are 10-year-olds, 18 are 11-year-olds and 18 are 14-year-olds. In addition we have video data on 96 children working in groups of three, each group using one set of tasks. Each set of tasks seeks to elicit children's ideas in a number of different ways, so that there is internal triangulation as well as triangulation across the three task-sets.

Understanding Children's Ideas about History

In research into children's ideas about history it is hard to escape linguistic behaviour as a source of data, or to find supporting evidence from other kinds of behaviour. Manipulation of objects can offer clues as to children's everyday understanding of the physical world, but not to their ideas about history. Changes in history teaching between the late 1960s and the mid–1980s emphasized the problem of accessing children's ideas. There was a partial shift in history education (both in teaching and research) from emphasis on substantive historical concepts (*monarch, peasant, church, revolution*) to an interest in second-order 'organizing' or 'structural' concepts like *historical evidence, explanation* and *change*. This shift made it easier for teachers to think of history as a discipline that challenged pupils' thinking as well as their memories, and at the same time offered researchers the possibility of investigating progression in children's ideas. But this reorientation was not without problems of its own.

Children are not analytical philosophers of history. They do not, on the whole, sit and reflect about historical explanation, or the nature of historical evidence. They do, on the other hand, tend to behave, in getting on with their history, as if they believed certain ideas, and those ideas seem to change. Such ideas are tacit, not merely because they remain unspoken, but because children seldom explicitly consider them. Researchers are therefore forced back onto an indirect approach, so that the way in which children tackle historical tasks is taken to index their working understandings. Research limits its aims to the generation of constructs that make sense of children's ideas. The best that researchers can hope to achieve is an internally consistent model that is not disconfirmed by what children do, and that allows conditional predictions about what range of moves a child is likely to make when confronted by certain kinds of historical task, *if* he or she has certain tacit ideas about (say) historical explanation.

Talk of progression in children's ideas requires some consistency of behaviour in the face of changes in substantive history; there should be signs of common strategies across different content. There should also be some sense in which ideas may be described as higher or lower level. CHATA makes the assumption, based on earlier work in the field, that it is possible to find sets of tacit ideas that allow or inhibit certain kinds of thinking (Lee, 1978; Dickinson and Lee, 1978, 1984; Shemilt, 1980, 1983, 1984, 1987; Ashby and Lee, 1987a, 1987b). Children who handle history, for example, as though they believe that historical agents are more stupid than we are, but share our goals, beliefs and values, will run into severe difficulties in dealing with certain kinds of historical problem, or even in making sense of certain passages of history. An assumption that people in the past might see things in a different way from us overcomes the conflicts posed by the lower-level ideas, and opens up new possibilities for further conflicts at a higher level. Ideas are higher or lower level because they create or solve more or fewer problems, because the ideas with which children work can have greater or less explanatory power. In particular, higher-level ideas can resolve problems created by the limitations of lower-level ideas. We will try to give substance to these remarks in what follows.

Children's Conceptions of Rational Understanding in History

One of the assumptions underlying the CHATA Project is that explanation of action is an important part of historical explanation and understanding. Looking at why people wanted to do certain things cannot in itself explain why things happened; but establishing what people were seeking to do, and why, is essential for understanding actions, and can help us to understand events. Such understanding involves establishing how agents saw the situation (their particular circumstances and their wider set of beliefs and values) and what they were trying to do (their intentions) in order to reconstruct their reasons for doing what they did. What clusters of ideas are pupils likely to bring to bear with regard to explaining and understanding people's behaviour in the past? And what progression is evident in these ideas?

Our interest in children's ideas (and skills) concerning rational understanding stretches over more than two decades. One of the tests used in the CHATA Project to investigate children's ideas about rational understanding is a further development of one used in our earlier investigations (Dickinson and Lee, 1984; Ashby and Lee, 1987b). In addition to this test (on the theme of Anglo-Saxon trial by ordeal), two new tests were developed (on Claudius' reasons for the invasion of Britain, and on the reasons for executing all the slaves in Pedanius' house following his murder by one of them in AD 61). On the basis of our earlier work, that of Shemilt (1984), and initial analysis of CHATA data, there seem to be good reasons for suggesting the following pattern of progression in children's ideas of what is involved in understanding other people's behaviour in the past.

The interim account of children's ideas employed in the research picks out six categories, but since previous work has paid some attention to the thinking of older children, and space is limited, it seems sensible to concentrate on the lower-level categories. Higher-level categories will be summarized very briefly with short examples. There is now a not insubstantial body of evidence to suggest that children's ideas go together in the ways suggested here, although much work remains to be done to refine the account further and to explore paths of progression in the tacit understandings that children employ to make sense of other people's behaviour in the past.

The baffling past

'You can't explain what they did – they just did it.' Actions and institutions and social practices in the past are seen as unintelligible. For children whose responses fall into this category it is hard even to conceptualize actions in any terms other than the description under which they are encountered in the first place: actions are not explained, even though they may be recounted in some detail.

Children thinking in this way typically said or wrote 'I can't explain', or repeated the words of the question (for instance, 'They used the ordeal to decide if someone was guilty of a crime'). When encouraged, they could usually recount what happened in the ordeal by cold water, the ordeal of hot water, and the ordeal of hot iron. Some children thought it appropriate to add comments such as 'Trial by ordeal would hurt my hand', and 'I would not put my hand in'. But this, of course, does not amount to explaining why the Anglo-Saxons used the ordeals to decide if someone was guilty of a crime!

In the following extract Aidan (Year 3) expresses interest in the ordeal, and recounts various details. In her responses to later questions there were traces of ideas characteristic of other categories, but in this particular excerpt there is evidence of difficulty, which seems to be characteristic of thinking in this initial category, in conceptualizing the ordeal further and constructing any reason for using the ordeal beyond simply restating what was said in the question.

Can you explain the ordeals, the cold water and the hot water?
Oh yes, this is what I liked as well. There's a story on the other page about that.
Right.
Yes, this is this one. Yeah. This one's the cold water.
Yes, we'll just do this one, you explain the cold water to me, the cold water ordeal.
Well, the person that had stolen something, well they might have done, they have to do an ordeal if they've proved to be . . . Well, no, no, don't worry about what I said just then. If they had stolen something or not, they would find it out by having an ordeal and there was a cold water, hot water or hot iron, and for the cold water it says, 'The accused (does that say 'accused'?) the accused person would drink some holy water, his hands would be tied and he would be thrown into deep water. If he sank far enough, 2 metres, he was innocent. If he floated he was guilty.'
Right.
Do you want me to read the whole of that one?
No, you did that one very well. Right, so the question we actually asked was 'Why did they use these ordeals to find out if someone was guilty or not?' Why do you think they did it?
I don't know. [long pause] To find out if they were guilty or not, I suppose.

The 'divi' past

Our investigations, past and present, have found examples in almost every class, regardless of age, of pupils who clearly assume a sense of superiority towards people in the past, who do not assume any need to find out about their particular values and beliefs and actually view them as intellectually and morally inferior. Thus Debbie (Year 9) began her written answer to the question 'Why do you think the Anglo-Saxons used the ordeal to decide if someone was guilty of a crime?' with the words:

It is pathetic!! The ordeals are stupid – especially the 'cold water' ordeal. If you sank you drowned. If you floated you were fined (or killed). You would probably sink and die!

Two Year 3 children were somewhat less forthright, but also dismissive, when they wrote: 'Because thay did kowe kone other way to punish them' (sic) and 'Because they had a law, and they couldernt think of another' (sic).

Actions in this category are thus reconceptualized in children's own terms, but an assumption of superiority leads them to be dismissive of the ideas and actions of people in the past. People in the past, they assume, were not as clever as us. (There is a sense in which they were mentally deficient – 'divi', 'thick' – because they failed to adopt obviously better courses of action.)

At the root of this is the inability of the child to recognize that people in the past often could not know what he or she now knows and takes for granted. Add to this an inability to envisage the inherent complexity of human institutions and interactions, and the past becomes a catalogue of absurd behaviour, to which a reaction of irritated incomprehension and contempt seems appropriate. At this level the additional difficulty that people in the past saw things very differently from us, and had different values, goals and expectations, scarcely begins to enter the pupil's calculations, and only makes the problem worse.

Indications of some of the assumptions that mark this category are to be found in what Kylie (Year 6) said about the cold water ordeal:

> Well I think it was really [stupid] because – I don't know about [the hot water and the hot iron ordeals] because I've never stuck my hand in hot water or carried a hot iron three metres, but I know that anyone who gets thrown into the bottom of the pool would float because I've tried it – but I think it really is ridiculous, though, because it's ... You can't expect people to prove not guilty when there are trials and ordeals like that because you know they're going to be guilty. They won't be innocent because it's just something that's impossible to think and, as I say, I don't know about the other two because I've never tried them, but it's, I think it's silly, it's ridiculous.

In similar vein, James (Year 9) wrote:

> The ordeal does seem like a stupid method of speaking the truth. I don't believe God would heal someone in three days or make them rise to the surface of a pond just to prove if someone is guilty or not. It puzzles me why they didn't just use evidence.

James' understanding of the ordeal might possibly be advanced by encouraging him to think further about the extent to which the Anglo-Saxons did and did not rely on evidence. And Kylie's oral comments suggest that she sees some need to consider the details of each ordeal. Thus there is evidence of at least a trace of an assumption that is characteristic of a higher-level category. One puzzle to be tackled in further analysis is that of the routes (linear or otherwise) that children's progress seems likely to take towards higher-level categories.

Generalized stereotypes

For some children understanding is characterized by reference to a 'conventional' or stereotypical account of people's intentions, situations, values and goals. This includes stereotyped role descriptions and the ascription of very generalized dispositions based on 'merely conceptual' understandings of intentions and situations. Thus David (Year 6) wrote that Claudius invaded Britain 'so that he could expand the Roman Empire, and also be one better than the previous Emperors', and that the Romans had the law about executing all the slaves in a household 'because they wanted to show them that they were powerful'.

In general no attempt is made in this category to distinguish what people now know and think from what people in the past knew and thought, or between their values and ours. Thus Claire (Year 7) wrote:

> Claudius decided to invade Britain because he wanted to show everybody how great and purposeful he was. He also wanted to prove that he was the best Emperor of all times, and wanted to have all the wealth and riches he could get, and wanted to be friends with the Romans so they would like him . . . Nothing puzzles me because all of the reasons are common today – that people want to be powerful and the best, that they want to be rich and happy, and that they want their citizens to like them and to have lots of friends to help them.

Everyday empathy

This kind of thinking differs from that of the previous category in its much closer application to the particular circumstances and people involved. Some responses make reference to evidence of the specific situation in which people found themselves. But the situation is seen in modern terms, assuming that late-twentieth-century ideas will provide all that is required to make sense of Anglo-Saxon justice. For instance Vicki (Year 9) wrote of the ordeal:

> Also it meant 'unpleasant experiences' so even if the person was guilty or not they wouldn't commit a crime after it, because of the risk of having to go through it again.

Fayad (Year 9) also saw the ordeal in terms of deterrence:

> It embarrassed the culprit if others saw his predicament, so he wouldn't try it again.

Louise (Year 7) made some reference to Claudius' situation, but essentially with regard to popularity:

> I think Claudius decided to invade Britain, because he could ensure a trade of pearls and other things. It would make Claudius more popular with the Romans (his own people) as well because it would put him above other great Emperors who had failed. Claudius needed this because he wasn't very popular at the time.

In response to the further question 'Does anything puzzle you about why Claudius decided to invade Britain?', she wrote:

> I'm puzzled that Claudius did not listen to Augustus when he said that they were 'too far away, too poor and too friendly'. I'm puzzled that he still wanted to attack even though they were very expensive to attack.

Thinking characteristic of the next two categories is needed to resolve such puzzlement.

Restricted historical empathy

More powerful ideas manifest themselves at the point where appeal is made to evidence of the specific situation in which people found themselves, but now with the recognition that this cannot necessarily be characterized in twentieth-century terms, because the beliefs, goals and values of people in the past were different from ours. Kirsty (Year 9) moves between present and past perspectives when she writes:

> No it doesn't puzzle me why the Anglo-Saxons used the ordeal. I think that in our society it would be hard not to find this sort of thing strange, but if you try and place yourself in their circumstances and with their beliefs, it does not puzzle me why they believe in the ordeal as a method of finding out if someone was guilty of a crime.

Children are able to understand that intentions are likely to be qualified, and to begin to follow some of their ramifications. In explaining why Claudius decided to invade Britain, Ben (Year 9) wrote:

> Claudius decided to invade because at the present time he was a new Emperor and fairly unpopular. If he were to invade and conquer Britain, he would have taken the land that had been out of the Roman realm for nearly 100 years. If he was successful, then he would have a new light of popularity and respect. If he failed, nothing would have changed and he might gain some respect for trying. After all, two Emperors before him had decided against it. The Britons also

might have had riches of gold and tin which were valuable to the Romans and would have improved their financial position.

Children whose responses fall into this category accept that people in the past saw things in a different way from us, but cannot take this much beyond the specific circumstances in order to relate these differences to other beliefs, values and material conditions. This means that they may still resort to exasperated criticism of what they see as futile beliefs, or ignorance (the very beliefs they have just cited in arriving at an understanding of the institution or action in question). This frustration will disappear only when everything can be seen in a wider context.

Contextual historical empathy

Some children assume that in order to explain the problematic action or institution they should set it in a wider context of beliefs, at the same time differentiating between the values, goals and habits enshrined in a past situation or social practice and those that are prevalent today. From our earlier work we know that some children can achieve this by Year 9, and there are further examples in the CHATA responses examined so far. Joel (Year 9) begins to fit the ordeal into a wider social context:

> Their different values and ideals would have meant that 'God would decide' about whether or not they were guilty. By using this system, they felt that God would definitely choose correctly. It also included the values they had in the social system (how much each man's oath is worth).

Children thinking in this way do not always give an entirely adequate or accurate explanation, but show clear signs of grasping what has to be done in order to achieve understanding. They differentiate between the position and point of view of the historical agent, and that of the historian; between the beliefs, values, goals and habits that define and surround a past institution or social practice, and those with which they are familiar in their own society. They see the problematic action or institution in a wider context of beliefs and values. Sometimes they attempt to link it with the material conditions of life. Children may still want to switch standpoint and apply current standards of rationality and knowledge in assessing actions or institutions, but they do so in the clear knowledge that their own standards cannot be assumed to be the same as those of the past.

Children's Conceptions of Causal Explanation in History

Children's ideas about causal explanation in history cannot be presumed to go hand in hand with their ideas about rational understanding. Both are central to giving explanations in history, but initial work on children's responses suggests that a child may have a sophisticated conception of one, and very limiting ideas about the other.

Our approach to children's ideas about causal explanation in history followed the same broad pattern as our approach to the other ideas under investigation. On three different occasions, children were given sets of tasks to perform. On each occasion the tasks were logically similar, but the substantive historical content of each set was different. Trials suggested that several elements were central to the way in which children handled explanatory tasks: some of these were pursued across all three sets of tasks, but in order to keep task-sets to a manageable size, others were investigated only in one. Within each set, some tasks demanded free-form or open-ended responses, and others were structured, demanding choices from, or links to be made among, items in a given list.

In this chapter examples will be taken from the first set of tasks, in which children were presented with basic information about the Roman Empire, most of it in both written and cartoon form. (We are greatly indebted to Phil Suggitt for his inspired and precisely targeted drawings, which were much appreciated by the children.) They were then given particular information about the Roman conquest of Britain. This was followed by a paradox:

> There were lots of Britons in Britain.
> The Roman army that went to Britain wasn't very big.
> The Britons were fighting for their homes.
> **So why were the Romans able to take over most of Britain?**

Information, purpose and cause

One aspect of children's understanding of causal explanation that we wished to explore was the degree to which children made distinctions between explaining by giving *purposes* for people involved in the Roman conquest, and explaining by offering *causal antecedents* – whether events, processes or states of affairs – that explain Roman success. We asked children to choose from a set of alternative sentences the two which best explained why the Romans were able to take over most of Britain. The six sentences from which the children made their selection exemplified three types of statement: causal antecedents (e.g. *The Roman army trained a lot and the Roman soldiers were used to fighting as a team*), reasons for action (e.g. *Claudius wanted to show that he was a great Emperor*), and statements of fact that matched some of those in the information that the children had been given, but had no direct explanatory value (e.g. *The Emperor Claudius had a limp*). Two sentences of each type were offered (see figure 10.1).

Early work on the responses suggests that there may be a patterned progression in children's understanding in this area:

1 Explanation and giving information are not distinguished.
2 Explanation is to be found in giving purposes: wanting makes things happen.
3 Explanation is given in terms of wants, but the link to outcomes is mediated by morale or strength of volition (you have to want something *really strongly*).
4 Explanation is a matter of finding causal antecedents.

Some children chose the two information boxes, perhaps following a simple matching strategy, as if explanation is simply providing more information (although this appears to be very rare even among 7-year-old children). Others were content to give reasons for the Roman invasion, making no distinction between wanting to take over and being able to do so. On the other hand, some children not only selected the two causal antecedents of Roman success, but explicitly ruled out the sentences giving reasons for action on the grounds that they did not explain why the Romans were *able* to take over. The situation is complicated, however, by the fact that when asked how their chosen (apparently non-causal) sentences explained the success of the Roman conquest, some children converted their choices into indirect reasons why the Romans chose to invade Britain, or even into reasons why they were able to succeed. A typical move in the latter case was to choose the sentence *The Roman Emperor Claudius decided to invade Britain in AD 43* (matching information) together with the sentence *Claudius wanted to show that he was a great Emperor* (reason for action). The sentences were combined in an implicit or explicit argument: Claudius had a strong reason for invading, Claudius was Emperor, Claudius gave his orders; therefore, Roman soldiers would fear failure and fight hard. Whereas some children behave as if there is a direct correspondence between wanting and achieving, so that reasons for action will suffice to explain outcomes, others mediate between wants and outcomes by reference to morale: wanting enough still makes things happen, but only indirectly. Roman soldiers wanted to win because Claudius did: their fear of Claudius' power made them fight harder or made them braver.

Why were the Romans able to take over most of Britain?
(You can take it that the sentences in the boxes are true.)

There were lots of Britons in Britain.
The Roman army that went to Britain wasn't very big.
The Britons were fighting for their homes.

So why were the Romans able to take over most of Britain?

Question 3.

Read Box A and Boxes 1 to 6 carefully.
Choose the TWO boxes which are best for making the Romans able to take over.
Draw lines to join them up to Box A (the one with the thick edges).

BOX 1
The Roman army trained
a lot and the Roman
soldiers were used to
fighting as a team.

BOX 2
The Roman Emperor
Claudius decided to
invade Britain in AD 43.

BOX 3
The Romans wanted to
make sure they could
get tin and pearls from
the Britons

BOX A
THE ROMANS WERE
ABLE TO TAKE OVER
MOST OF BRITAIN

BECAUSE:

BOX 4
Claudius wanted to show
that he was a great
Emperor.

BOX 5
The Britons lived in
different groups which
sometimes fought each
other.

BOX 6
The Emperor Claudius
had a limp.

Figure 10.1 Information, purpose and cause: the Roman conquest of Britain.

If further work confirms that there is a progression along these lines, it is important not to assume that it is tied directly to age. It is clear that some 7-year-olds perform at a higher level than some 14-year-olds. Whereas some 14-year-olds offered matching information, and justified their choice by declaring that 'it says it in the story', some 7-year-olds were very explicit in distinguishing between reasons for invasion, and causes of Roman success. One Year 3 girl, for example, ruled out Roman desire to get tin and pearls from Britain as 'not *very* good' because it 'doesn't *explain* it very well': it shows 'why they *wanted* to take over'. The trial version of the test included eight sentences, two of which were omitted from the final version. One of these (*The Romans were not pleased that the Britons were helping the Gauls*) elicited the response that while it might be '*some* good' for explaining why the Romans were able to take over, it 'wasn't *really* good'. In reply to the interviewer's question why this was, the girl replied: 'Well, I don't think it explains why they were *able* to take over most of Britain.' A Year 6 girl, having chosen the causal antecedents, explained that she rejected the other sentences 'because they didn't explain how the Romans could have conquered Britain'. She thought that other people might choose the wrong ones because 'they were the reason why he [Claudius] conquered Britain'.

Causal relations and causal structure

In another group of questions children were first asked to draw arrows linking boxes to show why a cup broke (see figure 10.2). It was explained that this extra-historical task was to help them with the next question, and it was indeed partly a device to familiarize them with a certain kind of exercise, but it was also a means of seeking evidence about their everyday causal notions. The boxes contained short sentences which might have some bearing on the breaking of the cup: some described events (*The cup hit the floor*), some referred to states of affairs (*The floor was hard*), and some described actions (*Jane and Fred both tried to grab the cup*). There were six possible explanatory boxes.

The next question asked children to do the same thing as they had done with the cups task, but this time to explain the Roman conquest. They were instructed to use arrows to join up some or all of six boxes containing statements about the Roman Empire or about the Britons to a centre box containing the sentence *So, the Romans were able to take over most of Britain*, in order to give the best explanation they could (see figure 10.3). In both the cup and the Roman take-over questions, children were told that an arrow from one box to another meant that the first box helped explain the second, and that they could have as many or as few arrows as they needed. They were also told that more than one arrow could go into or out of a box.

Part of the rationale behind these questions is an attempt to give a picture of

Question 11. This question is to help you do the one on the next page. Do this first.
WHY DID THE CUP BREAK?

HOW TO DO THIS QUESTION

Choose any boxes which help to explain why the cup broke.
Join them up to show in the best way you can why the cup broke.
(The boxes are not in any special order.)
Make the best explanation you can.
Draw in arrows to make the joins.
An arrow from one box to another means: *the first box helps to explain the second box.*

Like this:

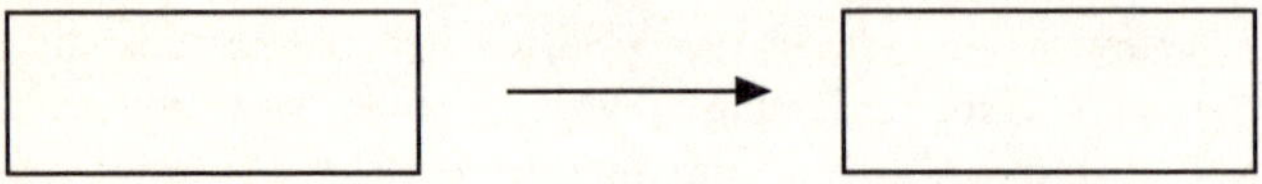

This box	helps explain	this box.

Use as many joins as you need. You can have more than one arrow to or from a box.
BUT don't make joins that don't help explain why the cup broke.

Make the middle box happen!

SHOW WHY THE CUP BROKE

Box 1
The cup was made of china.

Box 4
The floor was hard.

Box 2
The cup was very breakable.

SO: THE CUP BROKE.

Explain this box.

Box 5
Jane and Fred both tried to grab the cup.

Box 3
The cup hit the floor.

Box 6
Jane and Fred dropped the cup.

Figure 10.2 Causal relations: the broken cup.

Question 12. Why were the Romans able to take over?

(The boxes on this Chart are not in any special order)
Choose any boxes which help explain why the Romans were able to take over.
Join them up with arrows to show best why the Romans were able to take over.
Make the best explanation you can.
An arrow from one box to another means: *the first box helps explain the second box.*
Use as many joins as you need. You can have more than one arrow to or from a box.
BUT don't make joins that don't help explain why the Romans were able to take over.

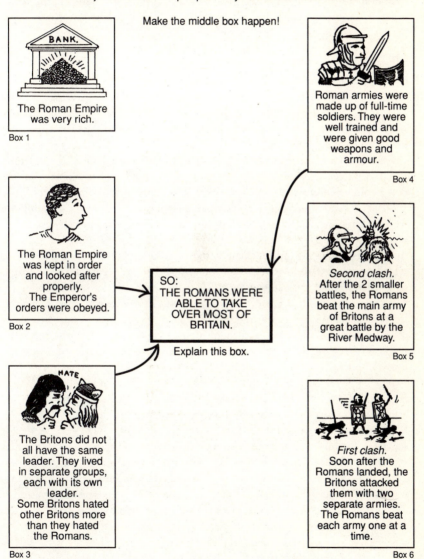

Make the middle box happen!

The Roman Empire
was very rich.

Box 1

Roman armies were
made up of full-time
soldiers. They were
well trained and
were given good
weapons and
armour.

Box 4

The Roman Empire
was kept in order
and looked after
properly.
The Emperor's
orders were obeyed.

Box 2

SO:
THE ROMANS WERE
ABLE TO TAKE
OVER MOST OF
BRITAIN.

Explain this box.

Second clash.
After the 2 smaller
battles, the Romans
beat the main army
of Britons at a
great battle by the
River Medway.

Box 5

The Britons did not
all have the same
leader. They lived
in separate groups,
each with its own
leader.
Some Britons hated
other Britons more
than they hated
the Romans.

Box 3

First clash.
Soon after the
Romans landed, the
Britons attacked
them with two
separate armies.
The Romans beat
each army one at a
time.

Box 6

Figure 10.3   Causal relations: an additive response by a Year 6 pupil.

children's ideas about causal relations, polycausality and causal structure, and in particular to discover whether there is any kind of depth-structure in children's handling of causal explanation. What follows is a tentative and preliminary characterization of children's strategies, based on a partial analysis. However, there is one feature of children's behaviour on the cause-box question that stands out already: there appears to be a high degree of consistency in the broad strategies employed in all three task-sets, regardless of content. We cannot yet say how far this consistency will survive more refined categorization of causal structure, but the broad picture may be illustrated with some examples.

Some children simply gave haphazard lists of causal factors in answer to the open question, and then in the box-questions made a few single joins to the centre box that had to be explained (see figure 10.3). They behaved as if causes are discrete and additive. Initial analysis suggests that children using this strategy were more likely to confine their choices to processes and states of affairs, and less likely to select events.

Other children gave a narrative of events in the open question, and then narrativized the box-question. This consisted in producing a linear sequence that could encompass all the cause-boxes, or just some of them (see figure 10.4). There appeared to be a range of ideas operating here, with some children treating processes and states of affairs as if they were events, and others using a narrativization strategy but showing some awareness of the different status of the connections they made. Typical signs of the latter were sets of links in which states of affairs or processes consistently preceded events. There appeared to be partitioning between items tacitly taken to be background conditions, and others regarded as precipitants (but these are our words, not theirs). At interview children using a narrativizing strategy sometimes talked in terms of 'beginning here', and used 'and then' or 'and next' as link expressions. Some marked 'start' for the beginning of the linear chain, and some numbered the boxes in order.

A completely different strategy was adopted by some children, who constructed a causal argument in answering the open question, and then used arrows to produce what can only be described as an analytical schema for the box-question (see figure 10.5). Background conditions were picked out as separate starting points for different, sometimes separate and sometimes interlinked, causal chains which led into the events for which they were conditions. Actions and events were usually treated separately from background conditions. Sophisticated ideas of causal structure seem to be operating here.

There is some evidence of movement from narrative to analytical strategies. On rare occasions spontaneously, and sometimes under pressure from the interviewer, some narrativizing children paused in dismay when they saw — during the course of explaining to the interviewer what they had done — that one box did not make another happen, but preceded it, or was part of a pattern

Question 12. Why were the Romans able to take over?

(The boxes on this Chart are not in any special order)
Choose any boxes which help explain why the Romans were able to take over.
Join them up with arrows to show best why the Romans were able to take over.
Make the best explanation you can.
An arrow from one box to another means: *the first box helps explain the second box.*
Use as many joins as you need. You can have more than one arrow to or from a box.
BUT don't make joins that don't help explain why the Romans were able to take over.

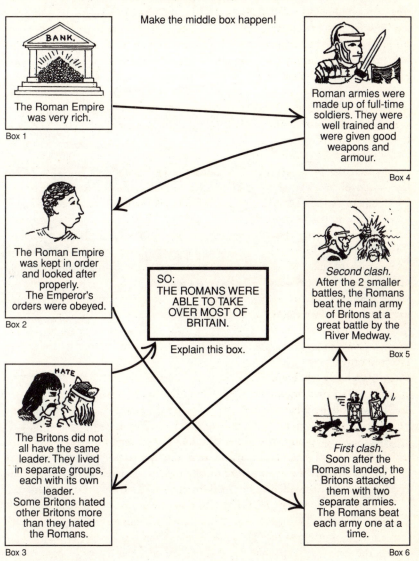

Figure 10.4   Causal relations: a narrativizing response by a Year 9 pupil.

Question 12. Why were the Romans able to take over?

(The boxes on this Chart are not in any special order)
Choose any boxes which help explain why the Romans were able to take over.
Join them up with arrows to show best why the Romans were able to take over.
Make the best explanation you can.
An arrow from one box to another means: *the first box helps explain the second box.*
Use as many joins as you need. You can have more than one arrow to or from a box.
BUT don't make joins that don't help explain why the Romans were able to take over.

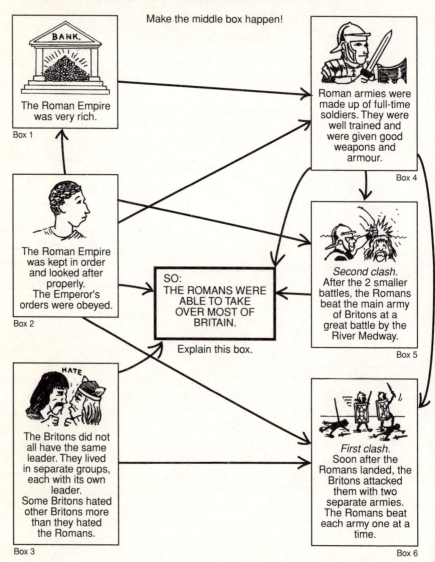

Make the middle box happen!

BANK.

The Roman Empire was very rich.

Box 1

Roman armies were made up of full-time soldiers. They were well trained and were given good weapons and armour.

Box 4

The Roman Empire was kept in order and looked after properly.
The Emperor's orders were obeyed.

Box 2

SO:
THE ROMANS WERE ABLE TO TAKE OVER MOST OF BRITAIN.

Explain this box.

Second clash.
After the 2 smaller battles, the Romans beat the main army of Britons at a great battle by the River Medway.

Box 5

HATE

The Britons did not all have the same leader. They lived in separate groups, each with its own leader.
Some Britons hated other Britons more than they hated the Romans.

Box 3

First clash.
Soon after the Romans landed, the Britons attacked them with two separate armies. The Romans beat each army one at a time.

Box 6

Figure 10.5   Causal relations: an analytical response by a Year 7 pupil.

of joint causes. Year 7 children were particularly likely to alter their approach between task-sets. One Year 9 child erased links in a narrativized chain in her pencil-and-paper response, and, appearing to recognize that the links were invalid because one box failed to explain its successor, altered her links to provide an analytical schema. (It remained invalid in its details, but recognized and avoided the initial problem thrown up by the narrative links.)

Alternative explanations

A subsequent question based on two alternative explanations sheds further light on children's ideas about causal structure (and also provides evidence about conceptions of the status of explanatory claims). Two different – very brief – explanations were offered to the children. One set out two simple background conditions for Roman success, and the other offered an event that was both a key step in the Roman conquest, and an immediate cause of their success:

The Romans were *really* able to take over most of Britain because the Roman Empire was rich and properly looked after.	The Romans were *really* able to take over most of Britain because they beat the Britons at the battle by the River Medway.

The children were then asked 'How can there be two different explanations of the *same* thing?' Follow-up questions asked whether one explanation was better than the other, how they could check to see if one was better than the other, and how they could check to find out if either explanation was a good or bad explanation.

Some children would only allow one explanation to be correct; others accepted both, but treated them as interchangeable and discrete. Some children decided that adding the two explanations together would give a better explanation, but still others argued that one made the other happen, or even, taking a more sophisticated line, that one was necessary for the other. They insisted that both explanations were valid, but treated them as exhibiting a structure that meant that they could not merely be added to one another, and were not interchangeable. One child characterized them as 'direct' and 'indirect' causes (a categorization not employed by any other child from the same school). Few children had any idea of how to test an explanation except by checking that the statements in it were true; for most, a cause was epistemologically speaking on a level with a statement of fact, and was either something that happened or existed, or was not. Nevertheless, some children (usually able 14-year-olds) suggested counterfactual thought experiments, and even comparisons with similar phenomena in different times or places as a means of evaluating explanations.

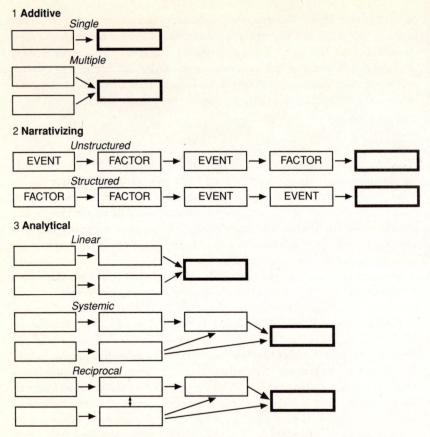

Figure 10.6   Causal relations and causal structure: schematic provisional model.

Any attempt to offer a clear-cut progression of ideas at this juncture would be premature. However, it is possible to point to certain patterns, and useful to summarize these in a systematic way, provided it is understood that the reality is likely to be much less tidy than the more or less speculative categorization offered here. The scheme set out in figure 10.6 is not to be taken as a model of linear (step-by-step) development. In particular, it is not to be assumed that the additive structure is necessarily less powerful than the narrative, and *a fortiori* there is no assumption that children who order causal links additively will necessarily move to a narrativizing strategy rather than an analytical one. The nature of the links is as important as the order in which they are made, and the latter does not provide conclusive evidence as to the meaning of the former. Nevertheless, there seem to be indications of a progressive structure in children's ideas. Children who approach the explanatory task as if the point is to put everything into a story run into difficulties that others solve by adopting a different strategy. (In the task given in figure 10.3, narrativization strategies could not cope with Box 3, whereas analytical strategies overcame the problem with ease.) In this area of historical ideas, as in others, an account of progression seems a realistic goal.

Conclusion

This chapter is intended only to make some tentative and even speculative suggestions about the development of children's ideas. As analysis of the responses proceeds, we should be able to say more about the consistency with which children operate 'the same' ideas in the face of different content and different tasks. This obviously has considerable importance for any claims to articulate progression in history in terms of 'levels'. We hope to improve the resolution of existing accounts of the development of children's ideas by examining the degree to which, and the ways in which, different but related ideas may be held by children as clusters. We shall also need to relate the development of children's ideas in different sub-strands of historical enquiry and explanation. This, too, is important for the notion of 'level', particularly if it is to be used as a practical basis for assessment in history. If, for example, there is little evidence that children's ideas about causal explanation are related to their ideas about reasons for action or the rational understanding of past social practices or institutions, then we should be cautious about throwing them together in an undifferentiated Attainment Target. Any effective assessment system based on progression must be based on empirical evidence of the ways in which children's ideas develop. It is unlikely that there is anything fixed or necessary about the development paths we find, and they are likely to change with different teaching approaches and objectives, or even as a result of wider shifts in assumptions about the way the world works. But this is not a reason for ignoring the patterns that may exist at present, so much as a reason for monitoring learning in a systematic and long-term way.

One particularly striking feature of early analysis is that some 7-year-olds perform at a higher level than some 14-year-olds on at least some of the tasks. (Similarly large variations in children's understanding in mathematics and science have already been described in chapters 8 and 9.) This has important implications for primary school history, where, until the advent of the National Curriculum, few teachers appear to have thought of history as offering any kind of progression. It is clear that there is a strong case for taking primary history seriously, and at least the possibility of developing the foundations of children's understanding of history in a more systematic way, and earlier, than has been traditionally attempted.

Past research and early work in CHATA suggest that progression in history, at least at the level of second-order concepts, is a profitable area of investigation. Researchers and history teachers agree in finding progression a valuable starting point for thinking about history teaching, and in this at least they are at one with the thinking behind the establishment of the National Curriculum.

Conclusions

Martin Hughes

Each of the ten chapters in this book stands in its own right. In each case, the authors have identified an issue that they consider to be of fundamental importance for understanding teaching and learning in times of change. They have described the methods chosen to explore that issue, and presented the findings that have emerged from their work; they have also, where appropriate, pointed out the implications of their findings for policy and practice. Readers interested in any of the ten topics addressed here will hopefully have gained further insights into the issues involved.

At the same time, the ten projects are part of a wider enterprise — a research programme supported by public funds in an area of major public concern. This final chapter therefore attempts to bring together what has emerged so far from the programme as a whole, and to point out some implications for policy and practice. It should be stressed, however, that the views expressed here are those of the editor and coordinator of the programme: there is no suggestion that the other contributors to the book would necessarily agree with the contents of this final chapter.

The structure of this chapter is based around the three main themes of the book — a concern with understanding the effects of the current reforms; a concern with understanding the nature of effective teaching and learning; and a concern with pupils' understanding and how it progresses. The chapter will, however, deal with these themes in reverse order. Thus we start by looking at what has been learnt about pupils' understanding; we then look at the kinds of teaching and learning experiences that are likely to foster this understanding; finally, we will look at the effects that the current reforms appear to be having on the processes of teaching and learning. The chapter ends with some implications for policy and practice.

Pupils' Understanding and How it Progresses

Several chapters in this book have been concerned – at least in part – with pupils' understanding within particular domains of learning. These domains have ranged widely both within and across the National Curriculum: they have included 'Knowledge about Language' (chapter 5); literacy and numeracy in the preschool period (chapter 7); knowledge about forces and measures (chapter 8); understanding scientific evidence (chapter 9); and ideas about historical explanation (chapter 10). The pupils' ages have also varied widely, covering the whole period from 4 to 16 years. Yet despite this variation in both domain and age-range, there are some interesting and important commonalities.

One common theme underlying several studies was the search for an underlying *progression* in pupils' understanding. Such progressions have indeed been identified, and have been reported in detail in chapters 7–10. These progressions appear to take two main forms. On the one hand, there is evidence of learners becoming more knowledgeable *within* particular domains – for example, the findings reported by Black, Brown, Simon and Blondel in chapter 8 indicate a clear progression in pupils' conceptual understanding of measures and forces. On the other hand, there is also evidence of learners becoming more knowledgeable *about the nature of* particular domains. Thus Duggan, Gott, Lubben and Millar indicate in chapter 9 that there is some progression in pupils' understanding of how evidence is used in science, while Lee, Dickinson and Ashby in chapter 10 outline a progression in pupils' understanding of historical enquiry. What is not clear from these findings is the relationship between these two kinds of knowledge – although it is highly likely (as Duggan and her co-authors suggest) that there is a close and complex relationship between them. What is also unclear is the extent to that the progressions identified here are reflected in current National Curriculum statements of attainment; there are clear suggestions in chapter 8, for example, that the match could be better than it currently is.

It is perhaps not surprising that this research has identified some clear areas of progression in pupils' understanding – one would, after all, expect learners to become more knowledgeable as they grow older. What is more surprising, however, are occasions when it appears that no real progression is taking place – or even where pupils' understanding appears to go backwards rather than forwards. There are at least two occasions in this book where the authors have pointed out what they consider to be significant *gaps* in key areas of pupils' knowledge or understanding. Thus Black and his colleagues report in chapter 8 on the lack of fundamental concepts in forces and measures, while Duggan and her colleagues suggest in chapter 9 that there are similar deficiencies in pupils' understanding of evidence. There are also indications from chapter 5, by Brumfit, Mitchell and Hooper, of serious gaps in certain areas of pupils' knowledge about language. In each case it is not so much that these concepts are being taught in the wrong place within the National Curriculum; rather, it would seem that they are not being taught at all.

The final common point emerging from these studies is that there is often greater variation *within* particular age-ranges than there is *across* them. Thus Black and his co-authors conclude, somewhat depressingly, that 'it must be profoundly disappointing that ideas that bright pupils can work out for themselves at age 6 or 7 when faced with more sophisticated contexts are still not understood by older pupils who have been in school for six more years'. Similarly, Lee and his colleagues suggest that 'some 7-year-olds perform at a higher level than some 14-year-olds' on some of their investigations into pupils' historical understanding. It is not clear from these studies what might underlie this kind of variation between pupils. However, the findings from Munn and Schaffer's chapter suggest that there are already significant differences in children's understanding when they start school: these authors suggest that differences in children's previous experiences of 'scaffolded joint activities' with adult caregivers might well be responsible. While such findings are hardly new – and are indeed acknowledged in the Dearing review – they still present substantial problems both for curriculum designers and for classroom teachers.

The Nature of Effective Teaching and Learning

The second main theme of the book has been a concern with the nature of effective teaching and learning. How, in other words, might schools help pupils overcome the kinds of gaps in their understanding indicated above? This issue is addressed – either directly or indirectly – by several contributors to this book.

The approach adopted by most contributors has been to explore the perceptions of those most directly involved in teaching and learning, and to observe teaching and learning as it takes place in the classroom (see Hughes, 1994, for further discussion of this approach). As a result, we now have some valuable insights into how teaching and learning are perceived and practised within a variety of different contexts. These contexts include the teaching and learning of cross-curricular themes (chapter 4); 'Knowledge about Language' in English and foreign language classrooms (chapter 5); the nature of effective teaching and learning in English and history (chapter 6); and the teaching and learning of numeracy and literacy at preschool level (chapter 7). In addition, the work described in chapter 3 allows us to consider teaching and learning within the broader perspective of pupils' overall school careers. As before, a number of common themes emerge from this work, despite the differences in context.

Perhaps the most striking area of commonality across these chapters is the view that learning is not primarily an individual process. Rather, it is most usefully seen as a social, interactive process involving the communication and negotiation of meaning between participants with varying degrees of knowledge or expertise. As several contributors have pointed out, there is a clear theoretical debt here to the work of Vygotsky and Bruner. At the same time, what is particularly interesting is the close correspondence between these theoretical views and the perceptions of teachers and learners themselves. This comes over most clearly in chapter 6, where Cooper and McIntyre argue that 'there is a strong sense in which both teachers and pupils see effective teaching and learning as "transactional" processes . . . The main contention of this view is that learners learn through a process of first being exposed to new knowledge, and then attempting to make sense of the new knowledge in terms of their existing knowledge'. One crucial role that teachers can play here, according to Cooper and McIntyre, involves providing an appropriate framework ('scaffolding') to support learners' efforts towards greater understanding – a framework that can gradually be removed as the understanding is achieved.

The notion of 'scaffolding' also proves useful in other chapters. In chapter 7, for example, Munn and Schaffer argue that children's initial introduction to numeracy and literacy does not occur in formal classrooms, but rather in the informal joint activities – such as sharing books or playing counting games – that take place between young children and adult caregivers (parents or preschool staff). In such contexts, they argue, adults can help children (through sensitive 'scaffolding') to a shared understanding of literacy and numeracy as meaningful social practices. The idea of scaffolding emerges again in the discussion of cross-curricular themes in chapter 4. Here, Whitty, Aggleton and Rowe describe how teachers can work out what 'lay theories' pupils possess in a particular subject area, and then use these – through a process of scaffolding – to introduce a subject principle. However, as Whitty and his co-authors point out, there is a further problem in teaching some cross-curricular themes, in that the subject knowledge still needs to be related back to pupils' own 'common-sense' understanding, if it is to be relevant to their life outside and beyond school. Again, it is helpful to see the learning process as a series of complex interactions between the different meanings and understandings possessed by teachers and learners.

Two further points of commonality arise directly from this perspective on teaching and learning. The first concerns the importance of social, emotional and motivational factors in education. As Cooper and McIntyre point out, if we accept that learning is dependent on communication and cooperation between teachers and pupils, then effective teaching and learning is more likely to take place in an emotionally supportive environment, in which the learner feels valued and respected by the other participants (teachers and fellow-pupils) in the learning process. The same point is taken up by Harris, Rudduck and Wallace in chapter 3. These authors conclude that 'the majority of Year 9 students really want to learn; they want to do well at school. Disengagement is sometimes the result of genuine boredom, and sometimes a strategy for masking loss of self-esteem . . . Above all, they want a fair chance of developing their confidence as learners'. These concerns are directly relevant to the point made by Whitty, Aggleton and Rowe in chapter 4 about the neglect of social education more generally within the National Curriculum, despite the clear intentions of the 1988 Education Reform Act in this respect. As Whitty and his colleagues make clear, the current treatment of the cross-curricular themes in secondary schools does not adequately address this fundamental problem.

The second point of commonality concerns *teaching methods*. Much public debate in education concerns the relative worth of particular teaching methods; a debate, moreover, which is often reduced to arguing the respective merits of two contrasting methods – direct transmission from the teacher as opposed to individualized, self-directed learning. Yet what emerges here, from the perspective of teachers and learners, is the widespread recognition that a *range* of methods is needed for effective teaching and learning – including, where appropriate, both direct transmission and individual study. To quote Cooper and McIntyre again: 'the critical issue for pupils appeared to be the degree to which the teaching created structures that fostered understanding, by enabling them to perceive personally meaningful connections between their existing knowledge and new knowledge'. In their study, this often involved activities that heightened pupils' interest and involvement, such as story telling by the teacher, drama and role play, discussion and collaborative tasks. A similar point is made by Brumfit, Mitchell and Hooper in chapter 5, where they report on the methods that pupils considered most effective in English and foreign language classrooms: here, pupils generally 'commended their teachers most often for telling pupils what to do, for explaining and making sure pupils understood, and for making learning fun and interesting'.

The Effects of the Educational Reforms

What has emerged from several chapters, then, is a common perspective on teaching and learning as an interactive process, a shared concern with affective as well as cognitive issues, and an indication that successful teaching and learning does not reside in a single teaching approach. This in turn raises the question of whether the changes introduced by the educational reforms are likely to encourage or inhibit the kinds of teaching and learning suggested by this research as being particularly effective.

It is hard to give a definitive answer to this question, on the evidence currently available. This is partly because the perspective on teaching and learning outlined above emerged only in the course of the research; none of the studies in the programme was specifically set up to address this particular issue. Nevertheless, several contributors have reported findings that bear – either directly or indirectly – on the question. Consideration of their findings suggests there are some substantial areas of concern, where it appears that the effects of the reforms may not be conducive to effective teaching and learning as described above.

One area of concern is the effect that the reforms have had on teachers' *workload*, and in particular, the pressures that teachers have experienced in trying to implement the reforms. These effects are particularly evident in the studies concerned with Key Stage One. Thus many of the teachers in Plewis and Veltman's study (chapter 1) expressed considerable difficulty in fitting in all the subjects of the National Curriculum to their school day; some of these teachers also suggested that teaching young children had become 'a less inspirational and joyful activity than it used to be'. Similarly, the teachers studied by Desforges, Holden and Hughes (chapter 2) reported little enthusiasm for standardized assessment; many considered that it took up too much of their time, and provided them with little useful information in return. The pressures experienced by these infant teachers were also evident in the preschool years: thus the nursery teachers whose views are reported by Munn and Schaffer in chapter 7 were concerned that downward pressure from the new curriculum would curtail their traditional attention to personal–social as well as cognitive factors.

These concerns, it should be said, are hardly novel. They are supported by other research on Key Stage One (e.g. Campbell et al., 1991; Pollard et al., 1994), and were explicitly acknowledged in the Dearing review of the National Curriculum. While it is hoped that the new, slimmer National Curriculum will make teachers' lives easier, at the time of writing it is still too early to say if this will happen. Our concern here, however, is with teaching and learning. If teachers are feeling as pressured as they report, and are preoccupied with issues of curriculum and assessment, then it raises serious doubts as to whether the reforms have enhanced their ability to provide the kind of sensitive, interactive teaching that this research suggests will be most effective for developing pupils' understanding.

A second issue of concern is that of *differentiation*. As was noted earlier, there is clear evidence from chapters 7–10 of widespread variation in understanding amongst pupils of the same age. Such variation inevitably presents considerable problems for teachers, particularly if they are to match their teaching to the individual characteristics of learners. One policy that many schools adopt to reduce these problems is that of setting – the grouping within particular subject areas of pupils with similar levels of achievement. The issue of setting is looked at in some detail by Harris, Rudduck and Wallace in chapter 3. Their study suggests that the changes introduced by the current reforms are likely to lead to increased competition and differentiation within schools, and that this will be reflected in an increase in the practice of setting. Yet their chapter also indicates that setting has mixed effects; while it may have a positive motivating effect on some pupils, it may have a serious negative effect on the self-esteem of others, and particularly the lower achievers. The implication of this work is that the reforms are acting to widen and accentuate variation between pupils, rather than reduce it.

A third area of concern lies in the emphasis placed within the National Curriculum on individual subjects, and the danger of a resulting *loss of coherence* in the curriculum as a whole (see Rudduck et al., 1994, for further discussion of 'coherence'). Within this book, the issue arises in a number of places. In chapter 4, for example, Whitty, Aggleton and Rowe focus specifically on the cross-curricular themes; they present clear evidence within this chapter that the themes, while ostensibly being taught through the core and foundation subjects, are in fact being given little attention as the core and foundation subjects are prioritized. Another example of lack of coherence is highlighted by Brumfit, Mitchell and Hooper in their study of 'Knowledge about Language' in chapter 5; as these authors point out, pupils are receiving contrasting messages on this topic from their English and foreign language lessons. Further indications of lack of coherence come from chapter 6, which suggests that history and English teachers are interpreting the requirements of the National Curriculum in very different ways. While it is, of course, inevitable that teaching and learning will take on a different nature within different subject areas, it is still important that the experiences offered to pupils across the curriculum as a whole have a certain degree of consistency, and in particular, that they are enabled to make links between their existing knowledge and new knowledge. The concern here is that the strongly subject-centred nature of the National Curriculum may inhibit rather than encourage them in doing this.

Implications

The 1994 Dearing review of the National Curriculum promised a moratorium on change. Once the proposed revisions to the curriculum had been made, then no further changes would be made for a period of five years. This moratorium, it should be pointed out, does not necessarily apply to other aspects of the reforms: there is no suggestion that the reforms as a whole will

be put 'on hold' for the foreseeable future. Nevertheless, the moratorium holds
out a promise of stability, of providing an opportunity for reflection on what
has been achieved so far, and the hope that any further reforms will be based
on careful consideration of the underlying issues. If this is to be the case, then
it is suggested that some consideration is given to the following issues, which
have emerged from the research described in this book.

1   There is a clear need to bring the curriculum closer into line with what is
    becoming known about progression in pupils' understanding. There are
    several examples in this book of clear disagreements between the assump-
    tions of the National Curriculum and the available evidence on what pupils
    know, believe or understand at different ages. Particular attention should
    be paid to 'gaps' in pupils' understanding – significant areas that currently
    appear to be neglected in the curriculum.

2   There is also a clear need to go beyond the current subject-centred nature
    of the National Curriculum, and to address the issue of coherence in the
    curriculum. Particular attention should be paid to the cross-curricular
    themes, which appear to be dropping out of sight in many schools, to more
    implicit cross-curricular issues such as knowledge about language, and to
    the wider neglect of social education within the National Curriculum. The
    overall aim should be to create a curriculum that helps learners make links
    between their own knowledge and new knowledge, rather than sending
    out conflicting and confusing messages.

3   Serious consideration must be given to the issue of differentiation. The
    evidence provided here shows that the differences between pupils of similar
    ages are extremely wide, and that current policies are in danger of
    exacerbating rather than reducing these differences. Schools and teachers
    need both policy guidance and practical suggestions: there is also a need for
    further research on how the problem should best be tackled.

4   Further attention should be paid to relationships between home and school.
    The current emphasis on parents as 'consumers' does not give sufficient
    recognition to their clear desire to be more closely involved in the
    education of their children. One area where parents could be more closely
    involved (as many already are) is in helping children learn to read – a
    recommendation clearly reinforced by Plewis and Veltman's finding that
    children spend only eight minutes a week reading aloud to their teacher.
    The case for drawing on parents' evident desire to help their children
    appears to be overwhelming.

5   Finally, it is time to give further attention to what we have termed,
    somewhat academically, the affective side of school life. On the one hand,
    there is clear evidence from this research that pupils value attempts by
    teachers to make lessons interesting, exciting and fun. On the other hand,

there is also evidence that the reforms have increased the pressure on teachers and decreased their enjoyment in their work. Rather than criticizing teachers for what they are not doing, we would like to draw their attention to the many examples in this book of successful lessons, which teachers and pupils described with both interest and excitement. Such episodes remind us that teaching and learning can indeed be worthwhile and rewarding pursuits, even in times of change.

References

Ader, J. 1975: *Building Implications of the Multi-option School*. Paris: OECD.

Apple, M. W. 1993: *Official Knowledge: Democratic Education in a Conservative Age*. New York and London: Routledge.

Archenhold, F., Austin, R., Bell, J., Black, P., Braund, M., Daniels, S., Holding, B., Russell, A. and Strang, J. 1991: *Profiles and Progression in Science Exploration*. Assessment Matters No. 5. SEAC.

Ashby, R. and Lee, P. J. 1987a: Discussing the evidence. In *Teaching History*, 48, London: The Historical Association, 13–17.

Ashby, R. and Lee, P. J. 1987b: Children's concepts of empathy and understanding in history. In C. Portal (ed.), *The History Curriculum for Teachers*. Lewes: Falmer Press, 62–88.

Baddeley, A. 1990: *Human Memory*. New York: LEA.

Ball, S. J. 1981: *Beachside Comprehensive*. Cambridge: Cambridge University Press.

Ball, S. J. 1993: Education, markets, choice and social class: the market as a class strategy in the UK and the USA. *British Journal of Sociology of Education*, 14 (1), 3–13.

Bastian, A., Bruchter, N., Gittell, M., Greer, C. and Haskins, K. 1985: *Choosing Equality: The Case for Democratic Schooling*. New York: New World Foundation.

Bernstein, B. 1971: On the classification and framing of educational knowledge. In M. F. D. Young (ed.), *Knowledge and Control*. London: Collier-Macmillan, 47–69.

Bernstein, B. 1977: *Class, Codes and Control*, vol. 3, 2nd edn. London: Routledge and Kegan Paul.

Bernstein, B. 1981: Codes, modalities and the process of cultural reproduction: a model. *Language and Society*, 10, 327–63.

Bernstein, B. 1990: *The Structuring of Pedagogic Discourse*. London: Routledge.

Biggs, J. B. and Collis, K. F. 1982: *Evaluating the Quality of Learning: The Solo Taxonomy*. New York: Academic Press.

Black, P. J. 1993: Progression in physics in the National Curriculum. *Physics Education*, 28, 351–5.

Black, P. J. and Simon, S. A. 1992: Progression in learning science. *Research in Science Education*, 22, 45–54.

Bliss, J., Ogborn, J. and Whitelock, D. 1989: Secondary school pupils' commonsense theories of motion. *International Journal of Science Education*, 11, 261–72.

Bowe, R., Gewirtz, S. and Ball, S. J. 1994: Captured by the discourse? Issues and concerns in researching 'parental choice'. *British Journal of Sociology of Education*, 15 (1), 63–78.

Bowey, J. A. 1988: *Metalinguistic Functioning in Children*. Geelong, Australia: Deakin University Press.

Brophy, J. and Good, T. 1986: Teacher behaviour and pupil achievement. In M. Wittrock (ed.), *Handbook of Research on Teaching*. New York: Macmillan.

Brown, S. and McIntyre, D. 1993: *Making Sense of Teaching*. Milton Keynes: Open University Press.

Brumfit, C. 1993: *Advanced Language Training for English Teachers*. University of Southampton: Centre for Language in Education Briefing Documents, 3.

Brumfit, C. and Johnson, K. (eds) 1979: *The Communicative Approach to Language Teaching*. Oxford: Oxford University Press.

Brumfit, C., Mitchell, R. and Hooper, J. 1992: Researching children's language awareness in the English and modern languages classroom. Paper presented at the joint Conference of the Association for Language Learning/International Association for the Teaching of English as an International Language. Edinburgh, April 1992.

Bruner, J. 1987: The transactional self. In J. Bruner, and H. Haste, (eds), *Making Sense: The Child's Construction of the World*. London: Methuen.

Bruner, J. and Haste, H. (eds) 1987: *Making Sense: The Child's Construction of the World*. London: Methuen.

Bryant, P., Bradley, L., MacLean, M. and Crosland, J. 1989: Nursery rhymes, phonological skills and reading. *Journal of Child Language*, 16, 407–28.

Campbell, R. J., Evans, L., St J. Neill, S. R. and Packwood, A. 1991: *Workloads, Achievement and Stress*. University of Warwick.

Carter, R. (ed.) 1990: *Knowledge about Language and the Curriculum: The LINC Reader*. London: Hodder and Stoughton.

Carter, R. 1992: The LINC project: the final chapter? Unpublished paper. University of Nottingham.

Case, R. 1985: *Intellectual Development: Birth to Adulthood*. New York: Academic Press.

Central Advisory Council for Education 1967: Children and their Primary Schools. [The Plowden Report]. London: HMSO.

Chandler, R. 1988: Unproductive busywork. *English in Education*, 22 (3), 20–8.

Clement, J., Brown, D. E. and Zietsman, A. 1989: Not all preconceptions are misconceptions: finding 'anchoring conceptions' for grounding instruction on students' intuitions. *International Journal of Science Education*, 11, 554–65.

Codd, J. 1993: Equity and choice: the paradox of New Zealand educational reform. *Curriculum Studies*, 1 (1), 75–90.

Cole, M. 1985: The Zone of Proximal Development: where culture and cognition create each other. In J. Wertsch (ed.), *Culture, Communication and Cognition: Vygotskian Perspectives*. London: Cambridge University Press.

Coles, M. and Gott, R. 1993: Teaching scientific investigation. *Education in Science*, 154, 8–11.

Connell, R. W. 1994: Poverty and education. *Harvard Educational Review*, 62 (2), 125–49.

Cooper, B. 1992: Testing National Curriculum mathematics. *Curriculum Journal*, 3, 3.

Cooper, P. 1989: Respite, relationships and resignification: a study of the effects of residential schooling on pupils with emotional and behavioural difficulties, with particular reference to the pupil perspective. Unpublished Ph.D. thesis: University of Birmingham, UK.

Cooper, P. 1993a: *Effective Schools for Disaffected Students: Integration and Segregation.* London: Routledge.

Cooper, P. 1993b: Field relations and the problem of authenticity in researching participants' perceptions of teaching and learning in classrooms. *British Educational Research Journal*, 19 (4) 323–38.

Council of Science and Technology Institutes 1993: *Mapping the Science, Technology and Mathematics Domain.* The Council of Science and Technology Institutes.

Crowley, T. 1989: *The Politics of Discourse.* Basingstoke: Macmillan.

Dearing, R. 1993: *The National Curriculum and its Assessment: Interim Report.* York/London: NCC/SEAC.

Dearing, R. 1994: *The National Curriculum and its Assessment: Final Report.* London: School Curriculum and Assessment Authority.

DeLoache, J. S. and DeMendoza, O. A. 1987: Joint picture book interactions of mothers and one year old children. *British Journal of Developmental Psychology*, 5, 111–24.

Department of Education and Science 1977: *Curriculum 9–16.* London: HMSO.

Department of Education and Science 1985: *Education for All: Report of the Committee of Inquiry into the Education of Children from Ethnic Minority Groups.* [Swann Report]. London: HMSO.

Department of Education and Science 1988a: *Education Reform Act 1988.* London: HMSO.

Department of Education and Science 1988b: *National Curriculum Task Group on Assessment and Testing: A Report.* London: Department of Education and Science and the Welsh Office.

Department of Education and Science 1988c: *Report of the Committee of Inquiry into the Teaching of English Language.* [Kingman Report]. London: HMSO.

Department of Education and Science 1989a: *English for Ages 5 to 16.* [Cox Report]. London: HMSO.

Department of Education and Science 1989b: *Mathematics in the National Curriculum.* London: Department of Education and Science and the Welsh Office.

Department of Education and Science 1990a: *English in the National Curriculum* (No. 2). London: HMSO.

Department of Education and Science 1990b: *National Curriculum and Assessment.* London: DES.

Department of Education and Science 1991a: *History in the National Curriculum (England).* London: HMSO.

Department of Education and Science 1991b: *Mathematics in the National Curriculum 1991.* London: Department of Education and Science and the Welsh Office.

Department of Education and Science 1991c: *Modern Foreign Languages in the National Curriculum*. London: HMSO.

Department of Education and Science, 1991d: *Science in the National Curriculum 1991*. London: Department of Education and Science and the Welsh Office.

Department of Education and Science 1991e, 1994: *The Parent's Charter*. London: DES.

Department of Education and Science 1991f: *Your Child and the National Curriculum*. London: DES.

Department for Education 1995a: *Mathematics in the National Curriculum*. London: HMSO.

Department for Education 1995b: *Science in the National Curriculum*. London: HMSO.

Desforges, C. 1989: *Testing and Assessment*. London: Cassell.

Desforges, C. 1992: Assessment and learning. *Forum*, 34 (3), 68–9.

Desforges, C., Holden, C. and Hughes, M. 1994a: Assessment at Key Stage One: its effects on parents, teachers and classroom practice. *Research Papers in Education*, 9 (2), 133–58.

Desforges, C., Hughes, M. and Holden, C. 1994b: Parents' and teachers' perceptions of assessment at Key Stage One. In Hughes, M. (ed.), *Perceptions of Teaching and Learning*. BERA Dialogues 8. Clevedon: Multilingual Matters, 26–34.

Dickinson, A. K. and Lee, P. J. 1978: Understanding and research. In A. K. Dickinson and P. J. Lee (eds), *History Teaching and Historical Understanding*. London: Heinemann Educational Books, 94–120.

Dickinson, A. K. and Lee, P. J. 1984: Making sense of history. In A. K. Dickinson, P. J. Lee and P. J. Rogers (eds), *Learning History*. London: Heinemann Educational Books, 39–84.

Donmall, B. G. (ed.) 1985: *Language Awareness*. NCLE Papers and Reports, 6. London: Centre for Information on Language Teaching.

Driver, R., Guesne, E. and Tiberghien, A. 1985: *Children's Ideas in Science*. Milton Keynes: Open University Press.

Duggan, S. and Gott, R. 1995: The place of investigations in practical work in the UK National Curriculum for Science. *International Journal of Science Education*, 17 (2), 137–47.

Ellis, R. 1990: *Instructed Second Language Acquisition*. Oxford: Blackwell.

Ellwein, M. C., Glass, G. V. and Smith, M. L. 1988: Standards of competence: propositions on the nature of testing reforms. *Educational Researcher*, 17 (8), 4–9.

Esland, G. M. 1971: Teaching and learning as the organisation of knowledge. In M. F. D. Young (ed.), *Knowledge and Control*. London: Collier-Macmillan, 70–132.

Fairclough, N. L. (ed.) 1990: *Critical Language Awareness*. Harlow: Longman.

Foulds, K., Gott, R. and Feasey, R. 1992: *Investigative Work in Science*. University of Durham.

Fowler, G. 1992: Non-hierarchical teaching: an ideological analysis of cultural transmission and a model for use in post-compulsory education and training. Unpublished Ph.D. thesis, University of Nottingham.

Frydman, O. and Bryant, P. 1988: Sharing and the understanding of number equivalence by young children. *Cognitive Development*, 3, 323–39.

Gewirtz, S., Ball, S. J. and Bowe, R. 1993: Values and ethics in the education market place: the case of Northwark Park. *International Studies of Sociology of Education*, 3, 233–53.

Gleeson, D. and Whitty, G. 1976: *Developments in Social Studies Teaching*. London: Open Books.

Goffman, E. 1961: *Asylums: Essays on the Social Situation of Mental Patients and Other Inmates*. Harmondsworth: Penguin.

Goodson, I. 1983: *School Subjects and Curriculum Change*. London: Croom Helm.

Goodson, I. (ed.) 1985: *Social Histories of the Secondary Curriculum*. Lewes: Falmer Press.

Gott, R. and Duggan, S. 1994: *Investigative Work in the Science Curriculum*. Milton Keynes: Open University Press.

Harley, B. 1993: Instructional strategies and SLA in early French immersion. *Studies in Second Language Acquisition*, 15 (2), 245–59.

Harris, S. 1993: CEG post National Curriculum: What future? *Careers Education and Guidance*, October, 2–3.

Harris, S. 1994: Entitled to what? Control and autonomy in school: a student perspective. *International Studies in Sociology of Education*, 4 (1), 57–76.

Harris, S. and Rudduck, J. 1993: Establishing the seriousness of learning in the early years of secondary schooling. *British Journal of Educational Psychology*, 63, 322–36.

Harris, S. and Rudduck, J. 1994: 'School's great – apart from the lessons': students' early experiences of learning in secondary school. In M. Hughes (ed.), *Perceptions of Teaching and Learning*. BERA Dialogues 8. Clevedon: Multilingual Matters, 35–52.

Hayes, P. J. 1979: The naive physics manifesto. In D. Mitchie (ed.), *Expert Systems in the Microelectronic Age*. Edinburgh: Edinburgh University Press.

HEA 1992: *Health Education Policies in Schools*. London: Health Education Authority.

Holden, C., Hughes, M. and Desforges, C.W. 1993: What do parents want from assessment? *Education 3–13*, 21, 3–7.

Holland, J. 1981: Social class and changes in orientation to meaning. *Sociology*, 15 (1), 1–18.

Hughes, M. 1986: *Children and Number*. Oxford: Blackwell.

Hughes, M. (ed.) 1994: *Perceptions of Teaching and Learning*. BERA Dialogues 8. Clevedon: Multilingual Matters.

Hughes, M., Wikeley, F. and Nash, T. 1994: *Parents and their Children's Schools*. Oxford: Blackwell.

James, C. and Garrett, P. (eds) 1991: *Language Awareness in the Classroom*. Harlow: Longman.

Johnson, P. 1993: Internal working paper. *Exploration of Science Project*, University of Durham.

Jonathan, R. 1990: Choice and control in education: parental rights, individual liberties and social justice. *British Journal of Educational Studies*, 37, 321–38.

Keddie, N. 1971: Classroom knowledge. In M. F. D. Young (ed.), *Knowledge and Control*. London: Collier-Macmillan, 133–60.

Kogan, M. 1971: *The Politics of Education*. Harmondsworth: Penguin.

Krashen, 1981: *Second Language Acquisition and Second Language Learning*. Oxford: Pergamon.

Lee, P. J. 1978: Explanation and understanding in history. In A. K. Dickinson and P. J.

Lee (eds), *History Teaching and Historical Understanding*, London: Heinemann Educational Books, 72–93.

MacBeath, J. and Weir, D. 1991: *Attitudes to School*. Glasgow: Jordanhill College.

Millar, R. 1989: Bending the evidence: the relationship between theory and experiment in science education. In R. Millar (ed.), *Doing Science: Images of Science in Science Education*. London: Falmer Press, 38–61.

Millar, R., Lubben, F., Gott, R. and Duggan, S. 1994: Investigating in the school science laboratory: conceptual and procedural knowledge and their influence on performance. *Research Papers in Education*, 9 (2), 207–49.

Mitchell, R. 1988: *Communicative Language Teaching in Practice*. London: Centre for Information on Language Teaching.

Mitchell, R. 1993: Diversity or uniformity? Multilingualism and the English teacher in the 1990s. In C. Kennedy (ed.), IATEFL Annual Conference Report 1993: Plenaries. Whitstable: IATEFL, 9–16.

Mitchell, R., Brumfit, C. and Hooper, J. 1994: Perceptions of language and language learning in English and foreign language classrooms. In M. Hughes (ed.), *Perceptions of Teaching and Learning*. BERA Dialogues 8. Clevedon: Multilingual Matters, 53–65.

Moore, R. 1995: Elementary commonsense – policies and deep structures in the primary school. Essay review of A. Pollard (ed.), *Look Before You Leap* (London: Tufnell Press). *Curriculum Studies Journal*, 3 (1), 96–104.

Mortimore, P., Sammons, P., Stoll, L., Lewis, D. and Ecob, R. 1988: *School Matters*. Wells: Open Books.

Munn, Pamela 1985: Accountability and parent–teacher communication. *British Educational Research Journal*, 11, 105–10.

Munn, P. 1994a: The early development of literacy and numeracy. *European Journal of Early Years Education*, 2 (1), 5–18.

Munn, P. 1994b: What counts as reading before school? Children's beliefs. In P. Owen and P. Pumphrey (eds), *Understanding, Encouraging and Assessing Children's Reading: International Concerns*. Sussex: Falmer Press.

Munn, P. and Schaffer, H. R. 1993: Literacy and numeracy events in social interactive contexts. *International Journal of Early Years Education*, 1, 61–80.

Munn, P. and Stephen, C. 1993: Children's understanding of number words. *British Journal of Educational Psychology*, 63, 521–7.

National Curriculum Council 1990a: *Curriculum Guidance 3: The Whole Curriculum*. York: National Curriculum Council.

National Curriculum Council 1990b: *Curriculum Guidance 5: Health Education*. York: National Curriculum Council.

Noss, R. 1990: The National Curriculum and mathematics: a case of divide and rule? In R. Noss and P. Dowling (eds), *Mathematics versus the National Curriculum*. Lewes: Falmer Press.

OFSTED 1994: *Taught Time*. London: Office for Standards in Education.

Peck, A. 1988: *Language Teachers at Work*. Oxford: Pergamon.

Pfundt, H. and Duit, R. (eds) 1991: *Bibliography: Students' Alternative Frameworks and Science Education*, 3rd edn. Kiel: IPN – Institute for Science Education.

Piaget, J. and Inhelder, B. 1958: *The Growth of Logical Thinking from Childhood to Adolescence*. London: Routledge and Kegan Paul.

Plewis, I. 1991: Pupils' progress in reading and mathematics during primary school: associations with ethnic group and sex. *Educational Research*, 33, 133–40.

Plewis, I. and Veltman, M. 1994: Teachers' reports of curriculum coverage in response to change. In M. Hughes (ed.), *Perceptions of Teaching and Learning*. BERA Dialogues 8. Clevedon: Multilingual Matters, 18–25.

Plewis, I. and Veltman, M. forthcoming: Opportunity to learn maths at Key Stage One: changes in curriculum coverage 1984–1993. *Research Papers in Education*.

Plewis, I., Mooney, A. and Creeser, R. 1990: Time on educational activities at home and educational progress in infant school. *British Journal of Educational Psychology*, 60, 330–7.

Pollard, A., Broadfoot, P., Croll, P., Osborn, M. and Abbott, D. 1994: *Changing English Primary Schools?* London: Cassell.

Powney, J. and Watts, M. 1987: *Interviewing in Educational Research*. London: Routledge.

Pramling, I. 1990: *Learning to Learn: A Study of Swedish Preschool Children*. New York: Springer-Verlag.

Protherough, R. 1989: *Students of English*. London: Routledge.

Public Attitude Surveys 1989: *Parental Awareness of School Education*. High Wycombe: Public Attitude Surveys.

Rowe, D. 1993: Citizenship, PSE and the French Dressing approach to curriculum planning. *Social Science Teacher*, 22, 2.

Roy, D. 1990: Improving recall by eye witnesses through the cognitive interview. *The Psychologist*, 4 (9), 398–400.

Royal Society 1985: *The Public Understanding of Science*. London: The Royal Society.

Rudduck, J., Harris, S. and Wallace, G. 1994: 'Coherence' and students' experience of learning in the secondary school. *Cambridge Journal of Education*, 24 (2), 197–211.

Saxe, G. B., Guberman, S. R. and Gearhart, M. 1987: Social processes in early number development. *Monographs of the Society for Research in Child Development*, 52 (2), Serial no. 216.

Scribner, S. and Cole, M. 1981: *Psychology of Literacy*. Cambridge, MA: Harvard University Press.

Sharwood-Smith, M. 1993: Input enhancement in instructed SLA: theoretical bases. *Studies in Second Language Acquisition*, 15 (2), 165–79.

Shemilt, D. 1980: *History 13–16: Evaluation Study*. Edinburgh: Holmes McDougall.

Shemilt, D. 1983: *The Devil's Locomotive. History and Theory*, vol. XXII, no. 4, 1–18.

Shemilt, D. 1984: Beauty and the philosopher: empathy in history and the classroom. In A. K. Dickinson, P. J. Lee and P. J. Rogers (eds), *Learning History*. London: Heinemann Educational Books, 39–84.

Shemilt, D. 1987: Adolescent ideas about evidence and methodology in history. In C. Portal (ed.), *The History Curriculum for Teachers*. Lewes: Falmer Press, 39–61.

Simon, S., Black, P., Blondel, E. and Brown, M. 1994a: *Forces in Balance*. Hatfield: Association for Science Education.

Simon, S., Black, P., Brown, M. and Blondel, E. 1994b: Progression in understanding the equilibrium of forces. *Research Papers in Education*, 9, 249–80.

Straddling, B. and Saunders, L. 1993: Differentiation in practice: responding to the needs of all children. *Educational Research*, 35 (2), 127–37.

Strauss, S. and Stavy, R. 1982: *U-Shaped Behavioural Growth*. New York: Academic Press.

Sulzby, E. 1988: A study of children's early reading development. In A. D. Pellegrini (ed.), *Psychological Bases for Early Education*. New York: Wiley, 39–77

Tizard, B., Blatchford, P., Burke, J., Farquhar, C. and Plewis, I. 1988: *Young Children at School in the Inner City*. Hove: Lawrence Erlbaum.

Turner, M. 1990: *Sponsored Reading Failure*. Warlingham: IPSET Education Unit.

Vygotsky, L. S. 1978: *Mind in Society*. Cambridge, MA: MIT Press.

Vygotsky, L. 1987: *The Collected Works of L. S. Vygotsky*, vol. 1, ed. R. Reiber and A. Carton. London: Plenum.

Vygotsky, L. S. and Luria, A. R. 1930; 1993: *Studies on the History of Behaviour: Ape, Primitive and Child*. Ed. and trans. I. Golod and E. Knox. Hillsdale, NJ: Lawrence Erlbaum Associates.

Wallace, G. (ed.) 1992: *Local Management of Schools: Research and Experience*. Clevedon: Multilingual Matters.

Wallace, G. (ed.) 1993: *Local Management, Central Control: Schools in the Market Place*. Dorset: Hyde Publications.

West, A., Davies, J. and Scott, G. 1992: Attitudes to secondary school: parents' views over a five-year period. *Research Papers in Education*, 7.

Whitty, G. 1985: *Sociology and School Knowledge*. London: Methuen.

Whitty, G. 1992: Integrated Humanities and World Studies. In A. Rattansi and D. Reeder (eds), *Radicalism and Education: Essays for Brian Simon*. London: Lawrence and Wishart.

Whitty, G., Rowe, G. and Aggleton, P. 1994a: Subjects and themes in the secondary school curriculum. *Research Papers in Education*, 9 (2), 159–81.

Whitty, G., Rowe, G. and Aggleton, P. 1994b: Discourse in cross curricular contexts. *International Studies in Sociology of Education*, 4 (1), 25–42.

Wood, D. 1988: *How Children Think and Learn*. Oxford: Blackwell.

Woods, P. 1971: *The Divided School*. London: Routledge and Kegan Paul.

Wynn, K. 1990: Children's understanding of counting. *Cognition*, 36, 155–93.

Index